50 MILITARY LEADERS WHO CHANGED THE WORLD

50 MILITARY LEADERS WHO CHANGED THE WORLD

William Weir

FALL RIVER PRESS

Fall River Press
122 Fifth Avenue
New York, NY 10011

ISBN: 978-1-4351-1444-9

Printed and bound in the United States of America

1 3 5 7 9 10 8 6 4 2

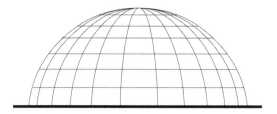

Dedication

For Henry, from "Grandpa white house"

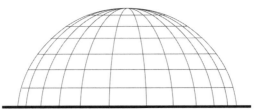

Acknowledgments

No author writing about military leaders from the time of Sargon the Great to the Korean War could rely on personal knowledge (although at times I've felt old enough to be Sargon's grandfather). This book, then, depends on the work of hundreds of persons, both living and dead. The fruits of their labors would not have gotten between these covers without the help of many people. Among them are the staff of the Guilford, Connecticut, public library (and everyone in the interlibrary loan system), who seem to be able to find any book published anywhere. (The authors of the books used to reference *this* one may be found in the bibliography.)

Illustrations as well as information are needed for a book like this, and when the subject matter covers a span of several thousand years, they are not always easy to find. The staffs of the Library of Congress, the National Archives, the British Museum, and the U.S. Naval Institute were most helpful.

Pictures and information then have to be turned into a book. Michael Pye, Adam Schwartz, and Jeff Piasky of Career Press/New Page got this book into production, and Astrid deRidder, my editor, proved to be extremely knowledgeable and most helpful.

My wife, Anne, who endured my interminable communing with a computer, and also humored me by reading every page and making many necessary suggestions.

To all of these people I am extremely grateful.

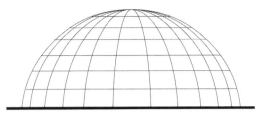

Contents

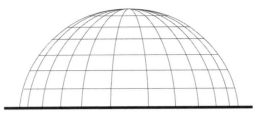

Introduction

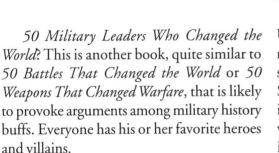

50 Military Leaders Who Changed the World? This is another book, quite similar to *50 Battles That Changed the World* or *50 Weapons That Changed Warfare*, that is likely to provoke arguments among military history buffs. Everyone has his or her favorite heroes and villains.

Not all of *these* leaders are heroes, though. Benedict Arnold is the infamous traitor of the American Revolution. And Sun Tzu, Carl von Clausewitz, Alfred Thayer Mahan, and Giulio Douhet had far more impact on history through their writing than through their actions. Jean Baptiste de Gribreauval made his mark with logistics. Ivan the Terrible was a mediocre general at best, but his reign was a major turning point in history. Adolf Hitler was a monster, but even monsters can change history. The two qualifications for getting on this list were: (1) being a military leader, and (2) being responsible for a major change in history. Most of the people on the list were generals and admirals, but some (especially the early ones) were kings, and there are a dictator or two among the more modern leaders. There is also a naval captain (sort of), who keeps the list from being populated exclusively by officers and rulers.

Considering that the United States is going into its third century, while many other countries represented on the list are well into their third millennium, it may seem that the United States has more than its share. And maybe it does. But there are two facts that should be taken into account: (1) the United States is (and has been for some time) a very important country with a major influence on world history, and (2) I am an American writing for an American audience. And most Americans (as with every other nation) consider their own history the most important.

Here, in roughly chronological order, are 50 military leaders who have made the biggest changes in history. They are in "roughly" chronological order because they are arranged by the dates of their big achievements rather than their birthdays. (That's why Admiral Yamamoto, who was older than Hitler, comes later.)

Transliteration from languages that use writing systems other than the Roman alphabet present a problem. For example, the Arabic alphabet has no symbols for vowels. When written in English, various letters have been used to represent those vowels. Thus "Muslim" in older writing is usually "Moslem." English spellings of Arabic words seem to go in and out of fashion. Therefore "ibn," as in Abdul Aziz ibn Sa'ud, the founder of Saudi Arabia, is now "bin," as in Osama bin Laden. (At one time, it was "ben.") According to the Associated Press, Osama bin Laden leads the al Qaida organization; but according to the

New York Times, his organization is al Qaeda. I have attempted to use the most current and commonly accepted spellings, but I ask for your understanding if you see alternate spellings elsewhere.

Transliterating Chinese causes the most problems. In the memory of many people, the same Chinese city has been Peiping, Peking, and Beijing. There is now a new system of transliteration applicable to all Chinese words. I've tried to use it when I know what the modern spellings are. Also Chinese, Japanese, and Korean names are usually given in the traditional way, with the family name first. The only exception here is Syngman Rhee, because that's the way his name has always been given in the United States.

At the end of this book is a list of honorable (and dishonorable) mentions—military leaders who were considered for this group of 50 but didn't make the cut, along with brief explanations of why they weren't included. Some of them are well known, but some aren't.

Some regular entries are longer than others. In most cases, that's because some of the subjects have done more noteworthy things than others, or because there's more information available about them. The chapter on Matthew Ridgway is longer because it concerns a war about which too few Americans have too little knowledge—the Korean War. It seemed necessary to me to explain how the Korean War started, how it ended, and the roles played by General Matthew Ridgway and General Douglas MacArthur.

I was an army combat correspondent and photographer (a soldier, not a civilian) with the 27th "Wolfhound" Infantry Regiment on Heartbreak Ridge and in Kumwha in the Iron Triangle, and I have learned repeatedly how little the public knows of this particular war. Most of the people I've spoken with don't know there was a war going on in the 1950s. That's partly because after the peace talks began and combat became a murderous kind of trench warfare, the news media lost interest. The yo-yo effect—two armies bouncing up and down the peninsula—had ended. The U.N. army had orders not to advance, and the Communist armies were blasted every time they tried to.

Another reason for the ignorance of this war is that the government consciously tried to downplay the hostilities. It became impossible for a regular army unit to get news of combat into *Pacific Stars and Stripes*, a paper owned by the Army. The Pentagon ascribed assaults by the North Korean Army to the Chinese (MacArthur supposedly having annihilated the North Koreans) and the *New York Times* put the Pentagon reports in fine print on page 2. Why the Korean War is the "Forgotten War" and why its casualties have been minimized is something of a mystery.

Changes in history are easier to discern at a distance. That is why the latest of these history-changers operated more than 50 years ago. As well as suffering from a lack of modern military leaders, the list also suffers from a shortage of women. It contains only one woman, Joan of Arc, and 49 men. The trouble is that, throughout history, there has been a serious shortage of women in military leadership positions, and therefore few women who were in a position to change history through military means.

Nevertheless, there are some fascinating women warriors, which would make a great book (which might be my next project). Possibilities include Ahhoteb I, an Egyptian queen who may have personally led troops into battle; the Scythian queen who allegedly assassinated Cyrus the Great; Artemisia, who commanded five ships on the Persian side at the Battle of Salamis; Boudica, the British queen who fought the Romans; Zenobia, Queen of Palmyra, who fought the Romans; and Lakshmi Bai, the Indian rani who fought the British in the 19th century. And we can't forget either Elizabeth I or Grace O'Malley (the pirate queen of Western Ireland), who treated each other as equals. There are also plenty of non-noble women, such as Molly Pitcher of the Revolutionary War, and Cathay Williams, a former slave who changed her name to William Cathay and pretended to be a man to fight in the Indian Wars.

Until I can get started on that though, you can enjoy *50 Military Leaders Who Changed the World*. Some of them were good and some of them were bad, but I guarantee that they are all interesting.

1

Sargon of Akkad

The King of the Four Corners of the Earth

(c. 2334–2279 B.C.)

Sargon of Akkad, sometimes named as Sargon the Great or Sargon I, is history's third emperor, and the first conqueror of a multi-ethnic empire. He lived so long ago, however, that many details of his life and conquests are unknown and exist only in legend, without much foundation in fact. The Sumerian text known as the "Sargon legend" is the only source of information describing Sargon's life, but much of the text is missing. We know he reigned for 56 years, conquered all the cities of Mesopotamia, and built an empire that extended through modern Iran, Turkey, and Syria. Some authorities date his reign to sometime around 3800 B.C., while others say it extended from 2334 to 2279 B.C.

Assyrian battering ram with movable tower.
Bible Encyclopedia

Mesopotamia (modern Iraq) was settled by the Sumerians, who spoke a language apparently unrelated to any other. They irrigated the land between the Tigris River and the Euphrates River, built independent city-states, and warred with each other and with the nomads of the desert. The nomads were Semites, who spoke languages similar to modern Arabic and Hebrew.

Sargon was one of these Semites; he was born in the city of Kish. According to one legend, his mother was either a princess or a priestess. Sargon's father is unknown, but it is likely that his parents were not married, because after the baby Sargon was born, his mother put him in a pitch-lined basket and put the basket in the Euphrates River. A gardener named Akki found the basket in some bulrushes, and raised the baby as his own. For a while, Sargon worked as a gardener, but he soon became cup bearer to an ambitious noble named Ur-Zababa, who became the king of Kish. One night, the legend says, Sargon dreamed that the goddess Inanna (Ishtar) said she favored him and that she then killed Ur-Zababa. He was foolish enough to tell Ur-Zababa about the dream. Ur-Zababa sent Sargon on a mission to Lugal-zage-si, a Sumerian king who had conquered many Mesopotamian cities. Unbeknownst to Sargon, the message he carried for Lugal-zage-si requested that Lugal-zage-si kill this dangerous young man. If Sargon was a favorite of a goddesss, Ur-Zababa didn't want his blood on his own hands.

For some reason, Lugal-zage-si failed to murder Sargon. The clay tablets inscribed with this part of the legend have not been found. When the story resumes, Sargon has overthrown Lugal-zage-si and has begun building his own empire. He probably managed to rally his nomad kinsmen. The nomads fought in a looser formation than the Sumerians, who depended on a phalanx of spearmen and heavy wooden war carts drawn by donkeys. The nomads used the bow extensively. A statue of Sargon's grandson, Naram-sin, shows him carrying a recurved, composite bow.

Sargon's tactics were effective. A cuneiform text quoted in *A Sourcebook of Ancient History* by George Botsworth says:

> *Sargon, King of Akkad, through the royal gift of Ishtar was exalted, and he possessed no foe nor rival. His glory over the world he poured out. The Sea in the East he crossed, and in the eleventh year the Country of the West in its full extent his hand subdued. He united them under one control; he set up his images in the West; their booty he brought over at his word. Over the hosts of the world he reigned supreme.*

After becoming emperor, Sargon supposedly washed his hands in the "lower sea" (the Persian Gulf) to symbolize his lordship over the entire region of Sumeria.

Sargon built the city of Akkad (sometimes spelled Agade) and made it his capital. If the ruins of that city are ever found, we may learn more about this great conqueror. We do know that he conquered everything

west of the Euphrates to the eastern shore of the Mediterranean, that his armies marched south to the end of the Sinai Peninsula and north to the mountains of Cappadochia in what is now central Turkey, and that he defeated and conquered the Elamites of southern Iran. Sargon took the title "King of the Four Corners of the Earth."

Sargon didn't allow Sumerians to administer to the governments of city-states in his empire. Sargon appointed Akkadians to rule the people. In this way, Akkadian, rather than Sumerian, became the common language of his empire.

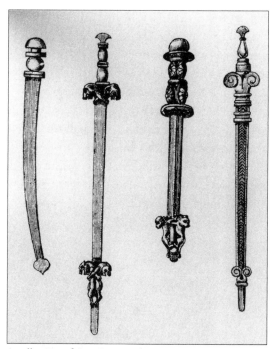

A collection of Assyrian swords.
Bible Encyclopedia

His conquered lands did not submit peacefully to his rule. According to an article by Barbara Nevling Porter in the collection *A Reader's Companion to Military History*, Sargon recorded the events of his reign on a clay tablet:

In my old age of 55, all the lands revolted against me, and they besieged me in Agade "but the old lion still had teeth and claws." I went forth to battle and defeated them: I knocked them over and destroyed their vast army. "Now let any king who wants to call himself my equal, Wherever I went, let him go."

Sargon's empire expanded under his grandson Naram-sin. But by 2095 B.C., the Akkadian Empire, struggling against civil war and wild tribesmen from the Iranian mountains, collapsed. The empire set the precedent, though, for a long succession of empires that engulfed the Land of the Two Rivers up to modern times—the Third Dynasty of Ur, which was overthrown by the Elamites and the Semitic Amorites; the First Babylonian Empire; the Assyrian Empire; the Second Babylonian Empire; the Persian Empire; the Arab Empire; and various Turkish empires.

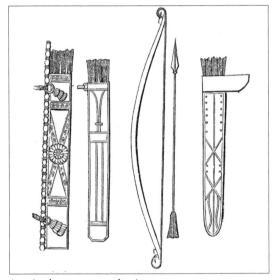

Assyrian bow, arrow, and quivers.
Bible Encyclopedia

The Sea Peoples

The Restless Isles

(c. 1200–1100 B.C.)

"The Isles were restless, disturbed among themselves at one and the same time." These words are carved on the wall of a temple at Medinet Habu. The "Isles" were Crete, the Cycladic Islands, Rhodes, Cyprus, and mainland Greece—the area the Hittite emperor called Ahhiyawa (the Hittite version of Achaea). The Hittite emperor recognized Achaea as one of the great powers of the civilized world, along with Egypt, Babylon, Assyria, and his own empire. From Hittite records on baked clay tablets made between 1339 and 1190 B.C., we learn that the high king of the Achaean Confederation and the Hittite emperor had friendly relations. We learn that Troy (Wilusiya to the Hittites) was a Hittite vassal, and Miletus (on the coast of Asia Minor) owed allegiance to the high king of Achaea. One of the Trojan vassal kings was named Alaksandrus (apparently a Hittite version of Alexandros—the alternative name of the Trojan prince, Paris). Both the Achaeans and the Trojans were descended from the ancient Minyans, a people identified by a distinctive type of pottery. The Dorians, a Greek-speaking people slightly less civilized than the Achaean, were also Minyan descendants. Although a vassal state of the Hittite Empire, Troy also seems to have had close ties to the Achaean Confederation.

Relations between Achaea and the Hittite Empire gradually began to cool. According to O. Gurney's book *The Hittites*, we learn that between 1250 and 1220 B.C., the king of Achaea began encroaching on Hittite lands and had to be driven back.

At that time in history, Egypt, Babylon, and Assyria were all unified empires, with a single monarch who brooked no rivals. Achaea (as we know from both the works of Homer and documents found at Pylos and Knossos) was ruled by a mob of petty kings who more or less followed the orders of the high king of Mycenae. The Hittite Empire was another collection of petty kingdoms, with neither a common religion nor a common language to unite them. The Hittites had one thing no other nation had—a near monopoly on iron working. (Note: Iron has been somewhat overrated as a material for weapons. Wrought iron is tougher than bronze, and it will hold an edge better, but bronze swords were still effective in the thousand years before iron became common. In a contest between a warrior using a bronze sword and one using iron, the skill of the warrior was far more important than the metal of his blade. Iron's greatest advantage was its wide availability.)

The "restlessness of the Isles" suddenly turned the eastern Mediterranean civilizations upside down. Around 1250 B.C., the armies of the Achaean Confederation defeated the armies of Troy and its many allies, and destroyed the city. Troy had allies on both sides of the Aegean Sea—Thracians, Ciconians, and Paeonians on the west side, and Dardanians, Mysians, Meionians, Carians, and Lycians on the east. The Dorian Greeks were Trojan allies.

Following the defeat of their Trojan vassal, the Hittites's relations with the Achaeans became even more strained. Both the Achaean Confederation and the Hittite Empire experienced internal troubles. In Achaea, a civil war shortly before the Trojan War resulted in the destruction of the city of Thebes. After the war, the heirs of Achilles remained hostile to the house of Agamemnon. The internal problems of the Hittite Empire were even worse. Madduwattas, a vassal of the Hittite emperor, turned against the emperor after a Hittite army rescued him from an Achaean force. Madduwattas convinced the powerful Hittite vassal state of Arzawa to rebel. With the help of Arzawa and the Achaeans, Madduwattas conquered most of the western provinces of the Hittite empire. At about the same time, the Phrygian people (who had moved from Thrace to northeast Anatolia) began attacking the empire.

Then around 1220 B.C., the people of the "Isles," (the nations the Egyptians called the "Peoples of the Sea") moved down the coast of Asia Minor and Syria and attacked Egypt. They coordinated their attack from the east with the Libyans (known to the Egyptians as the Meshwesh), who attacked Egypt from the western desert. Among the "Sea Peoples" named by the Egyptians in this first attack are the Akaiwasha (identified by modern scholars as the Achaeans), the Tursha (or the Tursenoi or Etruscans), the Luka (also known as the Lycians), the Shekelesh (believed to be the Sicilians), and the Peleset (or Philistines). The Egyptians, under Pharaoh Merneptah, defeated both the Sea Peoples and the Libyans. They celebrated the victory as a holiday for years afterwards as the "Day of the Slaying of the Meshwesh."

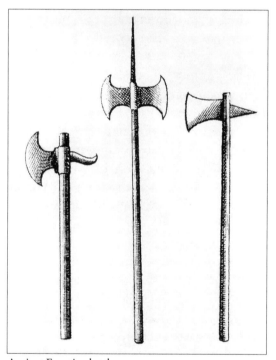

Ancient Egyptian battle axes.
Encyclopedia of Source Illustrations

Less than 30 years later, Egypt faced another invasion by the "Peoples of the Sea." This was bigger, and the attackers came by both land and sea. This time, there were no Achaeans among the attackers, but there was another Greek nation—the Dorians.

A carving on the wall at Medinet Habu relates what happened :

No land stood before them beginning with Kheta (the Hittite Empire), Kedi (Cilicia), Carchemish, Arvad and Alashiya (Cyprus). They destroyed them, and assembled in their camp in one place in the midst of Amor (Amurru, the old name of Palestine).

The Egyptian pharaoh, Ramses III, followed their progress down the eastern shore of the Mediterranean. He was prepared to meet them. The land army of the Sea Peoples was mostly infantry spearmen, and was burdened with ox carts carrying loot and captives. It was an easy foe for the Egyptian charioteers, with their powerful composite bows. Egypt, unlike the Hittites and other Asian powers, had not been weakened by civil war. The Sea Peoples fleet looked as if it might be more formidable, but Ramses predicted where it would enter the Nile before landing. He prepared an ambush with archers and spearmen on the shore, and galleys stripped for action hiding among the reeds. Of the Sea Peoples, the scribe wrote: "Their hearts were confident, full of their plans." They were traveling serenely under sail as they glided into the big river.

The Egyptian galleys attacked. They were using oars, which made them more maneuverable than the enemy ships. The invaders had no time to put their own oars in place. There was no ramming. The Egyptian ships were loaded with archers. They mowed down the Sea Peoples, who depended on swords and spears. The Egyptians boarded the enemy ships after most of their crews had been shot down. They capsized some by pulling down their masts. The Sea Peoples who tried to reach shore were shot in the water by the land-based archers.

Ramses' scribe recorded his master's boast:

Those who reached my frontier, their seed is not; their heart and soul are perished forever. As for those who assembled before them on the sea, the full flame was in their front, before the harbor-mouths, and a wall of metal on the shore surrounded them. They were dragged, capsized and laid low upon the beach; slain and made heaps.

The destruction of the Sea Peoples wasn't complete. Some of the Peoples of the Sea returned home, such as the Luka, who came from Lycia. Others settled in new lands. The Philistines, who claimed they came from Crete, went to Palestine (which, in fact, is named for the Philistines). The Tursha, who came from Asia Minor, went to Italy and became the Etruscans. The Shardana, islanders who had once been Egypt's favorite mercenaries but who fought with the attackers in the Battle of the Nile, ended up in Sardinia.

The passage of the Sea Peoples left the eastern Mediterranean shore depopulated and disorganized. Semitic tribes moved in from the desert. The Canaanites occupied what is now Lebanon and became known as Phoenicians. Hebrews crossed the Jordan to the south and began a long conflict with the Philistines. Arameans spread out all over the area, and Aramaic became a common language.

In Achaean Greece, the brilliant civilization of the Mycenaeans disappeared. For many years, this was believed to have been caused by an invasion by the Dorians from the north. But the discovery that clay tablets excavated at Knossos in Crete and Pylos on the Greek mainland in the "Linear B" script were in Greek (and could be read) destroyed that notion. The Pylos tablets show that the city was preparing for an invasion from the *south* just before its destruction. In the book

Rise of the Dorians, Ivor Gray Nixon presents a most plausible explanation. After the failure of the second attempt to invade Egypt, he argues, the Dorians in that expedition invaded Crete instead of returning home. From Crete, they struck at Pylos, then moved on the rest of the Achaean cities.

The first attack by the Sea Peoples, Nixon says, was organized by the Achaean victors of the Trojan War. Full of hubris, the Achaeans took advantage of the disintegrating Hittite Empire when they decided to move south and conquer Egypt. Their defeat hastened the disintegration of their own confederation. The heirs of Achilles joined the Dorians, who then attacked the Achaeans occupying Trojan territory. After liberating what was left of Troy, they gathered the Trojans and their allies together for a new attack on Egypt. The attempt failed, but it wiped out the Egyptian and Hittite possessions in Syria and opened the way for the desert tribes to take over.

Even more important than all the political reshuffling in the Middle East was the effect on technology. The Hittites had a near monopoly on iron working. Iron workers left the empire and spread around the Mediterranean. But it wasn't until the Sea Peoples gave the Hittite Empire in Anatolia the *coup de grace* that iron working became general. The Sea Peoples captured iron weapons from the Hittites and liked what they had found; they took iron workers with them. That was a revolutionary development. Bronze was always expensive. Copper is much more scarce than iron. And tin, the other necessary component of bronze, is fairly rare. Only the rich and powerful could afford bronze weapons and

Egyptian charioteers similar to this routed the Sea Peoples's land army.

armor. Most Bronze Age settlements (in places such as Greece and Anatolia) were castles—fortified residences for a chief and a handful of his retainers. In Troy, Mycenae, and Tiryns, the majority of the population lived outside the castle walls, with the understanding that they could seek protection from the castle should an attack come. The Mycenaean kings and nobles were buried with dozens of bronze swords, but the common soldier was lucky to have a bronze-tipped spear. Some Bronze Age warriors simply threw stones. Iron is one of the most plentiful minerals on earth, so it made weapons affordable. Cheap iron weapons changed society. Suddenly everyone could afford a sword and an iron spear.

The leaders of the two Sea Peoples expeditions (probably Achaean and Dorian warlords) are unknown, but they managed a mammoth organizing project by creating an army and a navy out of warriors from so many diverse nations. They failed to conquer Egypt, but few military leaders have contributed to such a major change in human history.

3

Cyrus the Great

The Shepherd King

(c. 576–529 B.C.)

They called him Kourash, which means shepherd. They did not call him this because anyone expected this infant boy, the son of Cambyses, the king of Anshan, Parsumash, and Parsa, would ever tend sheep, but because a Persian king was expected to be the shepherd of his people. We know him as Cyrus, the name the Greeks gave him after he became famous. Cyrus was a Persian, related to a people who entered what is now Iran many years earlier. The relatively minor tribes his father ruled were vassals of the Medes, another Iranian people, who conquered a considerable empire, extending from Anatolia well into Central Asia.

Cyrus's early life is obscured by myth. According to legend, Cyrus's mother was Mandane, daughter of Astyages, the high king of the Medes. Astyages supposedly dreamt that his grandson would overthrow him. Mandane had only just become pregnant, but Astyages sent for her and kept her in the palace until her son was born. Then he ordered his most trusted servant, Harpagus (steward of the palace and a general in the army), to take the baby and kill it. Harpagus, instead of killing the infant, placed the baby with a local herdsman and reported that Cyrus was dead. Years later, Astyages discovered the truth. He ordered Harpagus to explain what he had done with the baby, and Harpagus confessed that he did not kill the child. King Astyages was furious, and forced Harpagus to then eat his own son's body as punishment.

It makes a good grisly story, the kind the Greeks relished, because it shows the barbarity of the Medes and the Persians. It also sets the scene for Harpagus's revenge. Cyrus was allowed to return to his birth parents, and his rise to power began in earnest.

One source of Cyrus's power was that his country was the home of the Nisayan horses, the best cavalry mounts in the world. Another source of power was Cyrus's Persian highlanders. The Persians were illiterate farmers and herders. According to the Greeks, they learned only three things—to ride, to shoot, and to tell the truth. Their strength, as with the Scythians of the steppes, was that they were all horse archers. They also admired and followed clever war leaders.

Cyrus, being such a leader, was able to unite the Persian tribes. Astyages became quite worried. He summoned Cyrus to Ecbatana, his capital. Cyrus refused to come, because he felt the invitation was a trap. Astyages sent two armies against Cyrus. The first was led by Harpagus; the second (a week behind the first) was led by Astyages himself.

The first clash was a bloody draw. Cyrus had better troops, but Harpagus was a more experienced general. Then, as Astyages's army approached, Harpagus suddenly switched sides. He explained to Cyrus that a battle was necessary to get Astyages within reach; the Median king would think he would arrive in time to crush the Persians and gain all the glory. Instead, the combined armies of Cyrus and Harpagus crushed the forces of Astyages. Then Cyrus did something unprecedented for the time: He spared Astyages's life, and allowed him to live in luxury.

The reason for his merciful action is simple. Years before, Cyrus had visited the site of Susa, the capital of Elam. There was a stone tablet by the ruins of a palace, and Cyrus found someone who could read it to him. It said:

> *I, Assur-bani-pal, great king of all lands, took the carved furniture from these chambers; I took the horses and mules with gold-adorned bits from the stables. I burned with fire the bronze pinnacles of the temple; I carried off to Assyria the god of Elam and all his riches; I carried off the statues of thirty-two kings, together with the mighty stone bulls that guarded the gates. Thus I have entirely laid waste to this land and slain those who dwelt in it. I have laid their tombs open to the sun and have carried off the bones of those who did not venerate Assur and Ishtar, my lords—leaving the ghosts of those dead forever without repose, without offerings of food and water.*

A few years after setting up that tablet, Assur-bani-pal (the "great king of all lands") was dead, hounded in his last days by rebels. In another 15 years, Nineveh, his capital, was obliterated. Cyrus knew that the Assyrian way was not the way to build an empire. In his tradition, a king was a shepherd, not a wolf. Instead of laying waste to the land of the Medes and slaughtering its inhabitants, Cyrus appointed Median officials to share in the government of his new empire. And he made Harpagus one of his top officers.

The Shepherd soon learned that Astyages was not the only wolf in the world. The Median king's brother-in-law, the very rich and aggressive Croesus, the king of Lydia, saw an opportunity to expand his kingdom eastward. He consulted the Greek oracle at Delphi; if he crossed the frontier with Media, the oracle said, he would destroy a great empire. Convinced that the "great empire" was Cyrus's, Croesus sent his troops across the boundary. The Lydian cavalry, equipped with the long lance, was considered the best in Asia Minor, but Cyrus's horse archers engaged them in guerrilla warfare in the mountains of Cappadocia. With winter approaching, the Lydians headed home while Croesus called for his many allies—the Egyptians, the Babylonians, and the Spartans—to join him in a new offensive in the spring.

Cyrus did not wait for spring. He followed the Lydians out of the mountains, and when the two armies met on the plains, he had a surprise for his enemy. Cyrus's attack was led by archers riding baggage camels. The Lydian horses had never seen camels before. The unfamiliar sight and smell panicked them. The Persian army drove the disorganized Lydians behind the walls of Sardis, Croesus's capital. The Lydian capital was built on a hill, one side of which was so precipitous that it was only lightly guarded. According to the Greek historian Herodotus, a Lydian soldier accidentally dropped his helmet down the cliff. As a native, he knew the way down the cliff, so he climbed down to retrieve it. An alert Persian witnessed this, and noted the path the guard had taken. The Persians waited until there were no guards on the wall above the cliff, then they climbed up the cliff, scaled the wall, and took the city.

Croesus, Herodotus says, built a funeral pyre on which to immolate himself if the Persians broke in. He climbed to the top of it and ordered the torch bearers to light the fire. According to one report, he died in the fire. But Herodotus says Cyrus had the fire extinguished and made Croesus one of his advisers for the rest of his life. Cyrus's record of providing amnesty to his former enemies makes that story entirely possible.

Croesus had conquered the Greek cities on the shore of the Aegean. Cyrus reconquered them, and added these valuable ports to his empire. Then, because the nomad Scythians were troubling the eastern parts of his empire, he marched east. He drove the Scythians back and extended the empire north, deep into the steppes of the Caucasus and east to the border of modern India.

Ancient Persian shields and spears.
Sunday Book

While Persia's northern and eastern boundaries were temporarily secure, there was still a major threat in the west—the powerful Babylonian Empire. Cyrus's conquests in the east enabled him to enlist thousands of the nomad and semi-nomad horse archers. He felt strong enough to confront the Babylonian lion. The great Babylonian conqueror, King Nebuchadnezzar, was dead. The new king, old Nabu-naid, was busy changing modes of worship and oppressing his people.

Cyrus and his army appeared out of the mountains and attacked the Babylonian army commanded by Belshazzar, Nebuchadnezzar's son. They attacked behind a wind-whipped wildfire they ignited, and shot down the Babylonian charioteers from the backs of their Nisayan chargers. Babylonians stampeded through the gates of the Median Wall, Babylon's frontier fortification. Nabu-naid fled. Belshazzar and his troops prepared to defend the impregnable walls of Babylon. Then the mighty Euphrates, the river that ran through Babylon, became dry. Cyrus had diverted the river, and he and his men entered the city through the water gate. There was no battle. A short time later, the Persians captured the fugitive Nabu-naid. As he had done with other fallen enemies, Cyrus kept the old king in luxury until he died.

After being crowned as king of Babylon, Cyrus issued a decree that has been called the world's first charter of human rights. The decree was inscribed on a clay cylinder, which is currently displayed at the British Museum in London. Scholars there have translated the text on the cylinder:

I announce that I will respect the traditions, customs, and religions of the nations of my empire and never let any of my governors and subordinates look down on or insult them as long as I am alive.... I will never let anyone take possession of movable or landed properties of others by force without compensation. While I am alive, I will prevent unpaid, forced labor. Today I announce that everyone is free to choose a religion. People are free to live in all religions and take up a job provided that they never violate other's rights. No one will be penalized for his or her relatives' faults. I will prevent slavery, and my governors and subordinates are obliged to prohibit exchanging men and women as slaves within their own ruling domains. Such a tradition should be exterminated the world over.

The edict of Cyrus was inscribed in cuneiform on a large clay cylinder, often called the Cylinder of Cyrus, which is now housed in the British Museum. Cyrus also issued an edict to free all the Jews captured by Nabu-naid and the Babylonians, allowing them to return to Jerusalem and rebuild their Temple. The Shepherd King intended to end all kinds of oppression in his vast empire—the largest the world had ever seen. It extended from the Aegean and the Mediterranean to the Hindu Kush and the Indus, from the endless steppes of what is now Russia to the Persian Gulf and the Indian Ocean.

But Cyrus discovered that keeping the peace in such a vast area was almost impossible. In the east, the Massagatae (a Scythian tribe) had resumed raiding local settlements. Cyrus put himself at the head of his army and marched toward the rising sun. It was his last march. He was wounded in battle against

This clay cylinder relates Cyrus's great edict.
Photo courtesy of the British Museum

the Scythians. Like a good shepherd, he died protecting his flock. Cyrus created the largest empire of his time. But his greatest legacy is the "charter of rights" impressed on the Cylinder of Cyrus, which decrees the themes of his rule: respect for the gods of all people, just and peaceful rule, and the power and glory of the empire.

Legend states that Cyrus died in 529 B.C., while putting down a rebellion in the northeast region of his empire. Herodotus relates that Cyrus died during a fierce battle with the Massagetae. Croesus advised Cyrus not to continue in the attack, but Cyrus disregarded his counselor. Queen Tomyris assumed control of the Massagetae army after Cyrus killed her son. The Persian army suffered many casualties, including its leader, Cyrus. After the battle, Tomyris ordered that Cyrus's body be found. It is rumored that she dipped his head in blood to avenge the death of her son.

The tomb of Cyrus is now a UNESCO World Heritage Site, and lies in the ruins of Pasargadae. Although the city is in ruins, Cyrus's tomb remains mostly intact, and has been partially restored.

After the death of Cyrus the Great, his son (Cambyses II) succeeded him as king of Persia. Cambyses may have killed his own brother to cement his hold on the throne. After his death, the throne was taken by Darius the Great, a member of a collateral branch of the Persian royal family.

4

Sun Tzu

The Art of War

(544–496 B.C.)

Sun Tzu was born in a time the Chinese call the Age of the Warring States. According to legend, Sun Wu (Tzu is an honorific title bestowed upon him after death) was a member of the landless aristocracy and worked as a mercenary. He also wrote a military treatise, known as the bing-fa (*The Art of War*). His book attracted the attention of Helu, the king of Wu. The king asked Sun if he could command troops as well as write about strategy. Sun replied that he could. Helu sent him a company of 180 concubines and asked him to drill them. Sun lined up the women, put the king's two favorite concubines in command of two groups, gave them halberds, and explained how they were to face left, right, and to the rear at his command. He explained the movements five times and told them three times that they were to execute his orders when he beat a drum.

When he beat the drum, the women all laughed. "If the words are not clear and the commands not explicit, it is the commander's fault," Sun said. He then repeated everything he had said before. Again, he beat the drum. And again, the women only laughed. "If the instructions and commands have been made clear and are not carried out in accordance with military law, it is a crime on the part of the officers," he said. He ordered the king's two favorite concubines beheaded. The king tried to interfere. "When the commander is at the head of the army, he need not accept all the sovereign's orders," Sun said. The concubines were executed.

A portrait of the warrior and military strategist Sun Tzu.

When Sun tried the drill again, all of his commands were executed perfectly. "The king likes empty words," Sun Tzu said later. "He is not capable of putting them into practice."

King Helu made Sun Tzu the commander of his army. In that capacity, he defeated the armies of Chu, Qin, and Chi.

In spite of his bloody adventure with the concubines, Sun Tzu's aim in war was to achieve results with as little killing as possible. His emphasis was on subtlety and deception rather than brute force. The British military commentator Basil H. Liddel Hart said Sun's writings "have never been surpassed in comprehensiveness or depth of understanding." Each of the 13 chapters of *The Art of War* is a collection of verses. According to a translation by Samuel B. Griffith, the chapters are:

1. Estimates
2. Waging War
3. Offensive Strategy
4. Dispositions
5. Energy
6. Weaknesses and Strengths
7. Maneuver
8. The Nine Variables
9. Marches
10. Terrain
11. The Nine Varieties of Ground
12. Attack by Fire
13. Employment of Secret Agents

These ideas have been treasured by Chinese and Japanese commanders for centuries, but only in the 20th century have good translations become available. Sun Tzu has, of course, thoughts on using such things as chariots and crossbows, but most of his book is concerned with such matters as strategy, espionage, character, and leadership—factors in war that are timeless and unchanging. Sun Tzu's principles emphasize intelligence and creativity on the part of the commander.

Western military thought has traditionally been more concerned with overwhelming the enemy with firepower than deceiving them with maneuver and secret agents. And in modern war, because of often unbroken front lines, heavy equipment, and extreme dependence on supply lines, it is extremely difficult to apply Sun Tzu's precepts. That is not true of guerrilla warfare. Guerrillas make up for their lack of numbers and firepower by employing Sun Tzu's ideas. That's one reason Western military leaders should become more familiar with his writings. Sun Tzu's ideas are just as valid now as during the period of the Warring States.

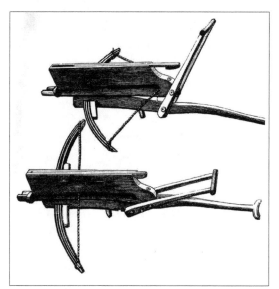

This type of repeating crossbow made Chinese armies a formidable foe in the time of Sun Tzu.
Natural History

5

Alexander the Great

The King Who Would Be a God

(356–323 B.C.)

A general at age 16, a king at 20, conqueror of the world's mightiest empire at 26, dead at 33—Alexander of Macedon (known as Iskander in Muslim lands) became a leading figure in the legends of both the East and West.

Alexander conquered an empire even larger than that of Cyrus, and he did it in a phenomenally short time. That, however, is not his greatest impact on history. Alexander established outposts of Greek civilization (Europe's most advanced) as far from its homeland as Central Asia and India. He also incorporated aspects of Persian culture into his court. His conquests created the "Hellenistic World," a remarkable blend of European and Asian culture.

Alexander inherited a magnificent military machine from his father, Philip II of Macedon. Philip had improved the traditional Greek phalanx and added other kinds of troops. He had, for example, field and siege artillery—machines to cast stones and spears using the elasticity of twisted ropes of sinew or hair. He had engineers. He had cavalry (the Macedonian nobles were all horsemen). He had light infantry (archers, slingers, and javelin men). His phalangites wore lighter armor than their Greek counterparts, carried smaller shields, and used spears that were twice as long as the Greek weapon. To connect the cavalry with the infantry, Philip had the hypaspists—elite infantry armed similar to the Greek phalangites, but trained to fight in small, mobile groups.

Philip II used his army to dominate the Greek city-states. Then he moved to invade Persia and established a bridgehead on the eastern shore of the Hellespont. But at the beginning of the operation, he was assassinated, and Alexander became king.

Alexander the Great.

Young Alexander had been given the best education possible; his tutor was none other than Aristotle. One lasting effect of his education was his love for the *Iliad*. He kept a copy of it at all times. His mother, Olympia, repeatedly reminded him that he was a descendant of both Achilles and Heracles, and his aim in life was to live up to the reputations of the heroes of the Trojan War.

As soon as he became king, he executed not only his father's assassin, but anyone (there were several) who might dispute his claim to the throne. Alexander intended to carry his father's plan to conquer Persia, but before he could cross into Asia, the city of Thebes (which had been incorporated into Philip's Hellenic League) revolted. Alexander besieged the city. When his troops broke in, they massacred the inhabitants. All the surviving Thebans were enslaved. The other cities in the League of Corinth (which had been on the point of joining the rebellion) hastily made peace with the young king. With his base secured, Alexander commenced with his father's plan of conquering Persia.

The King of Persia, Darius III, certainly had capable generals, but the first one to meet Alexander, Aristes, was not one of them. Aristes had 20,000 Persian cavalry and was supported by Memnon of Rhodes, a Greek mercenary with 20,000 infantry. Memnon advised retreating and leaving the Greeks and Macedonians nothing but scorched earth. Aristes overruled Memnon. Instead of retreating, he decided to hold the east bank of a small river, the Granicus. And for his first-line troops, he used his cavalry instead of the traditionally rock-solid Greek phalanx. But attacking—not holding positions—is the strong suit of cavalry.

Alexander took the Persian defensive posture as a sign of a lack of spirit. He led his own cavalry, better equipped for close fighting, into the river, up the bank, and through the Persian horsemen. The crest of Alexander's helmet was cut off and he barely escaped death from the sword of the Persian noble named Spithridates. But Alexander never feared death. A descendant of a hero and a demigod, he was sure he had the favor of the gods.

Alexander's charge put the Persian horsemen to flight; he didn't bother to chase them. The Persian soldiers he captured were released to go home. But when thousands of surrounded Greek mercenaries surrendered, Alexander killed 90 percent of them and enslaved the remainder. He decided they were traitors to the Greek cause, although Greek mercenaries had been fighting in Persian armies for decades, and few Greeks anywhere subscribed to Alexander's conception of his campaign as a crusade against barbarians. Years later, he found a Greek-speaking town in Central Asia. The inhabitants were descended from Greeks captured by Persians centuries before and transported to the heart of the Persian Empire. The town's citizens joyfully opened their gates to their countrymen. Alexander massacred them all.

Whether by design or good luck, Darius III placed an army behind Alexander, cutting him off from his supply bases. As soon as he heard the news, Alexander turned his army around and attacked the Persians, who were holding the opposite bank of a river that ran into the Gulf of Issus. Alexander again led the charge, this time on foot at the head of his infantry. He located where Darius was in the line and drove straight at him. Darius did not have Alexander's fearlessness. He fled in his chariot, leaving his wife, his mother, and his daughters to the mercy of the Greeks. Luckily for them, Alexander treated his captives as royalty, with all the respect due queens and princesses. The Macedonian king was unusual among ancient conquerors in that he generally forbade rape and abuse of women, except in cases where he ordered the massacre or enslavement of a whole town.

After the Battle of Issus, Darius offered to give Alexander the western part of his empire if he would end the war. Alexander, in reply, demanded that Darius address him as King of Asia and recognize him as an overlord. Darius stayed near Babylon and did little to impede Alexander as he moved down the eastern shore of the Mediterranean. The goal of this operation was to destroy the bases of the superior Persian navy, which was mostly Phoenician (with some Greek mercenaries, such as Memnon of Rhodes, a veteran of the Battle of Granicus). Memnon didn't survive long, and Alexander captured his wife, a Persian beauty named Barsine. He reportedly married a woman named Barsine, who bore him a son, but he divorced her after he discovered that she cherished a few pieces of jewelry inscribed, "The love of Memnon of Rhodes."

On his march along the coast, Alexander was generous to cities that submitted without a siege. At Smyrna, Alexander offered to pay for the reconstruction of the temple of Artemis, if the citizens would record his generosity with an inscription on the wall. The citizens told him it would be improper for a god to dedicate offering to other gods. The citizens were flattering the conqueror, but Alexander took them seriously.

He continued on into Egypt, while King Darius sat in Mesopotamia doing nothing. In Egypt, Alexander visited the temple of the god Ammon at the Siwah Oasis. The priests of Ammon received him with great ceremony and assured him that Ammon and Zeus were the same god, and that Alexander himself was the son of Ammon. Alexander considered the facts. He had twice defeated much

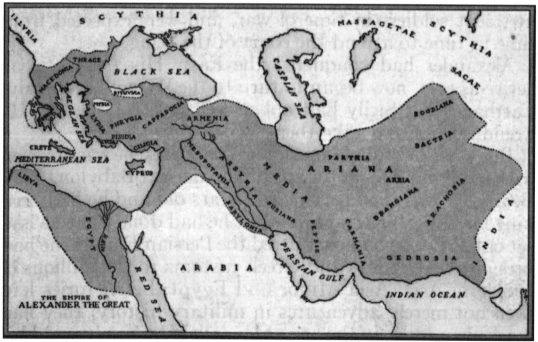

The empire of Alexander the Great.

larger armies and captured cities like Tyre, probably the strongest fortress in the world. He had narrowly escaped death numerous times. In two years, he had conquered half of the huge Persian Empire. He probably *was* a god. He began to adopt the manners of the divine Egyptian Pharaoh and the semi-divine King of Persia.

When Darius made no move against him, Alexander moved first. King Darius was waiting for him at a place called Gau Gamela (which means "grazing place of the camel") with an enormous army. It included elephants and chariots with scythe blades on their axles. The chariot had been obsolete as a weapon for centuries, but Darius had revived it. To use his chariots, the Persian king had cleared an enormous field of rocks and brush. When the Macedonians appeared, Darius planned to have his chariots and elephants break up their formation while his cavalry attacked them on both flanks.

Darius's preparation, however, destroyed his strategic mobility. His army was tied to the field and able to move in only one direction. Alexander's troops moved around the area and reconnoitered the situation from every angle. Alexander could easily have hit Darius from the rear or either flank, but he was looking for a definitive battle. Among other things, defeating such a huge army as the Persians fielded that way would demonstrate his divinity. His generals suggested a night attack, but Alexander said he wouldn't "steal a victory." This was more than bravado or chivalry. Alexander's strength was his ability to observe his enemies' movements and react to them: The Persians expected a night attack and stayed awake all night while the Macedonians and other Greeks slept.

Alexander's troops appeared on the edge of the prepared field facing the center of the Persian line. But instead of marching straight ahead, they marched obliquely to the right. Darius saw that they would strike his left flank and perhaps overlap it. And his chariots would not be able to drive over his painstakingly prepared field. The Persian king sent his left wing cavalry to stop the Macedonian flanking movement, which was led by Alexander and his elite cavalry. At the same time, he ordered the chariots and elephants to charge the king's Macedonian phalanx.

The charioteers demonstrated why the chariot was obsolete. It had originally been a mobile missile platform, with a driver and an archer. It was also useful for charging disorganized troops. But only the most highly trained horses *ridden* by highly trained troops could even hope to break through a steady line of spear points. Usually they couldn't. A driver standing *behind* a pair of horses had a hopeless task. The Macedonian phalanx stopped the chariots and the Macedonian archers shot down the charioteers. The elephants fared little better. The battalions of the phalanx opened lanes for them to pass through while the archers and javelin men shot both men and beasts.

The Persian cavalry pushed back some of the Greek cavalry, but Alexander's Macedonians pushed back the Persians. Alexander noticed that the movement of the Persian cavalry had uncovered the Persian infantry's left flank. That was where Darius stood in his chariot. Alexander rallied his men and charged directly at the Great King. Again, Darius fled. The Persian army started to disintegrate, but it delayed Alexander long enough to let the Great King get away.

A mural in Pompeii depicting the marriage of Alexander to Roxane in 327 B.C.

Alexander had himself crowned as Great King in Babylon, and had large numbers of his soldiers and officers take Persian wives, in an attempt to create lasting harmony between his Macedonian and Persian subjects. He also proclaimed a new doctrine. The Greeks had always believed that there were only two types of people: Greeks and barbarians. Alexander now proclaimed that all men were brothers. He aimed to unite all people in one harmonious kingdom. He then celebrated his coronation by plundering Persepolis, the Persian capital, killing all the male inhabitants, enslaving all the females, and burning the city.

He took up the pursuit of Darius, but never found him. The Persian king had been murdered by a man named Bessus, one of his nobles. Alexander caught the noble and had him crucified. He continued marching east and north. His army overran modern Afghanistan, and conquered most of what is now Tajikistan, Uzbekistan, and Pakistan. He wanted to go on through all of India, but his soldiers demanded to go home.

Alexander's last days were troubled. There were mutinies, and he murdered one of his own generals, Cleitus, in a drunken rage. In Babylon, he was stricken with a fever and died at the age of 33. After his death, his generals (after many civil wars) divided his empire among themselves. But even that fragmented empire carried Greek culture deep into Asia and stimulated international trade in products and ideas. Alexander's idea of the unity of humanity was centuries ahead of his time.

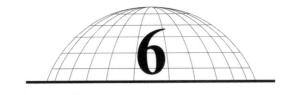

6

Chandragupta Maurya

East Meets West

(340–293 B.C.)

Alexander's incursion into India had effects in areas far beyond the places he actually visited. One such effect was in the kingdom of Magadha in northeastern India. Magadha was one of the two largest of the many small states that covered the Indian subcontinent. It was centered on the eastern portion of the Ganges Valley and was ruled by kings of the Nanda Dynasty.

Chandragupta Maurya was a general in the Magadha army and was born sometime in the fourth century B.C. His family origins are unknown, but there are a number of theories. One suggests that he was brought up by peacock trainers. Another theory is that he was the son of a Nanda prince. Legend has it that while simply a Magadha soldier, Chandragupta met Alexander the Great in the city of Taxila. Some historians believe that Alexander's uniting of the small states of what is now Afghanistan and Pakistan inspired Chandragupta to unite the states of India. First, though, he had to conquer the Magadha.

One Indian legend says Chandragupta got his idea for uniting India from a Brahman (a holy man) named Kautilya, who had been insulted by the king of Magadha. Kautilya has been called the "Indian Machiavelli." As with the Renaissance Italian, Kautilya was brilliant, cynical, and unscrupulous. He also wrote a book titled the *Arthasastra*, a guide to statecraft. Chandragupta led a revolt and ousted the Nanda dynasty in 322 B.C. to create the Maurya Empire in northern India.

Silver coins minted under Chandragupta Maurya in the third century B.C.

Alexander the Great died in 323 B.C. Theoretically, his heir should have been his son Alexander IV, born to his wife Roxane shortly after his death. However, an empire as vast as Alexander's could not be governed by a child, and the regions were soon divided among four generals. Seleucus was named governor of Babylon, but he soon began to move east. He began moving into Alexander's Indian conquests at the same time Chandragupta was making new Indian conquests, taking over the Punjab and other northwestern territories. Chandragupta declared war on Seleucus. In the penultimate battle, Chandragupta's army (which included a huge number of elephants) smashed the army of Seleucus. Seleucus surrendered all of Alexander the

Great's conquests in what is now Kashmir, Pakistan, and Afghanistan. To secure the peace, Seleucus gave his daughter to Chandragupta (or, according to some accounts, his son). In return, Chandragupta gave Seleucus 500 elephants.

Chandragupta's conquests did not end there. He created an empire that extended north to the Himalayas, west to include all of what is now Afghanistan and Pakistan, east to the delta of the Ganges, and south almost to the tip of India. For the first time in history, virtually all the states of India were united. The Mauryan Empire lasted 140 years.

Before Chandragupta united India, it was quite unfamiliar to Europeans. The Seleucid Empire sent diplomats to Chandragupta's court at Pataliputra (now Patna). Megasthenes, one of the envoys, sent back reports on the king's enormous palace, his highly organized bureaucracy, his secret service, and methods of government. For the country as a whole, it was an absolute monarchy. For cities, towns, and regions, it was democratic, with officials elected by the people.

Members of the Jain religious sect claim that towards the end of his life, Chandragupta Maurya became a Jain monk, abandoning the throne and moving to southern India. He meditated in a cave, where he practiced the most extreme form of Jain asceticism: He starved himself to death.

Elephants were an important part of Indian warfare. From India, their use spread to Persia, Macedonia, and Carthage.

7

Hannibal

Crossing the Alps

(247– c.183 B.C.)

Hannibal stood on the crest of a low range of hills that curved like a crescent toward the Roman lines. This was the moment he had spent his life preparing for, the moment he would repay Rome for all the injury it had done to his family and his empire. It was the spring of 216 B.C., and Hannibal was about to engage in the battle of Cannae.

In front of him, the Roman army stretched out almost endlessly. On their right wing, the Roman heavy cavalry was squeezed tightly between the Roman infantry and a river. The Roman commander, Gaius Tarentius Varro, was probably afraid of being flanked by the more numerous Carthaginian cavalry. To the left of those Romans, the bright sun shimmered on the iron armor of the Roman infantry, standing shoulder-to-shoulder, instead of in the usual Roman checkerboard formation. There were eight consular armies here—the largest force Rome ever fielded. On the far end of the line, almost out of sight, was the Roman light cavalry. Gaius Varro was stationed there. On the Roman right, the other consul, Lucius Aemilius Paullus, commanded. There were so many Romans that one man could not possibly command the whole army.

Consul Caius Terrentius Varro and Consul Lucius Aemilius Laullus commanded on alternate days of the battle. Paullus, similar to other Roman aristocrats, had an almost superstitious dread of Hannibal. The young Carthaginian general had already destroyed two Roman armies after doing the impossible: crossing the Alps (with an army that included elephants). He fought his way through the lands of the Gauls and managed to enlist thousands of them in his army.

This marble bust of Hannibal was found in Rome, and was apparently made during his lifetime.

The Romans finally defeated Hannibal, but his invasion of Italy changed the history of Rome and the history of the world. For many years afterwards, the phrase "Hannibal is at the gates!" meant death and disaster was near.

After Hannibal annihilated a Roman army on the shores of Lake Trasimene, the Romans elected Quintus Fabius Maximus, the most aristocratic Roman in public life, as dictator. Fabius then took his army around Italy, following Hannibal, hoping to cut off the Carthaginian foragers; and waiting for Hannibal to make a mistake.

But Hannibal didn't make mistakes. He marched through Italy, devastating farms and villages. Hannibal wanted to force the Romans into a major battle, but Fabius wouldn't oblige. Although Fabius's strategy was successful in avoiding a major confrontation, it was unpopular with many Romans, who considered it a form of cowardice.

The Roman citizens soon elected Varus and Paullus as consuls, and put each in charge of the two largest armies Rome had ever raised. When Hannibal began to approach Rome, the two armies joined together and prepared for battle at Cannae. Varus and Paullus were supposed to take turns commanding, and on the day of the battle the aggressive Varus (rather than the cautious Paullus) was in command.

Hannibal's desire for a pitched battle might seem strange. His army was less than half the size of the force Varus and Paullus commanded, and most of them were foreigners. His heavy cavalry were Gaulish and Spanish. His light cavalry were Numdians, Berber tribesmen from Africa. His best infantry were African, too, but few were Carthaginians. Much of his infantry were Gauls, Spaniards, and Italian hill tribesmen. He was taking this motley crew against a vastly larger army composed of the best soldiers in Europe.

But Hannibal was desperate, and his cross-country march to Italy from Spain was a mad enterprise. Rome and its Latin allies contained 6 million people. Carthage and all the African territory it controlled had a population less than 700,000. Hannibal had no way to use Carthage's meager resources; he was in the middle of hostile territory with no supply lines to Carthage or Spain. Besieging Rome was impossible.

Hannibal was following a different, and very subtle, strategy. He saw Rome as the oppressor of the people of Italy. Etruscans, Greeks, and Gauls had only recently been conquered. They wanted to be liberated from the Romans. Even the Latins were restive. If Hannibal could defeat the Romans in one great battle, the local people would turn to him as a liberator. Then he could enlist the trained, civilized soldiers of the Etruscan and Greek cities (and perhaps even the phalanxes of Latinium) and overwhelm the Romans.

Hannibal arranged his army with the Gaulish infantry—his most volatile troops—in the center. He made no attempt to hold the crescent of the hills. The center bowed out in front of the hills toward the Romans. On his left flank was the heavy cavalry. (They were "heavy" cavalry only because the cavalrymen, Gauls and Spaniards, were huge compared to the Romans.) They had little armor, and were armed with swords and javelins similar to the Roman *pila*—a spear point on a long iron rod attached to a heavy wooden shaft. Next to them were battalions of African heavy infantry, troops trained to fight as a phalanx. Then there were the Gaulish, Spanish, and Italian mountain infantry. More African infantry held the right end of the infantry line, and the Numidian light cavalry guarded the right flank.

The Romans clashed their spears on their shields and shouted their war cry. The Gaulish heavy cavalry exploded like an avalanche of flesh and crashed into the Roman heavy cavalry. The Gauls skewered the Roman with their javelins. They rode through them, over them, and disorganized them. The less numerous and more clumsy Roman heavy cavalry was soon annihilated.

On the other flank, the Numidians (who guided their horses with their knees and threw iron javelins with both hands) were swirling through and around Varus's light horse. One group of Numidians surrendered. Then, as the Romans were escorting them from the field, they pulled swords from under their long, white robes and cut down their attackers.

The Roman infantry had no idea that their cavalry was in trouble. They were busy pushing back the hated Gauls, who had advanced ahead of the rest of their army. The Gaulish center of the Carthaginian line slowly yielded, while the Carthaginian infantry on the flanks stayed immovable. The center of Hannibal's line, which once bowed outward, now bowed inward. The Romans became disorganized, so frantic were they to break through the Gauls. The Gauls fought back more fiercely as they were pushed up the slopes behind them. Parties of African regular infantry appeared from behind the hill crest to strengthen the line. And the heavy infantry on the flanks began to turn inward. The Romans were in a sack, pushed together so closely they couldn't use their weapons. At that point, the Carthaginian heavy cavalry, having finished off their Roman counterparts, charged the Roman infantry from behind.

That day, an estimated 70,000 Romans (out of an army of 86,000) perished. For the numbers of men engaged and the time it took, such a complete, slaughtering victory in a stand-up battle between two regular armies has seldom, if ever, been equaled. But Rome did not give up. The city strengthened its walls and raised another army.

Hannibal's elephants cross the Rhone River. They crossed the Alps as well, but the northern weather killed them off before Hannibal's big battles in Italy.

Hannibal stayed in Italy for years. He destroyed four more Roman armies and killed five more Roman consuls, but he could not win the war. He was eventually called back to Carthage, where his weakened army was defeated by a Roman army under Publius Cornelius Scipio.

But Hannibal inflicted more damage on Rome than either he or the Romans knew. The stalwart Roman farmers who were driven into the city by Hannibal became an urban proletariat who had to be appeased with free bread and circuses. The senators, such as Fabius, became obscenely rich from the troubles of the peasants, and demanded more and more slaves to work their estates. Leaders such as Marius and Sulla arose, enlisting the proletariat in their private armies, and the Roman Republic was plagued by seemingly interminable civil wars. One general, Julius Caesar, became so powerful that, under him, Rome was a Republic in name only. He was assassinated, but his heir, Augustus Caesar, became the first Roman emperor.

Hannibal spent the last years of his life fleeing from the Roman forces, taking refuge in Tyre and Ephesus. He committed suicide by poison on the eastern shore of the Sea of Marmera rather than surrender to his enemy, the Romans.

8

Qin Shih Huang

The Beast of Qin

(260–210 B.C.)

"He was a man with a prominent nose, large eyes, the chest of a bird of prey, the voice of a jackal, and the heart of a tiger or wolf." This description of the king of the northwest China kingdom of Qin was probably meant to be flattering. It was written by one of the king's counselors. The king, Cheng Wang, was only 13 years old when he mounted the throne. Long before Cheng Wang reached middle age, he dropped the title Wang (king) and resurrected the old title of emperor (Shih Huang). Unlike previous holders of the title, Qin Shih Huang was no figurehead. He would be remembered for millennia by the Chinese literati as the "Wild Beast of Qin."

Early China could be described as a country with a single culture and multiple governments. The earliest dynasty that we know of is the semi-legendary Hsia. The Hsia monarch was the first Chinese ruler to call himself *emperor*, but it seems that he had little more power than a feudal overlord, although he was revered as the choice of heaven. The Shang Dynasty (which began around 1600 B.C.), ruled in much the same way. As time passed, the Shang emperors grew less powerful. The last emperor, Chou Hsin, was hated for his debauchery and cruelty. In 1027 B.C., Wu Wang (leader of the Chou clan), defeated the Shang army. The Chou people were pioneers, farming virgin land in northwest China. They were also kept busy fighting off raiding nomads from the Mongolian steppes. The Shang army numbered 70,000; the Chou were only 45,000 strong. The Chou leader was also more realistic. He decided to title himself *king* rather than *emperor*.

Qin Shih Huang began many large projects, including building the precursor to the modern Great Wall of China.

In power, the Chou followed the traditional patterns. The feudal leaders had new faces, but they remained feudal leaders. China was in the process of switching from a bartering economy to a money-based economy, and peasants began to rent their land from the nobles instead of holding it by hereditary right. The nobles grew in power as the king's power shrank. In the end, the feudal lords became fully independent, resulting in governmental chaos.

The period the Chinese call the Age of the Warring States, an epoch of more than 200 years, was what historian Rene Grousset calls "a period of endemic warfare and appalling slaughter and massacres of whole civilian populations." The kingdom of Qin was the most troubled of those warring states. Qin had to contend not only with its Chinese rivals, but also with nomadic horsearchers from the steppes, particularly the ferocious Hsiung-nu, who a few hundred years later became known to Europeans as the Huns. To deal with the Huns and other nomads, the Qin kingdom developed horse archers of its own. The Qin horsemen, combined with infantry crossbowmen and spearmen, eventually drove the Huns into the Gobi.

The king of Qin saw that this powerful army could put an end to the warring in the Warring States. He absorbed the other kingdoms one after another and declared that he was now Qin Shih Huang. He accomplished this in spite of enemies (both external and internal). China in the third century B.C. was a tough place, and many people did not like the new king. Legend has it that one of the Qin generals presented Qin Shih Huang with 1,000 heads (of his enemies). The other generals grew despondent, thinking that they would never be able to match such a magnificent gift. The only solution apparent to the

generals was to assassinate the king. But Qin Shih Huang survived the assassination attempt, and promptly executed the rebelling generals.

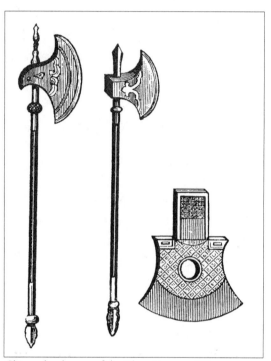

Chinese battle-axes of the Chou Dynasty, 500 B.C. *Arms & Armor*

But discontent manifests in many different ways. Many of the Qin generals expected to be made dukes and princes and given vast feudal holdings. They were disappointed. Qin Shih Huang turned Chinese society upside down. He divided the country into 36 districts (without regard for ancient feudal boundaries). Each was administered by three officials—a civil governor, a military governor, and a superintendent—each reporting directly to the emperor. He standardized the characters of written Chinese, so that although there were many different spoken dialects, the written language was the same everywhere in the empire. He standardized the weights and measures, and even the width of the axles of wagons and carriages so that all vehicles could travel in the ruts in the roads. He dug canals to drain swamps, making it possible to provide irrigation, and carry freight on canal boats. He linked a number of ancient walls to provide the basis of what became known as the Great Wall of China. His armies subdued the nomads of the north and conquered the barbarians of the south. In short, he founded the Chinese Empire. Many of his reforms can still be seen in the form of the modern Chinese government.

Today, Qin Shih Huang is remembered mainly for the army of life-size terracotta soldiers buried near his mausoleum. A total of 8,099 warriors and horses stand guard over the emperor's tomb. The figures were discovered in 1974 near Xi'an, in Shaanxi province. It is believed that it took 700,000 workmen nearly 38 years to complete the figures, each one appearing slightly different. They were armed with real weaponry, such as bows, swords, and halberds (which may have seen battle before being interred with the terracotta soldiers).

Interring these statues was a change from the earlier custom of burying *real* soldiers with the monarch. The substitution of statues for people may have been an act of humanity on the part of the emperor, or he may have just thought it was a terrible waste. The army, after all, was the basis of imperial power.

Qin Shih Huang was no gentle warrior. He was not a gentle emperor, either. But it was not because of his bloody conquests or his hard rule that later Chinese scholars denounced him as the "Wild Beast of Qin." It was because he burned all of the Confucian classics he could find. He believed that the classics were "backward-looking" and celebrated the ideals of feudalism. After his death, there was a revolution and a period of chaos. Order was restored and the empire revived by Liu Pang, who founded the Han Dynasty. The Han Dynasty was so successful that modern Chinese say they are the "sons of Han." And the name Han became a title of royalty among the Hsiung-nu and other nomads, pronounced in their guttural Turkish tongues as khan.

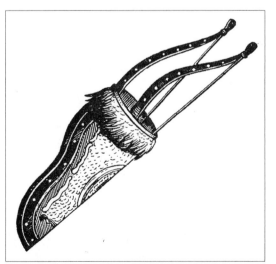

Bows, similar to these in a Chou dynasty bow case, were important weapons in ancient China.
Arms & Armor

9

Julius Caesar

Crossing the Rubicon
(100–44 B.C.)

When, after the Franco-Prussian War, the king of Prussia became emperor of Germany, he took for his title the name of a noble Roman family that thrived approximately 2,000 years earlier. Centuries before the German coronation, when Ivan the Terrible assumed the leadership of all Russian principalities, he took the same name for his title. Even earlier, the sultan of Turkey gave himself the same title. The German *kaiser*, the Russian *tsar*, and the Turkish *kaiser i rum* were all paying homage to a most remarkable man who became a major military leader late in life, learned generalship as he went along, and laid the foundations for one of the world's most influential empires.

Gaius Julius Caesar came from a patrician family, but he was also the nephew of Gaius Marius, a general who had once been a private soldier and became the champion of Rome's lower classes—the plebeians and the Italian non-citizens. The farmers driven off their land by Hannibal sold their farms to the landholding aristocrats—the patricians and the knights (nouveau riche plebeians)—for far less than they were worth. They could find little employment in the city, so Rome had to increase the taxes on conquered provinces to give the idle proletariat "bread and circuses." At the same time, the aristocrats

worked their greatly enlarged estates with slaves. With immense acreage and low labor costs, patrician wealth increased enormously. But with such quantities of land, greater quantities of fieldworkers were also needed. The demand for slaves was so great that sometimes Rome made war simply to obtain more slaves. According to General J.F.C. Fuller in his *Military History of the Western World*, "many of these rebellions and so-called wars were little more than slave hunts."

The more slaves who were imported, of course, the more Romans and non-Roman Italians became unemployed. Most of the farmers driven into Rome were not citizens, but allies from other Italian states. The Gracci brothers (tribunes for the plebeians), used their limited political powers to the utmost to get land for the plebeians and citizenship for the allies. For their pains, they were both assassinated, along with scores of their supporters.

Fed up with corruption in the Senate and oppression by the patricians, the people of Rome elected Gaius Marius, an old soldier and military hero, rather than a politician, as consul. Marius reorganized the army by consolidating the company-size maniples into battalion-size cohorts. Before Marius, the Roman military was a militia of all men who owned a certain amount of property and who were between the ages of 17 and 45. They served whenever needed in a war, and then returned to civilian life. Marius eliminated the property qualification and got soldiers from the proletariat. They were long-service troops. They took an oath to serve the general, not the republic. Marius also demanded that his veterans be given land after they retired.

Marius served as consul seven times—an unprecedented number. During that time, he often struggled with Lucius Cornelius Sulla, who was sponsored by the Senate and had his own private army. When he was in power, Marius was a ruthless military dictator. But Sulla was a monster. After Marius died, Sulla became the new dictator and reversed all of the liberalizing laws of the last century, while slaughtering anyone who might object.

When Sulla died, two of his lieutenants, Gaius Pompeius (also known as Pompey) and Marcus Licinius Crassus, became consuls and reversed many of Sulla's reactionary laws. Pompey was a young general who had won a number of astonishing victories and was awarded the title "Magnus" (the Great) by the senate. Crassus was a good journeyman general who had put down the slave revolt of Spartacus. Roman aristocrats automatically became officers during their military service, and the good ones became generals. More important than Crassus's military qualifications was that he was the richest man in Rome.

Julius Caesar, a young politician, managed to get along well with both Pompey and Crassus (the two ex-consuls), who hated each other. After serving as a governor of Roman provinces in Spain, Caesar returned to Rome to run for consul. He was supported by both Pompey and Crassus. But Caesar was always looking ahead. He didn't like his prospects after he finished his term as consul. It was customary for ex-consuls to be given governorships in the provinces. If the senate had its way, Caesar (the leader of the party of Marius) would go to the most remote parts of Africa. But Caesar proposed to the two ex-consuls—both powerful men, Pompey with his military reputation and his popularity, and Crassus with his money—that they divide the real power in Rome among themselves and take the governorships they wanted. They thus formed the First Triumvirate, an unofficial alliance of power. Crassus got Syria, home to an ancient civilization and gateway to the fabulously rich empires of the Orient. Pompey chose Spain, which was rich in silver and other metals; the gateway to the Atlantic; and the center of trade routes to Britain, Gaul, and Africa, and all of the rich Mediterranean.

Julius Caesar leads his troops into the mysterious island of Bretagne.
Library of Congress

Caesar was left with Gaul, a land of semi-barbarous tribes who still practiced human sacrifice and produced nothing a decent Roman would want, except field slaves. Roman holdings in Gaul amounted to little more than a strip of Mediterranean coast between the Alps and the Pyrenees, and Cis-Alpine Gaul, the northern tip of Italy. But like all good real estate, Gaul had position. It cut the land route between Pompey's province of Spain and Rome.

The First Triumvirate of Rome ended when Crassus attempted to conquer Parthia. The king of Suren, a vassal of the king of Parthia, was outnumbered four to one by the Romans. But he still killed Crassus and destroyed his army.

Caesar, on the other hand, conquered all of Gaul, tribe by tribe, and invaded Britain to keep the Britons from furnishing aid to their Gallic kinsmen. Caesar had some experience as a military leader in Spain, but his early campaigns in Gaul were marked by personal bravery and leadership rather than brilliant tactics or strategy. In his *Commentaries on the Gallic Wars*, Caesar (who always wrote in the third person) recorded one incident:

> The situation was critical and as no reserves were available, Caesar seized a shield from a soldier in the rear and made his way to the front line. He addressed each centurion by name and shouted encouragement to the rest of the troops, ordering them to push forward and open out their ranks so they could use their swords more easily. His coming gave them new heart and hope. Each man wanted to do his best under the eyes of his commander despite the peril.

Caesar's war reporting was aimed at the public. (Military heroes always seem to do well in Roman politics.)

Caesar had a highly trained, disciplined fighting machine to use against undisciplined Gauls, Teutons, and Britons. His opponents were less well armed, much less well trained, and had no ability to maneuver on command. His engineers built a bridge spanning the Rhine, something his enemies considered impossible. He used mechanical artillery to shoot from a distance. His troops had endlessly practiced using the pilum (a heavy javelin), the scutum (a huge, semi-cylindrical shield), and the gladius (a short, pointed sword) in combination—probably the most efficient close-quarters combat system in pre-gunpowder times. In Gaul, Caesar didn't have to be very innovative.

It was different after Pompey proclaimed himself the sole consul. Caesar crossed the Rubicon River, the boundary between his jurisdiction and Italy, thus making himself a rebel. He had only one legion with him; the rest were in various parts of Gaul. Theoretically, Pompey had 10 legions in Italy and eight in Spain. But eight of the Italian legions consisted of little but centurions and eagles. The senate ordered all magistrates to draft citizens and incorporate them into the legions. Caesar's legion was composed of veterans of real and recent combat. Pompey's troops were not; most of them, in fact, had never worked together.

But Caesar took no chances. He marched down the Adriatic coast (the least direct route and, therefore, the least guarded). He moved fast. As he marched, the troops being assembled for Pompey's army joined his. Caesar had always been the favorite general of the common people. Caesar's march became an avalanche. Pompey left Rome and retired to

Capua. Caesar flanked Pompey's advance guard and cut it off from the main body. The advance guard joined his army. Pompey and his remaining men sailed to Greece from Brundisium (Brindisi).

Instead of following, Caesar attacked Pompey's troops in Spain. He calculated (correctly) that Pompey would concentrate on building up his strength in Greece rather than attack Caesar's base in Italy. In Spain, Caesar conducted a series of brilliant flanking moves that forced his opponents into a position without water. Instead of trying to annihilate his enemies, he let his men fraternize with their fellow Romans. These enemies, too, joined Caesar's army.

Caesar now turned to Pompey. Eager to meet his rival, he crossed the Adriatic although he was short of ships and, unlike Pompey, had no navy. He managed to get only half of his men across. After the rest of his army, under Marc Antony, arrived, there followed months of fruitless maneuvering around the Balkans. Finally, Caesar and Pompey met in battle at Pharsalus. Pompey was defeated and fled to Alexandria, where he was assassinated.

Caesar returned to Rome with much pomp and circumstance, and was given many honors by the senate. He also began to reform the city of Rome: he passed a law preserving the operation of local farms and businesses, established rules to confiscate the wealth of a murderer, and cancelled 25 percent of all debt, endearing him to the general population.

Caesar also reformed the dole. He forbade those citizens wealthy enough to purchase their own grain from taking free grain from the government.

Caesar also took care of his former soldiers. He established veteran cities throughout Italy and the Roman Empire. He also made provisions for future soldiers to be provided for after their service ended.

One of the most influential reforms that Caesar institute was the revision of the Roman calendar. In 46 B.C., Caesar established the 365-day year (which required a leapyear every fourth year). This calendar was named the Julian calendar. Caesar also declared that the seventh month should have 31 days, and the senate then named that month July in honor of Julius Caesar.

Julius Caesar was immortalized by William Shakespeare, who erroneously claimed that Caesar's last words were "Et tu, Brute? Then fall, Caesar." In reality, Caesar's last words are unknown.

In addition, great works of public architecture were begun, including construction on the Curia Julia, the Forum of Caesar, and the Temple of Venus Genetrix. The senate, however, was not pleased with Caesar's actions. They felt that he was spending money too freely, and that he was planning to proclaim himself "King of the Romans"—a title and position that the senate feared.

In the year 44 B.C., a group of senators attacked Caesar on the steps of the Theatre of Pompey, and stabbed him to death. Caesar was deified by the Second Triumvirate of Rome (Octavius, Marc Antony, and Lepidus) in 42 B.C. Caesar's murderers were punished by proscription, an act that had not been used in the Roman Republic for many years.

Caesar's adopted son and heir, Octavian Caesar, took his father's place as head of the state and ruled as an absolute monarch, while preserving all the forms of republican government. Although called the "Imperator," or commanding general, he was the first Roman emperor.

10

Attila the Hun

The Scourge of God

(A.D. 405–453)

He was a man born to shake the races of the world, a terror to all lands, who in some way or other frightened everyone by the dread report noised abroad about him, for he was haughty in his carriage, casting his eyes about him on all sides, so that the proud man's power was to be seen in the very movements of his body. A lover of war, he was personally restrained in action, most impressive in council, gracious to suppliants, and generous to those to whom he had once given his trust.

According to C.D. Gordon in his book *The Age of Attila*, this description comes not from a friend, but an enemy, a Roman. It describes Attila the Hun.

Attila, to be sure, was no gentle warrior. But in the fifth century, plunder and massacre were common in all military operations, and assassination was a tool of statecraft. Priscus of Panim, an east Roman historian, left a record of one diplomatic mission to Attila. Its ostensible purpose was to negotiate with the Hunnish king over the return of fugitives who had fled to the Roman Empire. Its real purpose was to hire a Hunnish noble to kill Attila.

Priscus and the ambassador, Maximinus, with their party were invited to dine with Attila. After the Hunnish king graciously greeted each guest individually, servants brought in the food. Priscus described the feast:

While sumptuous food had been prepared—and served on silver plates—for the other barbarians and for us, for Attila there was nothing but meat on a wooden trencher. He showed himself temperate in all other ways, too, for gold and silver goblets were offered to the men at the feast, but his mug was of wood. His dress, too, was plain, having care for nothing other than to be clean, nor was the sword by his side, nor the clasps of his barbarian boots, nor the bridle of his horse, like those of other Scythians, adorned with gold or gems or anything of high price.

Priscus and Maximinus were not in on the murder plot, which was hatched by Chrysaphius, the Roman emperor's chamberlain; and involved Edeco, a Hunnish noble who was Attila's bodyguard and who was to do the killing; and Bigilas, the Roman mission's interpreter, who was to pay Edeco 50 pounds of gold. Attila discovered the plot, because Bigilas could not account for all the gold he was carrying. Instead of executing the treacherous diplomat, Attila kept him in chains until the Romans sent another 50 pounds of gold for his ransom.

Attila seems not to have acquired his fearsome reputation because his conduct was any more atrocious than the conduct of contemporary rulers. Actually, compared to leading Romans at the time, he was almost saintly. Attila's one-time friend and final opponent (the Roman general Aëtius) once thwarted a possible alliance of the Visigoths and the Vandals by convincing the Vandal king that the daughter of the Visigothic king was unworthy of his son. The Vandal king had the girl's ears and nose cut off and sent back to her father!

Attila was feared because he led a united Hunnish nation that appeared to be truly undefeatable. The Huns had defeated the Alans (Iranian nomads) whom the Romans considered the most formidable warriors in the world, and incorporated most of them into their nomad nation. The other Alans fled west, with some even joining the Ostrogoths. Next, the Huns let their Alanic vassals attack the Ostrogoths, another powerful barbarian nation. The surviving Ostrogoths fled in panic and, with their Visigothic cousins, entered the Roman Empire to seek protection from the Huns.

The Hunnish military establishment was the result of centuries of development by the Eurasian nomads. When they arrived in eastern Europe late in the fourth century, the superiority of their system became evident. Similar to the ancient Scythians, the Huns's prime weapon was the recurved composite bow. Though only about 3 feet long, it was flexible enough to fully draw a yard-long arrow. Bows with a draw weight of 100 pounds were not unusual. Bows such as this far outclassed any weapons to be found in western Europe. Even the famed English longbow, which appeared a thousand years later, was no match for the horsearcher's weapon. For close fighting, the Huns used the lasso and a long, straight, single-edged sword called an *urepos*. Each Hunnish warrior had several horses. The Huns had saddles and stirrups with leather loops—equipment unknown to the Greeks and Romans. In addition to all that, the Huns had a sophisticated organization. They were divided into squads of 10, companies of 100, and regiments of 1,000. When the usually scattered clans united for war, they also had divisions of 10,000. The all-cavalry Hunnish armies could easily stay out of reach of infantry and concentrate their arrow fire on any selected point of an infantry line. They were not only more mobile than the infantry, their bows outranged any in western Europe. When faced with a massive charge of lancers (which was a Gothic specialty), the small Hunnish units scattered on their fast horses, regrouped, and shot at the lancers from all sides.

Attila's uncle, Rugila, managed to unite the Hunnish clans after their victory over the Alans, but it was a shaky confederation. Attila and his brother, Bleda, inherited leadership of the Huns. Bleda died a few years later. (One story is that Attila murdered him, but there is no evidence for that other than the word of biased writers who were convinced that Attila was either the emissary of Satan or a man chosen by God to scourge the sinners of Rome.) Attila, an administrator of talent, turned the Hunnish confederation into an empire. His aim was to unite all the nomads, and then all of the tribal peoples outside the Roman and Persian Empires. He took tribute from the empires, which pretended they were paying him as a general in their armies. He took his army north, east, and west in search of fighting men he could conquer and assimilate.

The Roman emperor, Valentinian, planned to marry his sister, Honoria, to an old senator in a political alliance. Desperate to avoid the marriage, Honoria sent a message and a ring to the only man powerful enough to thwart Valentinian's plans.

Attila chose to believe that the message from Honoria was a proposal of marriage. And he felt that Gaul, filled with Goths, Vandals, Alans, and other tribesmen who fled from the Huns, would be an appropriate dowry. So he marched into Gaul with his whole army, an army in which the true Huns were a minority. There were Goths, Gepids, Heruls, Bavarians, Alans, Slavs, and a motley array of German tribes. It may have occurred to Attila that there was a flaw in his policy of collecting barbarian tribes. The only horse archers in his force were Huns and Alans. All the rest, though mounted, were lancers.

The invasion posed a real problem for Flavius Aëtius, the Roman Master of Soldiers.

Attila's campaigns set the stage for the Middle Ages.

As a boy, Aëtius had been a hostage at the Hunnish court. There he struck up a friendship with the young Attila. And because of that friendship, he was able to acquire Hunnish mercenaries to keep the German tribesmen in Gaul from causing too much damage. If Attila won, all would be lost. But if Aëtius won, he might never again be able to hire Hunnish horsemen.

Aëtius's army resembled Attila's. In the Roman army, Romans were a minority. The Visigoths made up the largest part, but there were also Franks, Vandals, and other Germans. And, of course, there were Alans, who fought on both sides of just about any battle in the fifth century.

Attila led his Huns and Alans against the center of the Roman line, which was held by Frankish infantry and other Alans. He may have thought the Alans might not fight hard against their kinsmen, and he certainly despised all infantry. But the Alans spent most of their time fighting their kinsmen, and the Franks had learned that a solid line of infantry spearmen could stop any cavalry. The Romans pushed back the Hunnish center. Attila deftly slipped his Huns and Alans to the right to help the Ostrogoths, who were pushing back the Visigoths on the Roman side. And then old Theodoric, the king of the Visigoths, was killed. His tribesmen went mad and drove back the Ostrogoths. Attila signaled a retreat, and the Hunnish army streamed back to the shelter of their circled wagons. Aëtius did not pursue. There was a chance he could still use Attila's warriors in the future.

But Attila didn't settle down. The next year, he invaded Italy. The Roman government fled, and Aëtius was nowhere to be found. His Visigothic allies decided they had better things to do than to defend Italy.

But the pope, Leo I, confronted Attila. The details of their meeting are unknown, but Attila turned around and left Italy.

In the early months of A.D. 453, Attila the Hun died from an apparent nosebleed or a burst artery after a night drinking to celebrate his wedding to a new bride. His men buried him in an unmarked grave so none of his enemies could defile it. The great khan has no monument other than legend.

The Hunnish Empire broke up without Attila. Attila's greatest feat was uniting the nomad clans into a stable organization that accelerated the stampede of Germanic barbarians into the Roman Empire and brought about the fall of the western empire. The last Roman emperor, Romulus Augustulus, was the son of Attila's secretary, Orestes, a renegade Roman who organized an army of Germans who once belonged to Attila's horde.

Attila's invasion of Italy made another change to history. When the Roman government fled, Pope Leo confronted the Hunnish king. What they said is irrelevant. The important thing is that a church leader—here and in other places—stayed with the people while the government officials fled. People began to put their faith in priests instead of politicians. This changed the mindset of the Roman citizen to that of Medieval peasant. The Middle Ages had begun.

Attila became friends with Aëtius when Aëtius spent part of his childhood as a hostage at the court of the Huns.

11

Muhammad
The Prophet
(A.D. 570–632)

In A.D. 603, Chosroes II of Persia (called by his people Chosroes the Conqueror) began a war with the Roman Empire of the East, a war that was to last more than 20 years. Chosroes captured Jerusalem, slaughtered huge numbers of people, and enslaved the rest. He seemed about to attack Constantinople when a new emperor, Heraclius, appeared. Heraclius deposed the old emperor, and led his armies deep into the heart of Persia. The war ended in a Roman victory, but with both of the great powers exhausted. The war had barely ended in A.D. 628 when Heraclius received a message from the Arabian Desert. It demanded that he acknowledge the one true God and follow the law He had dictated to His prophet, a man named Muhammad. Heraclius had too much on his mind to worry about men living on the fringes of civilization. He hadn't been following events in Arabia.

During the Romano-Persian War , an Arab merchant in Mecca was preaching against the customs of his people. Drunkenness was wrong, he said, as was the murder of female babies. So was the worship of idols in the Ka'aba, the small temple in Mecca that housed a black meteorite that the Arabs believed had been a gift from the gods. There was only one God, Muhammad said, and He didn't reside in man-made idols.

As a young man, Muhammad was often called Al-Amin, a common Arabic name meaning "faithful and trustworthy." He was often sought out to adjudicate minor debates between his neighbors and friends. As he grew older, Muhammad often traveled to a cave outside Mecca (called Hira) for meditation. In A.D. 610, when Muhammad was 40 years old, he said he was visited in the cave by the Angel Gabriel. The angel recited verses sent from God. These revelations continued for the next 23 years, until his death. Collected, these works have become known as the Qu'ran, or the Muslim holy book.

Muhammad's wife was the first to believe that his visions were prophetic, and soon the rest of Muhammad's family supported his claim that God sent him these visions to purify and correct the misconceptions of other monotheistic religions. Muhammad began preaching his message from God in A.D. 613 to the people of Mecca.

For centuries Mecca profited from the thousands of pilgrims who came to the city every year to pray to the idols in the Ka'aba. Muhammad's preaching against drunkenness and infanticide was bad enough, but the idols were a major source of the city's wealth. In A.D. 622, Muhammad was driven out of Mecca. He traveled to Yathrib (modern Medina). The city of Yathrib had a large

Jewish population, and the people there were not offended by Muhammad's monotheism. The people of Yathrib were so impressed with Muhammad's preaching that they changed the name of their city to Medinat an Nabi—the City of the Prophet. Muhammad inspired many followers. They later adopted a calendar starting with the date of the Prophet's journey (*hijra* in Arabic) to Medina.

Muhammad's teachings especially pleased the nomadic Bedouin. Temperance appealed to people who never had enough of anything. So did making hospitality a religious duty. One never knew when his life would depend on the kindness of strangers. Muhammad's method of fighting appealed to them, too. He decided to make war on Mecca because that city's inhabitants had, by throwing him

out, shown that they were enemies of God. Also, when Muhammad and his followers left the city, all of their possessions were confiscated. Muhammad considered military action acceptable as a means to retake their rightful property. Mecca was a rich and powerful city, but its riches depended on the caravan trade. Muhammad led his armies against the caravans approaching the city of Mecca. Nothing could please the Bedouin more than knowing that by robbing caravans and enriching themselves, they were also glorifying God.

After years of campaigning, Muhammad united all the Bedouin tribes, con-quered Mecca, and converted all of southern Arabia. He established the city of Mecca as his capital and placed members of his tribe, the Quraysh,

Arab Muslims engage and defeat Roman troops at the Yarmuk. Almost simultaneously, they destroyed the Persian Empire.

in positions of authority. Muhammad declared that the Ka'aba stone was a gift to the people of Mecca from the angel Gabriel.

Muhammad sent commissioners to the Bedouin tribes to collect taxes and spread his teachings. Muhammad was a great organizer; under him, the tribes of Arabia were united for the first time in history.

One thing that helped keep the tribes united was war. The keystone of Muhammad's foreign policy was to make war on any nation that refused to submit to the law of God as he saw it. After the unification of Arabia, one of the first calls for submission was to the Roman Empire. Although his followers considered Mecca (Muhammad's birthplace) the holiest city in the world, the Prophet himself believed Jerusalem to be the holiest. Jerusalem was a Roman city.

Muhammad died in 632, before he could move against the Romans, but the Arab leaders elected his father-in-law, Abu Bakr, caliph (meaning successor). Abu Bakr sent Muslim armies against both the Roman and Persian empires. Neither empire was well prepared to meet an Arab invasion. Both were exhausted and weakened by their long war, and each was suffering from internal dissention.

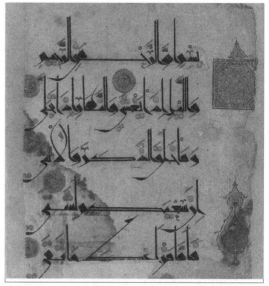

A page from an 11th century Qur'an in kufic script. *The Smithsonian*

The man, who began as a poor merchant, began one of the greatest religious movements in history. Muhammad became very ill in A.D. 632, and died on Monday, June 8, in the city of Medina. He was 63 years old.

After his death, the caliphs assumed authority of the Muslim movement. Under their leadership, the Islamic Empire expanded into Palestine, Mesopotamia, Syria, Persia, North Africa, Egypt, the Iberian peninsula, and as far as Anatolia.

12

Charlemagne
The Carolingian Renaissance
(A.D. 742 or 747–814)

He was named Charles after his grandfather Charles Martel (Charles the Hammer), who stopped the Arabs and Berbers at Tours and drove them back across the Pyrenees. He became a national hero in both France and Germany. The Germans call him Karl der Grosse. His French name is Charlemagne, which is preferred by English-speakers to its translation, Charles the Great. (There are too many "the Greats" in history.) Charlemagne deserves a more distinctive name, because he was a most distinctive king.

In 768, when Charles and his brother Carloman became joint kings of Frankland, little of the Roman Empire remained. The barbarians who had invaded the western Roman Empire had mostly settled down, but in their roaming back and forth, fighting Romans, fighting each other and sacking cities, they almost destroyed civilization in Europe. North Africa was conquered by the Muslims, who then invaded Spain and were known as the Moors. In the northern parts of Europe, the Scandinavians and Saxons who remained on the continent were mostly pagan, as were the Slavs and Avars in eastern Europe.

Enemies surrounded the kingdom of the Franks. Muslim raiding parties and pirates harassed it on the south. Saxon raiders harried the north, and on the eastern frontier there was always the threat of war. All the trouble was not external. The Bavarians, vassals of the Franks, were on the brink of revolting. And Charles's father, known as Pepin the Short, compounded all the troubles by naming both of his sons heirs to the kingdom.

Portrait of Charlemagne from the 16th century.

Carloman sickened and died in A.D. 771, before civil war erupted. Charlemagne was able to persuade the nobles in the other half of the kingdom to accept his rule. The Franks had a great military system for fighting in swamps and forests along the lower Rhine. Of all the Germanic invaders of the Roman Empire, they alone had an all-infantry army. They fought in a compact mass, using the angon (a spear similar to the Roman pilum), a long sword, and a throwing ax called a francisca. With this formation and these weapons, they defeated many Roman and Gothic armies, and they stopped the Huns at Chalons.

There was no standing army. When war threatened, every free man had to appear at the king's muster with his own weapons and armor (and reportedly, supplies for three months). Charles Martel had a mostly infantry army when he beat the Muslims at Tours; he was lucky to catch the mobile Muslims at all. After he had beaten them, he couldn't pursue them. So Charlemagne ordered all soldiers reporting at muster to bring a horse, if they could afford one.

Charlemagne's mixed cavalry-infantry army proved its worth against the Saxons. The Saxon war, however, lasted more than 30 years. It was a guerrilla campaign, which led to Charles developing the best intelligence service to be seen in Europe since the heyday of Rome. Before it ended (with the conversion of the Saxon king and his followers), Charlemagne rescued Pope Adrian from the Lombards and added Lombardy (northern Italy) to his empire. He invaded Spain to support the Christians there, but accomplished nothing. When returning through the Pyrenees, his rear guard (led by his nephew Roland) was attacked by the Christian Basques and wiped out. (This was his only major defeat.)

Charlemagne's tactics were standard for the time—a charge of mounted lancers followed by infantry using the traditional Frankish phalanx of ax-throwing spearmen. His strategy, however, was most effective. He used his intelligence service to track his enemies' movements, and he often divided his army into two or more columns to confuse the enemy. He concentrated his troops at the last moment and attacked. In his campaign against Bavaria, he employed grand strategy.

Charles the Great believed that he was restoring the Roman Empire of the west.
Library of Congress

Charles's cousin and vassal Tassilo, Duke of Bavaria, allied himself with both restive Lombard elements in Italy and with the Avar nomads in the east. Charles then summoned Tassilo to come to his court to answer the charges of oath-breaking and desertion. He then called on the Frankish nobles to bring their troops for what all expected to be an invasion of Bavaria. But instead of leading his army into Bavaria, he took it into Italy. He marched the length of the peninsula and into the lands of the duke of Beneventum, Tassilo's Lombard ally. The duke, Arichis, was unprepared for an invasion. He fled to Sicily and asked for help from the east Romans. The east Romans hesitated to antagonize the powerful Charlemagne, and Charlemagne soon offered peace terms. If the duke of Beneventum agreed to shave his beard and wear a mustache in the Frankish fashion, if he took an oath of loyalty to Charlemagne, and if he paid a tribute in gold, he could have peace. The duke accepted, and Tassilo lost an ally.

Charlemagne then massed his armies to invade Bavaria from three sides. Tassilo called on the Bavarian chiefs to appear with their armies, but the chiefs refused. They, as well as Tassilo, had taken oaths of loyalty to Charlemagne, and they would not be oath breakers. Tassilo called on his Avar allies, but the Avars were not going to support a leader whose own followers would not do so. Tassilo surrendered to Charlemagne, at whose court he was tried, found guilty, and sentenced to death. Charlemagne, though, commuted the sentence and had Tassilo enter a monastery.

But the Avars were still a menace. Known to the Chinese as Juan-juan, they were driven from the Gobi region and migrated west. The Juan-juan recruited Uighur Turks as they traveled. In the Ukraine. and later in Hungary, they incorporated several clans that had once been part of Attila's empire. These central Asian marauders became known to western Europe as the Avars, and Charlemagne was worried about their constant raids on his eastern borders. The Avars conquered many Slavic tribes and made them unwilling vassals. On the rich grasslands of Hungary, they became less nomadic.

Charlemagne's army at Tours, France.

Charlemagne called up all of his vassals, including the Lombards and the Bavarians. They crossed what are now the Austrian Alps in three columns. But the Avars saw them coming and made themselves scarce. Winter began to close in, and the Franks withdrew.

While Charlemagne was in Avarland, the Muslims in Spain raided what is now southern France. A Frankish noble named William of Toulouse defeated them in front of Carcassonne and killed their commander, but the invaders sacked Narbona and slaughtered thousands of people.

Then Charlemagne barely escaped a plot to kill him (led by one of this own sons). His troubles continued to multiply. He had to deal with a revolt by the Saxons, another revolt by the Frisians, and attacks by the Slavs. While his armies were putting down rebellions and Slavic attacks, Charlemagne began cultivating Avar diplomats sent to Frankland. He built up a pro-Charlemagne party among the Eurasian nomads.

Frankish armies again marched into Avarland. They forced the nomad warriors into constricted space and defeated them in close-range fighting. Some Avar clans rebelled and killed their khagan. Serbs and Croats, who had once been Avar vassals, turned against their masters. When the Franks took the main Avar fortress, they discovered an immense treasure, the booty from thousands of plundering raids by the Avars.

Charlemagne was crowned by Pope Leo III as the emperor ruling the Roman Empire in A.D. 800. The Roman Empire did not include former Roman lands conquered by the Muslims (Spain, North Africa, Egypt, Syria, Palestine, and Mesopotamia). It did not include Greece and Anatolia (which belonged to the eastern Roman Empire). It did not include Britain (although Charlemagne maintained cordial relations with the English kings). However, it did include modern France, Belgium, Luxemburg, Netherlands, Italy, Switzerland, Germany as far as the River Elbe, the Czech Republic, Slovakia, Austria, and Hungary.

Charlemagne did not merely unite all these different lands. He imported scholars from Ireland and England to establish schools. Towns began to be resettled. Arts and crafts flourished.

Charlemagne's resident scholar, Alcuin of York, standardized written script. Churches and other buildings showed original design, influenced as much by the Orient as by Rome. Miniature painting and illustrations, among the age's finest achievements, developed in the Rhineland and radiated throughout the empire. Metalworking for both decorative and useful objects flourished. Charlemagne began what has been called the Carolingian Renaissance.

Charlemagne tried to restore the western Roman Empire; he wanted to revive the dream of a political union of all civilized Europe, or at least the lands in which the Roman Empire was rooted. And he wanted to expand the civilization. The Irish, the Anglo-Saxons, and the Italians had begun the civilizing process. Charlemagne accelerated it. He shifted scholars around his empire, and he fought the Muslims and pagans who were attacking it from all sides. Those enemies and internal disputes brought the empire down after 30 years.

But the dream lived on, and the empire was revived again and again until Napoleon I laid the ghost of the Roman Empire to rest.

13

Otto the Great
The Holy Roman Empire
(A.D. 912–973)

Charlemagne's empire disintegrated just one generation after his death, but the cultural unity he inspired remained. The new Roman Empire was divided into several large pieces, which were themselves little more than conglomerations of autonomous duchies and principalities. The Vikings began raiding throughout western Europe. They stole horses so they could raid farms and villages far from the sea. The Vikings eventually seized an entire province in France, and settled in the British Isles. (Many castles/towers in Ireland were built to withstand Viking raids.) The Vikings also raided farther south, sailing through the Strait of Gibraltar and attacking southern France, Italy, and Greece. Europe was chaotic, and no one appeared capable of stopping the threat from the north. A strong leader was desperately needed.

Otto succeeded his father as king of the Germans in A.D. 936. He was an experienced soldier, given to leading wild cavalry charges (which made many think he was impetuous; he was anything but). Otto slowly centralized power in his kingdom. When the throne of a duchy became vacant, Otto would add its territory to an adjoining duchy, or he would give the throne to a close relative. The inhabitants of duchies often protested violently, but Otto won all his wars. He extended his power beyond Germany, into France and Italy.

While Otto was busy rebuilding Charlemagne's empire, the Magyars (a race of nomads from Hungary) struck at Otto's power. In A.D. 937, they raided Italy south of Monte Cassino and looted, burned, and slaughtered across Germany and into modern Belgium and central France. In A.D. 954, they again traversed Germany and attacked cities west of the Rhine. The next year, 100,000 Magyar horsemen laid siege to Augsburg.

Otto the Great was crowned as king of the Holy Roman Empire in Charlemagne's capital city of Aachen.

Otto collected a small army of mailed cavalry, reportedly only 4,000 men. (The numbers of Otto's army may have been revised downward, while the number of the invading Magyars was probably revised upward.)

The army was in eight divisions, in a loose column. Three Bavarian divisions were in the front; followed by a Frankish division; then a Saxon division; two Swabian divisions; and at the end of the column, a division of lightly armored Bohemians.

The Magyars raised the siege and disappeared into the broken country around the city of Augsburg. Then, on August 10, 955, as Otto was approaching the city, they suddenly crossed the Lech River and attacked the Bohemians at the tail of the column. The Bohemians fled, but the Magyars stopped to loot their baggage. While they were pillaging, Otto sent his Frankish knights against them. The Magyars dashed across the Lech. But the main Magyar army was in front of Otto's troops. The Germans formed a line and charged. Perhaps their early successes or their superior numbers made the Magyars overconfident, because they tried to meet the charge of the armored knights. A few years after this, Leo the Wise (a Byzantine emperor who wrote a book on military tactics) stated that a charge by the heavily armed Western knights on their huge horses was impossible to withstand.

The Magyars couldn't withstand it. The Magyar leaders tried to fight, but they were all killed. So were hundreds of their followers. Finally, the Magyars fled in panic while the Germans followed and killed as many as they could.

The battle of Lechfeld (the fields of the Lech) ended the Magyar menace. Most of the Magyar leadership died in the battle. Almost 15 years later, they agreed to become Christians. Two months after Lechfeld, Otto won another decisive victory, beating the Slavic Wends at Recknitz.

Fifteenth century Magyars on the march. These Eurasian nomads settled in Hungary and ravaged central and western Europe before Otto destroyed their power.
Historian's History

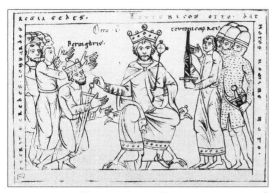

An engraving celebrating Otto's victory over Berengar of Ivrea.

In A.D. 962, Otto achieved his dream. He marched into Italy and had Pope John XII crown him Emperor of Rome. The pope also declared that he was the emperor's subject. Otto then took missionary activity out of the pope's hands and instituted a reform of the clergy, which he said had been corrupted by simony and commercial exploitation of shrines and relics. In A.D. 962, Otto deposed the pope and replaced him with Pope Leo VIII.

By taking over the government of the Church, Otto set the stage for a long and bitter struggle between the popes and the emperors. He also reestablished the Roman Empire, which was called the Holy Roman Empire.

Toghril Beg
Enter the Turk
(C. A.D. 990–1063)

In northeastern Asia, the Turks were a mighty power. As one of the kha'khans of the Blue Turks had recorded on an inscription (found in Siberia):

Amidst the sons of men arose my ancestors, Bumin Kha'khan and Ishtemi Kha'khan.... In the East, they conquered as far as the forest of Qadir Khan in Manchuria, and in the West, they conquered as far as the Iron Gates of Transoxiana. Over all the land between these two uttermost points the Blue Turks held sway.... The land of Byzantines, Sassanians, Chinese and others were beaten flat by the hooves of horses.

The claim is only a little exaggerated. The Byzantines were never attacked by the Blue Turks, but the Chinese and Sassanian Persians certainly were. The Blue Turks had ended China's Tang Dynasty. And the Empire of the Blue Turks flourished from the sixth through the eighth centuries, but the Mediterranean world and Europe would not feel the power of the Turks until the 11th century.

After a revolt by the Uighurs and other Turkish nations destroyed the empire of the Blue Turks, the clans that composed the empire went back to grazing their livestock and acting as mercenaries in the armies of other powers. Among those scattered Turkish nations were 24 tribes collectively called the Oghuz, or Ghuzz. Some believe the Ghuzz tribes were the founders of the empire of the Blue Turks. The Ghuzz tribes became Muslim in the 10th century and became known as Turkmens. A Turk named Seljuk (an officer in an Arab army) led a revolt by other Turkish officers, joined the local Turks, and became a tribal leader. His tribe was called the Seljuks. The Seljuks established themselves firmly in Central Asia.

In 1038, Toghril Beg, grand nephew of Seljuk, was crowned tribal sultan of the Turks in central Asia. He began building his empire at once. By 1040, Toghril Beg had conquered Khorasan, and by 1042, all of the Persian plateau, defeating every Arab or Persian force sent against him. In addition to Persia and Turkestan, he conquered Armenia, a Roman territory. Toghril Beg was just a simple soldier, but he studied the Persian administrative procedure and the bureaucracy that employed it. He then used the same methods to control his fledgling empire. In 1055, the Caliph Qaim (who was a virtual prisoner of a local strongman in Baghdad) asked Toghril Beg to rescue him. Toghril and his army entered Baghdad and took over the city. In 1056, the caliph married Toghril's niece, and in 1057, the caliph proclaimed Toghril Beg "Sovereign of the East and West."

Qaim was the Sunni caliph. There was also a Shi'a caliph. When Toghril went back to Persia, Basaseeri, a follower of the Shi'a caliph, captured Baghdad. Toghril hurried back to the caliph's city and was joined by his nephew Alp Arlan, with another Turkish army. They recaptured the city, and Basaseeri fled, only to be killed in a later battle alongside the Euphrates River. In 1062, Toghril married the caliph's daughter. He died the next year, but he was succeeded by Alp Arslan.

In 1068, Roman Emperor Romanos Diogenes decided to evict the Turks from Armenia. Three years later, Alp Arslan led the emperor into a trap, routed his army and captured him. Romanos Diogenes agreed to the terms Alp Arslan imposed: the Turks were to keep Armenia and part of Anatolia. The sultan released the emperor, but Romanos's stepson blinded the emperor and threw him into a dungeon, where he died a few days later. Alp Arslan was assassinated within a year. He was succeeded by a ruler of the west called the "Seljuk in Rum (Rome)," and another in Persia called the "Great Seljuk."

Toghril Beg changed the history of the Middle East by establishing the Great Seljuk Empire, and by relegating the Abbasid Caliphs to state figureheads. Unfortunately not much is known about Toghril's personal life, but none can argue that his actions did not change the political and social landscape of the Middle East.

Turkish horse archers were feared the length and breadth of Eurasia.

15

William the Conqueror
The Battle of Hastings
(C. A.D. 1028–1087)

For centuries, the British Isles were considered wild and barbarous, and were barely recognized as part of Europe. Britain was one of the first provinces the Romans abandoned when the empire was threatened. The Angles, Saxons, and Jutes from northern Europe conquered and settled in Britain, and established a firm Anglo-Saxon presence.

Then the Danes under Sweyn I (Sven) and his son Canute (Knut) conquered England in 1013 after a 10-year war. King Aethelred the Unready of Wessex, the paramount Anglo-Saxon power, fled to Normandy. His wife was the daughter of the duke of Normandy. The next year, Aethelred died attempting to retake England. His son, Edmund Ironside, continued the fight, but he soon died, and Canute became the undisputed king of England.

After a considerable amount of fighting among Canute's heirs, his son Harthacanute became king of England. Harthacanute had no children, and his nearest relative was his half-brother, Edward, who was living in exile. Edward was the logical heir. Edward's father was Aethelred the Unready, and his mother was Emma, grand aunt of Duke William of Normandy and the widow of both Aethelred and Canute. Harthacanute invited Edward, who was living in Normandy, to return to England.

Edward returned to England and, after Harthacanute's death, was elected king by the Witan, the council of English nobles. A little later, Earl Godwin of Wessex, one of Canute's nobles, and his son Harold Godwinsson rebelled and were forced into exile. Edward later pardoned them and allowed them to return, but Harold Godwinsson began intriguing with the Witan to take control of the kingdom.

Duke William successfully claimed the English throne and crown for himself at the Battle of Hastings, despite his illegitimate birth.

Edward (known to history as Edward the Confessor) had no children, and he didn't want Harold Godwinsson to succeed him. Harold was too much a man of the north. Edward's years in Normandy had convinced him that Scandinavia, even if it became Christian, was a backwater. He believed that the culture of France, Germany, and Italy was the future. He began grooming his nephew Ralph to succeed him, but the boy lacked courage in battle.

Edward the Confessor died in January of 1066 without an heir. Duke William II of Normandy was Edward's cousin, and decided to claim the English throne for himself, despite his illegitimate birth. William claimed that Edward had promised him the throne in 1052, and that Edward's brother-in-law (Harold Godwinson) had pledged his support while shipwrecked in Normandy.

Norman knights received the lions share of estates and offices once William conquered the Anglo-Saxons.

Harold had been caught in a fierce storm while fishing in the English Channel. He was driven ashore in France and taken prisoner by Count Guy, a vassal of Duke William. William freed Harold, and Harold took an oath to support William's claim to the throne of England. When Edward died, however, the Witan elected Harold Godwinsson king.

William began gathering an army to enforce his claim. The Norman duke found volunteers from all over western Europe to join his feudal levies. John Beeler estimates in his book *Warfare in England 1066–1189* that about 3,000 mounted men, 4,000 infantry spearmen, and 1,000 archers joined William in his expedition to conquer England.

A short digression on archery may be helpful at this point, because archery played such a key role in the Battle of Hastings. General J.F.C. Fuller, in his book *A Military History of the Western World*, says William's archers used "the short Norman bow." Many other historians have also written of this alleged short bow, although the famous Bayeux Tapestry (which chronicles William's conquering of England) shows Norman archers shooting with a fairly long bow. The Norman use of a short bow seems to be based on a couple of misconceptions: that the English (or maybe the Welsh) invented the longbow several centuries after Hastings; and that it was the length of the longbow that gave it the power to be so effective at Crecy, Poitiers, and Agincourt.

First, longbows, both with flat limbs or half-round limbs like the English longbow, have been found that date back to the Stone Age. Viking raiders used a longbow very similar to the traditional English weapon centuries before Hastings. Those bows, similar to the English weapon, were long, because a solid wood bow is brittle. To get a full draw with the traditional "clothyard shaft" (which was about 28 inches long), a wooden bow had to be long. But there is *no* evidence that a short bow made solely of wood was *ever* used in European warfare. Such a bow would have to shoot a short arrow, which would definitely affect its total power.

But length alone does not make a bow powerful. The power of a bow depends on two things: (1) the speed with which its bent limbs reassert themselves, and (2) the distance over which the bowstring pushes against the arrow. All other things being equal, shorter bow limbs reassert themselves faster than long ones. But if the limbs are too short, the bowstring can't give the arrow as long a shove.

Early in the 20th century, Saxton T. Pope (an American archer) made an exact replica of an English longbow found on the sunken 16th-century warship *Mary Rose*. It was 6-feet, 4.75-inches long. When drawn 28 inches, the draw weight was only 52 pounds and it shot a flight arrow only 185 yards. Pope cut it back to 6-feet. It now weighed 62 pounds and shot the flight arrow 227 yards. Pope trimmed the bow again, this time to 5-feet, 8-inches. When he shot this shorter bow, it weighed 70 pounds and shot the flight arrow 245 yards.

The success of the English longbow in the later Middle Ages probably depended more on the English tactics and the skill of the English archers than on the weapon itself. Edward III's tactics at Crecy in 1346 greatly resembled those of the Roman general Narses the Eunuch at Busta Gallorum in 552 B.C., but they were vastly superior to any use of archers since Hastings in 1066. Further, the English archers were the pick of yeomen who practiced archery every Sunday afternoon. The English longbow probably had a heavier draw

weight than the European bows of the time, which meant that its limbs would snap back faster and its bowstring would give the arrow a faster shove. The draw weights of the Norman bows are unknown, but they certainly had enough power to penetrate a coat of mail.

In England, William had to face the army of Harold (who had broken faith with William and escaped back across the English Channel to be elected king by the Witan). King Harold's army was probably larger than William's. Just three days before William's army landed, though, Harold's army defeated an invasion force from Harald Hardraada, the king of Norway. It was a fierce battle, with heavy losses on both sides. When they heard about William's landing, the Saxon soldiers under Harold mounted their horses and rode south. Harold's force was both depleted and exhausted when it confronted William's. Both armies were now about the same size.

Harold's force was all mounted infantry. The best armed were the king's "housecarles," professional soldiers making up his bodyguard. The rest were militia—citizens who appeared with their weapons when danger threatened. Similar to the Normans, most of them wore mail shirts and iron helmets and carried large shields. For weapons, they had spears, javelins, swords, the small "taper ax" (which was thrown), and the large "Danish ax" (which was not).

Harold occupied the crest of a chain of hills near the town of Hastings. A steep ravine protected each flank. The Normans had to cross a swamp, using a narrow strip of dry land in the middle of the wetlands. If Harold had attacked before William's army had completed the crossing, British people today might still be saying things such as, "Gespraec pa se goda gylp-worda sum." But Harold liked his defensive position.

The Normans opened the action with a volley of arrows, but the archers had to shoot uphill, so many of their arrows passed over their enemies' heads. Most of the rest were caught on the shields of Harold's soldiers. The Norman spearmen had no better luck. The "Danish axes" sliced through the Norman mail. The spearmen on William's left turned and ran. Harold's forces chased them into the swamp. William, commanding the center, led his Normans against the disorganized center, who suffered heavy losses before they regained their hilltop. William now sent his cavalry against the shield wall, but they, too, were forced to retreat. Harold's soldiers broke their formation to chase the Normans. According to Norman sources, the cavalry retreat was merely a ruse to provide the Normans another opportunity for a counterattack. Modern commentators, however, doubt that an army with the rudimentary communications of William's force could have accomplished that deliberately. They guess that the Norman aristocracy wouldn't concede that lowly foot-soldiers could drive back Norman knights.

The fighting continued. After six hours, significant losses prevented Harold from holding the line from ravine to ravine. The line could be flanked. William ordered a new attack with both infantry and cavalry. Again, the archers prepared the way. But this time, they aimed high into the air so that their arrows would fall on the enemy from the sky. Harold's soldiers had to hold their shields above their heads while the Norman cavalry and infantry charged them from all sides. Unfortunately, not all the men were able to raise their shields in time. Harold was hit in the eye by an arrow. It disabled but did not kill him. With no one commanding the line,

the Normans broke through. A Norman knight finished off Harold by cutting off his leg. By the end of the day, it was all over. William would still be campaigning for several months, but the Battle of Hastings decided the future of England.

But William was not yet proclaimed king. The conqueror traveled to London, where he was welcomed by the Archbishop of Canterbury. The few remaining Anglo-Saxon noblemen surrendered to William shortly after. William was proclaimed king of England at Berkhamsted, Hertfordshire. He was then crowned at Westminster Abbey on December 25, 1066. In less than 12 months, William the Bastard became the king of England.

Although living in England, most knights were of Norman-French descent, and still spoke the langue d'oc or langue d'oil languages of medieval France.

Many changes occurred during William's reign. He commissioned the Domesday Book, the first attempt to take a complete census of a country's people. He also ordered the construction of many castles, including the Tower of London. He had the language of the court changed to Norman-French. Anglo-Saxon, which would later become English, was used only by the commoners for the next 300 years.

Some scholars believe that to consolidate the Norman-French hold on Britain, William deported many of the Anglo-Saxon land-owning classes into slavery. (Many of these people ended up in Spain.) William then turned over the titles of all lands and public offices to his Norman-French supporters.

William had earlier married his cousin Matilda of Flanders, against the express wishes of the pope. Together they had four sons and six daughters. William was succeeded in England by his younger son William Rufus. His elder son took the title duke of Normandy upon his father's death. William's youngest son, Henry, became king after William Rufus died without an heir.

William the Conqueror died at age 59 near Rouen, France, on September 9, 1087.

Reportedly, his body was so corpulent it wouldn't fit in the stone coffin prepared to adorn his tomb. The assembled bishops attempted to prod the body into the sarcophagus, but the body burst, filling the chapel with a smell so foul that it scattered all of William's mourners.

An image from the Bayeux tapestry depicting William as the King of England.

16

Saladin
The Battle of Hattin
(A.D. 1138–1193)

Yusef ibn Ayyub (Joseph, son of Job) was born in 1138, in what is now modern Iraq. He was the son of a Kurdish officer in the army of Sultan Nur ed Din. When he became famous, his people called him el Malik en Nasr—the Conquering King. He took a name for himself, Saleh ed Din—the Honor of the Faith. His enemies called him Saladin.

Westerners often associate Saladin with England's Richard I (the Lionheart). Actually, he was quite different from Richard. Richard spent most of his time out of his kingdom, fighting in lands near and far. He was a knight of uncommon skill and strength, and he seemed to have no fear. Richard was an amateur troubadour and immersed in all the conceits of European chivalry, but he had little use for books or scholarship.

Saladin hated war and loved books, but he was dragged into war by family duty and the disintegration of the Seljuk Empire. Once involved in war, he proved to be a successful strategist, but unlike Richard, he never led his own troops. In spite of medieval legends of Richard and Saladin meeting in battle, that never happened. Saladin lacked Richard's skill with weapons, but as a ruler, he was far ahead of the English king. He was a wise and generous ruler who united Egypt, Syria, Mesopotamia, and much of North Africa into a single state. He even temporarily united the Shi'a and Sunni branches of Islam.

The Kurd and the Norman resembled each other in some ways. Both were cool, cautious and successful strategists. Both were famous for their chivalry, but both were capable of the most appalling cruelty. Once, growing impatient with Saladin's delays in the negotiating process, Richard ordered the massacre of 2,000 to 3,000 Muslim hostages in full view of Saladin's army. Saladin, too, could be impatient. If ransoms of his prisoners were not paid promptly, he usually had them slaughtered for the entertainment of his dinner guests.

Saladin united warring Muslim factions and defeated the Crusaders from Europe in the decisive Battle of Hattin.

This drawing depicts the Crusaders conquering Jerusalem before Saladin's reign, when the city remained under Muslim control.

Saladin accompanied his uncle Shirkuh (commander of Nur ed Din's army during the sultan's campaign) to consolidate his position in Syria. That accomplished, Nur ed Din sent Shirkuh and Saladin to Egypt. The Shi'a caliph paid Amalric, the Crusader king of Jerusalem, to head them off. After Amalric stopped the Syrians a second time, Shirkuh instigated a palace coup and installed a caliph who would not hire Christian protection. Shirkuh entered Egypt and took control of the country. Two months later, he died (probably of poison). Saladin accused several Shiites of Shirkuh's murder and had them crucified, but there has always been the suspicion that it was Saladin himself who poisoned his uncle. The puppet caliph appointed Saladin as sultan of Egypt.

In 1174, both Nur ed Din and Amalric died. Saladin marched to Syria and took over Nur ed Din's lands. He put Egypt (along with his Syrian conquests) under the authority of the Sunni caliph of Baghdad, although it was the Shi'a caliph of Cairo who had made him a sultan. Then Saladin turned to the Crusader states.

The Kingdom of Jerusalem was having a crisis. Amalric's heir was his 13-year-old son Baldwin, who suffered from leprosy. Raymond of Tripoli, a cousin, was appointed regent for three years. Raymond was an astute general, but after his regency ended, young Baldwin proved he didn't need advice from an older man. In 1177, soon after he began ruling in his own name, Baldwin surprised Saladin's invading army and wiped it out. Saladin barely escaped capture. Saladin recruited a new army and renewed the war in 1178. For the next two years, Baldwin, with a much smaller force, continually outmaneuvered the great Saladin. In 1180, Baldwin and Saladin agreed to a two-year truce.

One of Baldwin's internal problems was Reynald de Chatillon (formerly prince of Antioch) who had spent 16 years in Nur ed Din's dungeons. Reynald would recognize no agreement with an "infidel" such as Saladin. Moreover, he once put galleys on the Red Sea to attack Muslim pilgrims traveling to Mecca. He sacked Muslim cities on both shores of the Red Sea and landed troops in Arabia, where he threatened to march on Mecca. Saladin's fleet and army eventually defeated Reynald, but the ex-prince got back to his castle, Kerak, astride a main caravan route. Reynald went back to robbing caravans. He attacked one caravan (in spite of the truce), in which a sister of Saladin was traveling. Saladin and his army suddenly appeared and laid siege to Kerak.

Reynald was hosting a wedding. His stepson was marrying a daughter of King Amalric I. When Saladin and his army appeared, Reynald sent out (under a flag of truce) a portion of the wedding feast. In return,

Saladin ordered his engineers not to shoot at the tower where the newlyweds were staying.

Meanwhile, Baldwin's leprosy had grown much worse. He had neither fingers nor toes, and could not even sit up. He agreed to have his brother-in-law Guy de Lusignan stand as regent. It didn't take him long to realize that Guy was utterly incompetent. He fired his brother-in-law and took back the royal power. Then he heard that Saladin had besieged Kerak. He called up his army and accompanied them in a litter. Saladin saw the Crusaders coming, and went back to Egypt.

But then Baldwin died. Raymond of Tripoli arranged a new truce with Saladin, and Baldwin's 7-year-old nephew succeeded him as Baldwin V. But the child died after 18 months. His mother, Sibylla, had herself crowned queen and then crowned her husband, Guy de Lusignan, king.

Reynald de Chatillon again broke the truce, and Saladin invaded the Crusader territory. Guy de Lusignan rounded up all the fighting men he could and marched to meet the approaching force. It was the middle of summer. Saladin's army was large, and he could find no fodder for its horses and little to no water in the scorched hills of Palestine. Raymond of Tripoli advised Guy to wait. Saladin could not long maintain an army at this time. But Guy listened not to Raymond, but to firebrands like Reynald de Chatillon. Saladin blocked the Crusaders' access to water. Raymond and a few followers managed to cut their way through the Muslim lines, but the main Christian army succumbed to heat

Defeated Crusaders returning from a later expedition. After Saladin's victory, Christian Crusaders were never again able to capture Jerusalem.

and thirst as much as to Muslim arrows. Saladin let King Guy go without asking for a ransom, only his promise to no longer bear arms. "Kings do not kill kings," he said.

But Saladin swore to kill Reynald de Chatillon with his own hands. He went through the formality of asking Reynald if he would embrace Islam. When the Christian refused contemptuously, the sultan swung his sword. But, inept with weapons as always, he cut off Reynald's arm instead of his head. Saladin's embarrassed servants quickly finished off the Crusader. Saladin didn't bother asking the military monks (the Templars and the Hospitallers) to become Muslims. He knew the answer, so he had them all beheaded. The common soldiers went to the slave markets. The nobles he held for ransom. Saladin then retook most of the Crusader strongholds, including Jerusalem.

Guy broke his promise to Saladin as soon as he felt safe, and helped lay siege to the city of Acre. He was joined by Richard of England and Philip of France. (They were accompanied by Eleanor of Aquitane, who was currently the queen of France. She would shortly convince Philip to divorce her, however, and marry Richard's younger brother, Henry, founding the Angevin Dynasty.) After the fall of Acre, Richard led an army down the coast, using the traditional Crusader formation: the sea and Italian galleys protected his right flank, while infantry spear carriers kept the Muslim cavalry at a distance. Backing up the spearmen were crossbowmen, using weapons that outranged the Muslim bows. Behind these lines of footmen were the knights, walking their huge war horses. When the Muslim cavalry got close enough, the infantry lines would part and the knights would gallop out

with leveled lances. This formation cut through the Muslim forces, but Richard did not attempt to retake Jerusalem. He knew the Muslim horse archers could cut it off from the sea, and the city could only be resupplied by a full-scale field army. He signed a truce with Saladin. For centuries to come, Crusaders would try to retake Jerusalem and fail.

Saladin achieved great recognition for his chivalry. Despite the brutal murders of thousands of Muslims at the hands of the Crusaders, Saladin granted amnesty and free passage to all Christians. Saladin died on March 4, 1193. When they opened the Royal Treasury, his councilors found there was not enough money to pay for Saladin's funeral. He had given most of it away in charity.

Richard the Lionheart faced Saladin in battle many times, but maintained a strong respect for the Islamic leader's sense of honor.

17

Genghis Khan

One God in Heaven, One Khan on Earth

(A.D. 1162–1227)

"What is the greatest pleasure life offers?" the nomad chieftain asked his companions. "To ride out on the steppe when the grass is green with a fast horse beneath you and a falcon on your wrist," one old friend answered.

"No," the chieftain said. "The greatest pleasure is to break your enemies, to drive them before you, to take all the things that have been theirs, to hear the weeping of those who cherished them, to press in your arms the most desirable of their women."

The chieftain, once named Temujin, now called Genghis Khakhan (the Emperor of All Men) had already tasted such pleasure, and he was to enjoy more. He was nothing if not confident. On his jade seal, engraved in Uighur script, were the words "God in Heaven and the Khakhan on Earth, the Power of God. The Seal of the Ruler of All Mankind." Actually, in spite of the seal, Genghis Khan never referred to himself as "khakhan," the khan of khans. The reason, he said, was that there is only one God in heaven and one khan on earth, and he was it.

Genghis Khan's life now was quite different from what it had been a few years earlier, when he was simply Temujin. He was born the son of Yesukai the Strong, khan of the Yakka Mongols. But when he was 13, leaders of a rival clan poisoned Yesukai. Targutai, the khan of the Taidjut Mongols,

claimed the part of the steppes that belonged to Yesukai. Most of the families in Temujin's clan decided they could not follow a mere boy and joined other clans, especially Targutai's. Temujin's enemies attacked his clan, and the young khan became a fugitive fleeing for his life, dodging from one hideout to another on the edge of the Gobi Desert. At one point, he was captured but managed to escape. Temujin learned that life on the steppes was a dog-eat-dog affair, and mercy or compassion equals weakness.

Temujin persuaded a few of his father's followers to join him, and he led them with enough skill and cunning to win a series of tribal wars. He became strong enough to ally himself with Toghrul Khan, chief of the Keraits and his father's sworn brother. (Toghrul Khan's people were largely Nestorian Christians, and he may have inspired the medieval legend of Prester John, a Christian king in eastern Asia who might help the European Christians against their Muslim enemies.) During periods of peace, Temujin worked to turn his tribe into an army.

All the peoples of the Gobi area (Mongols and Turks) were horse archers. Their principal weapon was the short, powerful, composite bow, supplemented by lances and swords. They wore armor made of hardened leather, and they rode small, shaggy horses that could subsist on the sparse vegetation of the steppes. All of the clans, when they went to war, used squads of 10, companies of 100, squadrons of 500, regiments of 1,000, and divisions of 10,000. Whenever war broke out, the nomad warriors returned to the same units they had first joined. When peace returned, the clansmen scattered to their pastures and went back to herding horses and cattle. Temujin changed that way of life.

Temujin had a small group of friends who stuck with him during the bad times. They would officer his divisions. He gathered picked men into a personal bodyguard. They were fulltime soldiers. Instead of herding animals, they would practice military skills such as archery and horsemanship. Temujin trained them to respond to signals given by his standard of nine yak tails and by kettle drums. He extended military administration to civilian life. A leader of 10 cavalrymen became the leader of 10 tents during peacetime. The khan established military discipline over his tent villages as well as his army.

Eventually, Temujin had a showdown with Targutail and his Taidjuts. Targutai had twice as many warriors (having persuaded many uncommitted clans to join him). But when the armies met, Temujin's denser formations cut through Targutail's. The Taidjuts attacked Temujin's wagon camp, believing it undefended. But the wagon fort was defended by women who handled their bows and arrows well enough to stop Targutai's army. Then Temujin's riders, responding to a signal, wheeled and struck the Taidjut army in the rear. The Taidjut army fled, leaving behind 6,000 dead.

Temujin and Toghrul Khan warred against other steppe tribes as allies of China. When they took captives, Toghrul made them slaves. But Temujin enlisted them in his army.

Temujin grew in strength, arousing the jealousy of Toghrul's son, Sengun. Sengun invited Temujin to visit the Keraits to discuss a wedding. He planned to poison the Mongol leader, but Temujin learned of the plot and did not come. The Keraits then planned a surprise attack. Two herdsmen told Temujin they had seen a Kerait army approaching. Temujin didn't have time to gather his scattered tribe. He sent all the women and children in his camp far to the rear, led the men out of camp to a defensive position, and left the tents in place with the fires burning.

Genghis Khan's conquests united the Far East and Europe. Trade flourished, ideas were exchanged, and gunpowder came to Europe for the first time.

The Keraits rode into the camp and shot hundreds of arrows into Temujin's tent. Then they discovered it was empty. Still they enormously outnumbered all Temujin's warriors in the area. They attacked Temujin's men. In the most desperate time of the battle, Temujin sent some of his men around the Kerait's flank to take a position at their rear, at a place called Gupta Hill. It was an act of sheer bravado, but "the standard stood on Gupta," as the old Mongol chronicle put it, and the Keraits withdrew. The steadfastness of the Mongols impressed the other nomad clans. They flocked to Temujin's standard. The Mongol khan then attacked the Keraits and defeated them. Toghrul Khan and Sengun fled to the west, where both were killed by hostile nomads.

Temujin sent messengers to all the nomads around the Gobi asking for a kurultai, a council of tribes. They came and elected Temujin leader of all the nomads and gave him the name Genghis Khakhan. Genghis turned his domain into a military empire. The whole population was divided into the left wing (the eastern portion); the center (just north of the Gobi); and the right wing (the west). All men between the ages of 14 and 70 were soldiers. The best were combat troops, others (able-bodied but less talented in warfare) were responsible for roads and supplies. The least robust took care of the herds. Women and children managed the villages. For the first time, the centuries of inter-tribal raiding had ended. The tribes themselves had almost disappeared, merged into one Mongol army. The Mongol army was often called Genghis Khan's *ordu*, Mongol for camp. *Ordu* is the origin of the English word horde, which has come to mean something quite different from the highly trained, intricately organized, and extremely disciplined army of Genghis Khan. In addition to his troops, Genghis had a secret service of merchants and others who acted as

intelligence spies. The Mongols had, in fact, one of the most competent intelligence services.

Genghis began raiding southward into modern China. Against these settled people, the Mongols had a variety of tactics. They were far more mobile than the infantry-cavalry armies of the urban peoples. They could easily encircle them. They could concentrate men and arrows against weak spots in the enemy line. Sometimes they feigned flight to lure the enemy into an ambush. Another tactic was to allow the enemy to break through the encircling line, and then attack them when, scattered and retreating, they thought they were safe. The Mongols at first were not equipped for siege warfare. At one city, Genghis Khan offered to lift the siege if the city's ruler would give him thousands of cats and doves. The puzzled Hsian commander did that and hoped the Mongols would go away. Instead, they attached miniature torches to the animals and released them. The cats dashed for their homes in the city and squeezed through gaps in the wall. The doves flew back to their nests in the city. The city burned down.

Another siege weapon was terror. If a city submitted, its inhabitants were well treated. If not, they were all killed. The Chinese had been masters of siege warfare. In his six years of campaigning in China, Genghis Khan learned Chinese techniques, picked up Chinese siege engines, and recruited Chinese engineers. Nomad mercenaries of the Chinese were welcomed into the Mongol army, particularly if they fought bravely. He also welcomed Chinese if they had skills he could use.

West and south of the empire of Genghis Khan was the Khwaresmian Empire. It was a recent construction of conquering Muslim Turks, founded by former vassals of the Seljuks, and included Turkestan, Persia, Mesopotamia, Afghanistan, and what is now Pakistan. It was big enough and powerful enough to give pause even to Genghis Khan, whose left wing was deeply immersed in the attempted conquest of China. To the Khwaresmian king, Ala ed Din Muhammad Shah, Genghis Khan sent an invitation to trade. All went well for a while, until Muhammad Shah's officers decided that some of the merchants were spies. The shah had them executed.

Legend has it that Genghis Khan murdered his half-brother over a dispute about hunting spoils. Although severely reprimanded by his mother, he never showed remorse for the killing.

To Genghis Khan, killing envoys was an intolerable breach of custom and had to be avenged. He called up 250,000 men in 25 divisions. One of them was a Chinese division armed with siege engines. He split the army into three parts. One, under his oldest son, Juchi, marched south through the passes of the T'ien Shan mountains. Another kept to the valleys leading west. The third, under Genghis Khan himself, disappeared into the western steppe.

When Juchi emerged from the mountains, he saw the whole Khwaresmian army, under the shah himself. Juchi charged through the narrow pass and hit the center. The Mongols had no room for their normal horse archer tactics, and although vastly outnumbered, they severely shook the Muslims. They almost killed the shah, in fact. Muhammad Shah did manage to get troops around both Mongol flanks, however, and Juchi had to retreat. The shah prepared to attack the Mongol camp at first light. But Juchi had left his campfires burning and marched around the shah's army to attack the cities at his rear. He laid siege to Khojend.

Muhammad Shah did not try to raise the siege. He took up a position behind the Syr River and waited for reserves. He thought he was blocking the Mongol advance. Then he learned that the Mongols had crossed another part of the mountains about 200 miles to his right and almost at his rear. Chepé Noyon, one of the khan's most trusted generals, had taken two divisions from Juchi's column, and surprised the Turks watching other approaches. He was advancing on Samarkand. He threatened to cut the shah off from his main line of defense, the Amu River. Then two sons of Genghis Khan appeared farther up the Syr and attacked the cities there. The shah sent troops to reinforce the garrisons of his major cities and shut himself up in Samarkand. He believed the Mongols would not be able to take the cities. He was wrong. One by one the cities fell. The Mongols kept a few useful slaves and killed the rest of the population.

With three Mongol armies approaching from the east, Genghis Khan, with the largest Mongol force, appeared in the west, marching on Bokhara. The shah fled. Genghis Khan detached three divisions, put them under the command of Chepé Noyon and Subotai Bahadur (another trusted general) and sent them after the shah. The shah escaped to an island in the Caspian Sea, where he soon died of exhaustion. Chepé and Subotai sent a messenger to the khan, asking permission to return by riding around the sea. Genghis approved such enterprise.

What followed was one of the greatest cavalry marches in history: 30,000 horsemen rode into the Caucasus, defeated the army of the Kingdom of Georgia, defeated a second army of mountaineers (Alans and Circassians), wiped out an army of Kipchak Turks, stormed a Genoese fortress in the Crimea, annihilated a Russian army, and rode back to the Gobi. Chepé died on the way home, and Genghis Khan died soon after that, but Subotai returned to Europe 15 years later, leading a Mongol army that destroyed and burned Krakow and Pest. The Mongols returned to the Gobi only because Ogotai Khan, Genghis's son and heir, had died.

Genghis Khan left an empire that stretched from the Pacific Ocean to Poland.

Unlike the empire of Alexander, it did not fragment after his death. His sons and grandsons continued to expand it, and his grandson, Kublai Khan, ruled all of China as well as being lord of Turkestan, Persia, and Russia. Genghis Khan set another record; he is credited with having killed 20 million human beings.

Genghis Khan's importance, however, does not depend on his military brilliance, the extent of his empire, or his horrendous body count. For a while, he united the East and the West. Couriers and caravans crossed his empire from border to border in complete peace. Roger Bacon wrote his famous letter containing the formula for gunpowder just 11 years after the Mongols burned Krakow. Paper made from rags and wood pulp appeared in Europe about the same time. So did movable type. Ideas and merchandise traveled freely the length of the Eurasian continent for the first time.

Marco Polo appeared before Genghis Khan's grandson, Kublai Khan, at his court in Mongolia.

18

Enrico Dandolo
The Fine Italian Hand
(A.D. 1107–1205)

The new customers posed a serious dilemma for Doge Enrico Dandolo. The new customers were Crusaders (mostly French) and had come to Venice to arrange passage for their whole army—men and horses. That was a lot of transportation: there were 33,500 men and 4,500 horses. It meant building a whole fleet of ships to carry the Crusaders. And it meant a contract for Venice that would be the biggest in several lifetimes.

Enrico Dandolo had spent 80 years in service to Venice as a statesman, admiral, and general. In a battle with his city's Byzantine rivals, he suffered a wound that deprived him of sight. The wound did not affect either his foresight or hindsight, however, and he was now serving as doge in the republic of Venice. He helped make Venice the greatest naval power in the Mediterranean—greater than Genoa, greater than Pisa, greater even than Constantinople.

This Crusader contract would be a big step forward. In addition to providing transportation, the Venetians would loan the Crusaders 50 warships with their crews and supply the army with food and fodder for nine months. In return, the Crusaders would pay the Venetians 85,000 silver marks, a staggering sum, and give them half of all the spoils of conquest. There was only one hitch: the Crusaders planned to go not to the Holy Land, but to Egypt, which they considered the most vulnerable of Muslim lands on the Mediterranean. But Egypt was Venice's biggest trading partner.

First, Dandolo arranged to put the Crusaders up on the island of St. Nicholas of Lido, several miles offshore. He was not going to have thousands of armed men disrupting the life of Venice. Then he wrote to the sultan of Egypt, Saladin's brother, telling him not to worry. Then he put the Venetians to work building the needed ships.

When the ships were ready, Dandolo asked for his money. As he suspected, the Crusaders could not come up with 85,000 silver marks.

"You won't leave the island until we are paid," the doge told the warriors. There was something they could do, however. The king of Hungary, he said, had stolen the city of Zara from Venice. If they took it back for Venice, Venice would forgive their debt.

So the Crusaders successfully attacked Zara. They asked for their transportation to Egypt. But it was too late, Dandolo told them. The winter storms would make crossing the Mediterranean impossible. They'd have to wait until spring. While they were waiting, the Crusaders learned that the pope had excommunicated all of them for shedding Christian blood (during the fight to take back Zara for Venice), while they were sworn to fight for the faith. The pope finally realized that the men from France and Germany, had been taken in by his wily Italian countryman. He forgave the Crusaders, but warned them never to do it again. However, Dandolo introduced them to a young man named Alexius Angelus, the son of the Byzantine emperor, who had recently been deposed by a usurper. Alexius begged them to help him recover his throne.

According to Geoffroi de Villehadoin, one of the Crusader leaders, Alexius promised that if the Crusaders restored his inheritance, he would "put his whole empire under the authority of Rome, from which he has long been estranged." He would also give them 200,000 silver marks and provisions for every man in the army. And he would add 10,000 men to their army and would maintain, as long as he lived, 5,000 men to guard the holy places.

The knights thought ending the schism between Rome and Constantinople would overcome the pope's objections, and 200,000 silver marks and 10,000 more men made the deal irresistible to them. Taking the city and port of Constantinople would do two things for Dandolo: (1) it would turn a rival into a Venetian vassal, and (2) it would eliminate the danger to his principal trading partner. But Constantinople was no easy nut to crack. The Goths, Avars, Slavs, Vikings, Russians, Arabs, and Turks had all tried and failed. But Dandolo controlled the largest army in Europe and probably the largest navy in the world. He could not let this opportunity slip away.

The Byzantine army was lined up on the shore outside the city walls when the Crusaders arrived. Dandolo's galleys launched a storm of missiles from their catapults and crossbows. The Greeks fell back, and the landing ships dropped their ramps and the knights rode ashore. The Byzantines retired behind their walls. Constantinople had double walls on the landward side. A breach in the outer wall left attackers at the mercy of archers on the higher inner wall. There was not enough space between the walls to allow easy use of a battering ram or a scaling ladder. Nevertheless, the Crusaders wanted to attack from dry land. They could not imagine attacking a wall from the heaving deck of a ship. Dandolo wanted to attack the single wall on the sea side.

Constantinople defied all its enemies until Crusaders, led by a blind, 80-year-old Venetian, captured the city—twice.

So the Venetians and the Crusaders attacked simultaneously from land and sea. The land attack failed. Dandolo had built siege towers on the decks of some of his ships. The Venetian ships moved in, but fire from the archers and catapults on the wall was too hot.

The galleys backed water. The ancient, blind doge was furious. He seized a Venetian flag, wrapped it around himself and screamed, "Put me ashore, you craven dogs!"

The Venetians, fearing their doge more than the Byzantine stones and arrows, ran up on the shore. Dandolo jumped out and waded to dry land with the aid of Venetian soldiers. The drawbridge on a siege tower slapped down on the wall, then another, and another. Venetian soldiers gained a foothold and expanded it. The Greeks counterattacked, but the Venetians set fire to the city while the wind was blowing toward the Byzantines. The emperor led his troops out of the city and tried to attack the Crusaders, but was driven back. That night he left the city. For the first time in history, Constantinople was captured by an enemy.

Prince Alexius was crowned emperor, but he didn't have the 200,000 marks he had promised to pay (half of which would have gone to Venice). There was rioting between the Greeks and the Westerners, and the Byzantines tried to lock the Venetians and Crusaders out. Dandolo and the Crusaders captured Constantinople a second time. The pope was furious, but he learned that his own papal legate had blessed the enterprise, so he couldn't excommunicate the attackers.

The Crusaders established feudal domains throughout the Byzantine Empire, and the Venetians built bases on the Aegean islands. The new order on the mainland did not last long. The principal result of the Fourth Crusade was the fatal weakening of the Byzantine Empire and the fortress of Constantinople, Europe's main bulwark against Muslim invaders. It also deepened the split between the Western Churches (both Catholic and Protestant) and the Orthodox Churches of the East.

19

Joan of Arc
The Maid of Orleans
(A.D. 1412–1431)

The year 1428 was not a good one for France. In addition to the interminable, off-and-on war with England, there was a civil war. One powerful faction, led by the Duke of Burgundy, refused to recognize the King; the Burgundians claimed that he was illegitimate. Normally, that might not have been a great problem. Illegitimacy was no handicap to the duke of Normandy (known as William the Bastard before he became known as William the Conqueror). One of the great nobles of France, Jean Dunois, was known as the Bastard of Orleans. His men's battlecry, "Long live the bold Bastard," still delights high school boys compelled to read Scott's *Quentin Durward*.

The trouble was that the King of England (the ruthless young Henry V) had decided, once again, to lay claim to the kingdom of France. That gave people such as the duke of Burgundy an excuse to say that Henry had a better claim to the throne than the dauphin, who would normally become Charles VII on the death of his father.

Henry V landed an army in France and, near Agincourt, inflicted a crushing defeat on the supporters of the dauphin. The old king, Charles VI (who was subject to recurrent fits of madness), agreed to the marriage of Henry to his daughter, Catherine. He then confirmed Henry as the heir to the crown of France. Henry's claim to the French crown by inheritance was outstandingly flimsy, and many doubted that the old king had the right to disinherit his son in favor of his son-in-law. But then there was the chance that the would-be Charles VII was illegitimate. His mother, the queen, was a confirmed adulteress, so there was some reason to believe that young Charles was not his father's son.

But Henry V complicated the situation by dying young and leaving an infant son, who was to be King Henri in France and King Henry in England. The government of northern France (where the English and Burgundians were established) was in the hands of the duke of Bedford, Henry V's brother. The dauphin and his followers held out south of the Loire. Bedford sent an army to take Orleans, which guarded the best route across the Loire and into the dauphin's territory.

Things looked bad for the dauphin. Bedford had an experienced, well-trained army, while Charles had a rabble of knights who knew nothing of tactics or strategy. The whole art of war, they seemed to think, consisted of charging the enemy like a mad bull. That was how the French had fought early in the war at Crecy in 1346. The French knights had charged the dismounted English knights, ignoring the peasant archers on the flanks who were shooting from behind a hedge of pointed stakes. When they met the English again, 10 years later at Poitiers, the French thought they had learned the English secret—using knights as infantrymen. The dismounted French knights trudged over a muddy field in full armor while the English archers shot them down. Those who reached the English lines were too exhausted to fight. Later, some decided that the English secret was the longbow (which was closer to the truth), and that only Englishmen could handle the weapon (which was ridiculous). The English were good shots, able to draw heavy bows, because the law required all Englishmen of the yeoman class to practice archery every week.

The other English secret was that they formed a strong defensive line; usually a phalanx of knights, supported by archers and protected by pointed stakes, and let the French come to them. Under Bertrand Du Guesclin (a mercenary captain who became the Constable of France), the French adopted an effective counter. They refused to fight the English in the field. Instead, they attacked English castles and outposts. The English weakness was that they had a hard time keeping a field army supplied. When they couldn't get enough food or had too many wounded, they had to return to the ports.

Du Guesclin was long dead when Henry V landed, and the French chivalry reverted to the disastrous tactics they used at Crecy, with the same result.

The English at the siege of Orleans were still having trouble getting supplies. Bedford dispatched a convoy under Sir John Fastolf (whose name Shakespeare twisted into Falstaff) carrying barrels of pickled herrings. The French charged the convoy, but Fastolf circled his wagons, and the English archers

shot down the French knights. This encounter is remembered as the Battle of the Herrings.

Through much of this time, a peasant girl in Champagne was hearing voices and seeing apparitions. She had been a happy-go-lucky (but unusually pious) girl until she was about 13 years old. Then the voices began talking to her. She said the voices came from Saint Michael, Saint Catherine, and Saint Margaret, and she was later able to see them. "I saw them with these very eyes, the same as I see you," she would later tell her judges. This girl we call Joan of Arc; the French call her Jeanne D'Arc. Recent scholars have suggested the apostrophe is a grammatical error. Her real name was Jehanne (the old spelling of Jeanne) Darc.

Although she sat for one portrait during her lifetime, it has not survived.

The voices told her that God had a special mission for her. As Joan grew older, they became more specific. When she was 16, they told her she was to help the dauphin. They told her to see Roger de Baudricourt, commander of the dauphin's troops in the area. She did so, accompanied by a cousin. The dauphin was not impressed. "Take her home to her father and give her a good whipping," he told the cousin.

The voices became more insistent. "I'm just a poor girl. I know nothing about fighting," she told the saints. "It is God who commands it," they told Joan.

Joan returned to de Baudricourt and told him she had to see the dauphin, because the situation had become grave. She claimed that the dauphin's troops had just lost a great battle. Several days later, de Baudricourt learned that the Battle of the Herrings had occurred just before he spoke with Joan. He took her to see the dauphin.

The dauphin received her in a crowd of courtiers. He was dressed as an ordinary courtier, not a prince. Joan had never seen a picture of Charles and should not have known about the test of deception. But she unerringly located the true dauphin, disguised as a common courtier, and told him something secret. She never revealed what it was. (She probably reassured the dauphin that his secret worry about his legitimacy was unfounded.) He had her examined by a large panel of bishops and scholars. They said she could be safely employed.

The dauphin put her in charge of his army and offered her a sword. Joan begged that he give her an ancient and secret sword that was buried behind the altar in the chapel of Saint Catherine de Fierbois. The dauphin's men dug it up in exactly the spot Joan said it would be found. With the army, Joan chose to wear men's clothes, both to protect her modesty and for practicality.

On April 22, 1429, Sieur de Rotslaer wrote a letter to someone in Brussels, and said that "the Maid" had predicted:

> ...she would save Orleans and would compel the English to raise the siege, that she herself in a battle before Orleans would be wounded by a shaft but would not die of it, and that the King, in the course of the coming summer, would be crowned in Rheims, together with other things that the King keeps secret.

The letter was delivered to Brussels before any of those predictions came true.

Before she began her campaign, Joan sent a message to Bedford, the English regent, calling on him to withdraw all English troops from France. The English had heard about Joan, and they were sure she was a witch—a servant of Satan. If so, she was a most peculiar witch. With the dauphin's army she acted more like the mother superior of a convent. She forbade swearing and drunkenness, and she drove the whores out of camp.

Although Joan dictated her correspondence, she did sign her name on three of the letters, which still exist.

The English had not established a solid siege line around Orleans, and on April 30, 1429, Joan and a contingent of troops entered the city during a storm. The next day, while Joan was asleep, the commandant of Orleans, the Compte de Dunois (the Bastard of Orleans) led an attack on an English outpost. The French were repulsed, but the noise of the battle woke up Joan. She put on her armor, mounted her horse, and rode out to meet the retreating troops.

"Go boldly in among the English!" she shouted. They did, and they took the fort. In an attack on another English fort, she was wounded by an arrow. She told Dunois not to retreat, but to storm the fort as soon as they saw her standard against the wall. She was unable to carry the standard herself, but she had a soldier carry it up to the wall. When it reached the wall, the French attacked from all sides, scaled the wall and took the fort. The English raised the siege soon afterward.

Half of Joan's mission was completed. The remaining part was crowning the king in Rheims. Joan and her army took the English-held towns along the Loire one after another. A large English army under Lord John Talbot was at Patay when Talbot learned that Joan and her troops were nearby. Other officers advised Talbot to retreat, but he decided to attack. He ordered his archers to take up positions. The English soldiers frightened a deer. Joan saw the deer, knew that the English were near, and ordered an immediate attack. She yelled that they should not try to form a straight line but dash into the woods and into the English at once.

The English archers had no time to fix their protective stakes. A third of Talbot's army was killed, and he was captured. Fastolf came up with more troops just as the French crushed Talbot's army. Fastolf's troops panicked. Fastolf got away, but he was later unjustly charged with cowardice. He was acquitted, but his reputation was ruined, and Shakespeare (with a slight change in his name) turned him into the buffoon Falstaff.

Joan had shown a new way to beat the English in the field: do not give them time to establish a defensive position. The French proceeded to Rheims, and Charles VII was crowned. That was a decisive moment. Few in France now had any doubt that Charles was king, rather than the infant Henri, living overseas in the safety of London. The Duke of Burgundy might resist, but his faction was weakening rapidly. Six years later, Burgundy recognized Charles as sovereign. Joan's mission was finished.

The victories of Joan of Arc nullified those of England's Henry V, and France remained independent.

The king and the army, however, begged her to stay on. She did, but she was soon captured by the Burgundians, who sold her to the English. She was tried as a heretic by theologians of the strongly Anglophile University of Paris under Pierre Cauchon, bishop of Beauvais, a creature of the Burgundian faction. At one point she signed a retraction, but with the stipulation that she was retracting only what God wanted her to retract. Because she "adjured her heresy," Joan was sentenced to life imprisonment instead of death.

The English were furious that she had not been executed, but Bishop Cauchon assured them hat Joan would be punished. One of Joan's crimes was to wear men's clothing. The court's claim that this was sinful was contrary to church law, which approved cross-dressing under certain circumstances. At her trial, Joan testified that the English guards had tried to rape her, and witnesses said that one time the Earl of Warwick had to drive would-be rapists away. The court ordered to her resume female clothing on May 24, 1431. She complied, but the next Sunday, her English guards refused to give her any clothing but male attire. On May 29, she was condemned as a relapsed heretic and burned at the stake on May 30.

In September of 1435, France and Burgundy were reunited under Charles VII by the Peace Arras. The union was significant, because both France and Burgundy had been developing a new type of artillery—mobile field guns that could be towed by horses and put into action immediately. The English, confident that the longbow was the ultimate weapon, had neglected artillery. In 18 years, the new French army (based on infantry and artillery) drove the English out of all the positions they had gained in more than 100 years.

20

Mehmed II

The Door to Europe

(A.D. 1432–1481)

Constantinople was often called Europe's bulwark against a Muslim invasion. It was, but sometimes it acted more like a revolving door. In 1446, when Sultan Murad II of Turkey was fighting a coalition of Christian states, the government of Constantinople ferried the Sultan's troops across the Bosporus for the cost of 1 ducat per man. The eastern empire was in pretty sad shape as a result of Dandolo's invasion two-and-a-half centuries earlier, and it needed the money; which was a source of great annoyance to the Turks. Murad's son, Mehmed, decided to take action.

When Mehmed decided to do something, he didn't fool around. As soon as he became sultan at the age of 21, he sent an assassin to drown his infant half-brother so there would be no rival for the throne. He then executed the assassin and married the baby's mother to a slave. His soldiers called him the "Drinker of Blood." They had reasons. One of the few people he admired was an enemy, Vlad the Impaler of Transylvania. One legend claims that Vlad (better known today as Dracula) was offended by Turkish envoys who refused to remove their turbans in his presence, so he had the turbans nailed to their heads. "It is impossible to drive out of his country a prince who does such grand things as that," Mehmed commented.

To deal with the walls of Constantinople, Mehmed (now 22) hired a renegade Hungarian gun founder named Urban. Urban cast the largest guns every seen; some of them could fire stone balls weighing more than 1,400 pounds. They were so heavy they had to be cast right outside the walls to avoid the problem of moving them long distances. Mehmed's army of 200,000 far outnumbered Constantinople's 8,000, and the Turkish army included 12,000 Janissaries, the best infantry in Europe. Janissaries—the word is a corruption of the Turkish *yeni cheri*, or new soldiers—were slaves.

Except for the two Crusader attacks early in the 13th century, Constantinople had never been taken. The walls were still standing. But there was weakness behind the walls. The bitter hatred between Greek and Latin Christians—a result of Dandolo's attack—caused much of it. The Genoese, who settled in the town of Galata (across the Golden Horn from Constantinople), declared their neutrality. The pope wanted the Italians to defend Constantinople, because the city prevented Turkish hordes from invading western Europe, but the Orthodox hierarchy opposed any help from Italians. An Orthodox priest named Gennadius organized a mob that rioted outside the Emperor's palace, shouting

"Death to the excommunicated (Italians)!" Orthodox priests said they would refuse absolution to anyone who had any dealings with the Italians.

Of 25,000 Constantinopolitan men of military age, only 5,000 agreed to help defend the city. A sprinkling of mostly Italian volunteers and mercenaries brought the number of defenders up to 8,000. Two men, both foreigners, were the defenders' greatest assets. One, Giovanni Giustiani (a Genoese) arrived with 700 men and two galleys. He was a master of artillery tactics, and the emperor put him in charge of the defense. The other, Johann Grant, was a German engineer well versed in siege tactics. Nothing though, could make up for the defenders' lack of men. If Giustiani spread his men evenly along the wall, each man would be defending 18 feet of wall.

Mehmed took a number of Byzantine outposts. In some cases, he used poison gas— pots of burning sulfur. Then he set up his guns. To drag one of those monsters a short distance took 50 oxen and 450 men; to load one took two hours. So the defenders had plenty of warning as to where an attack would take place. They had plenty of time to take countermeasures, too. Each gun could fire only seven or eight shots per day.

The Turkish gunners aimed at a single spot on the wall and hit it repeatedly. But when they made a breach in the wall, they found the defenders had built another barrier behind it. Enraged, Mehmed ordered a general assault. Giustiani had no big guns, but he had

The Siege of Constantinople was completed when Mehmed rolled his ships on greased logs across the boom that blocked the entrance to the Golden Horn. Once he did so, he was able to disrupt the supply lines to the city and force the citizens to defend more length of city wall.

plenty of crossbows, catapults, arquebuses, small cannons, and wall guns that could fire five bullets with one shot.

Three Genoese galleys loaded with soldiers and munitions sailed into the harbor. A Turkish squadron of 145 ships tried to capture them. The Genoese cut through the Muslims, and the Christians lowered the chain blocking the harbor to let them in. The frustrated Mehmed beat his admiral, a renegade Bulgarian, with a heavy stick.

As the siege went on, Mehmed's super-guns accomplished nothing. Each time a hole opened in the wall, the Turks found that Grant's engineers had built a new wall behind it. Each infantry assault failed, cut to pieces by Giustiani's skillfully handled weapons. Mehmed's men rolled a siege tower up to the walls, but Giustiani rolled barrels of gunpowder into the dry moat and blew the tower up. Mehmed tried mining, but Grant had half-buried drums along the wall. The vibrations of dried peas on the drumheads showed where

the Turks were digging. The defenders then attacked the mines. Some mines they flooded, some they blew up, and some they filled with poisonous sulfur dioxide.

Finally, some Janissaries found an undefended postern gate. They entered the city and hit the defenders from the rear while the main Turkish army was attacking from the front. Giustiani and Grant were killed. So was the emperor, who led a last, hopeless charge.

The fall of Constantinople in 1453 ended the original Roman Empire, although the revived western empire of Charlemagne and Otto the Great would struggle on for another three-and-a-half centuries. The scholars from the destroyed city fled, carrying with them the documents that fueled the Renaissance in Italy. The Turks invaded the Balkans and dominated much of eastern Europe. That domination continued until the First Balkan War (1912–1913). Turkey became the strongest power on the Mediterranean, supplanting Venice.

Constantinople controlled the access to Europe from Asia Minor until it fell to the Turks under Mehmet II. After the city fell, the Hagia Sophia was converted from a church to a mosque.

21

Francisco de Almeida

The First Viceroy of India

(A.D. 1450–1510)

Dom Francisco de Almeida was a Portuguese gentleman, soldier, and explorer. He was a counselor to John II of Portugal, and fought valiantly at the battle of Granada in 1492. One of his most significant achievements was the battle he fought, which marked a reversal in the relative prosperity of the Muslim and Christian worlds.

For centuries—even before the birth of Muhammad—Arabs, Africans, and Indians had been crossing the Indian Ocean with goods to trade. This trade became vastly more lucrative after the Crusades, when the Europeans became familiar with the riches of the East. Dhows from Arabia and East Africa crossed the ocean to India, the islands of the Indies, and even China. They brought back jewels, precious metals, silks, and spices. They sailed up the Red Sea and sold the goods in Egypt. The Egyptians sold the goods to merchants from Venice, Genoa, and other cities, who distributed them throughout Europe. Egypt reaped enormous profits from this trade, and that Egyptian wealth spead through the Muslim lands in the near east and North Africa.

In the far west, the Portuguese (having driven out the Muslims who had occupied their country for seven centuries) were looking for new adventures. Slowly, methodically, Portuguese navigators worked their way down the west coast, rounded the Cape of Good Hope, and sailed north. Then, similar to the Arabs before them, they crossed the Indian Ocean and began cutting into the traditional Muslim trade.

Everything was not peaceful. Muslim traders attacked the Portuguese and incited Indian princes against them. Portuguese seamen helped the rajah of Cochin in his war against the Calicut, defeated the Muslim warriors sent against them, and began sinking Muslim ships.

The government of Venice implored the sultan of Egypt to send a fleet to the Indian Ocean and destroy the interfering Portuguese. They were joined by the Muslim rulers in East Africa, South Arabia, and India. To put an overwhelmingly powerful fleet on the Indian Ocean, the sultan of Egypt asked the aid of his rival, the sultan of the Ottoman Empire. The Muslim fleet consisted of a huge number of galleys, each mounting three or four cannons on the bow. (In modern warfare, these cannons took the place of the ram, which had been the galley's main offensive weapon for centuries.) The galleys were propelled by sails and by hundreds of rowers who became fighting men when the opposing ships got too close and boarding began. There were also 1,500 marines who had no duty but fighting. They had bows and matchlock guns, as well as swords and spears. The galleys were also equipped to throw fire pots at enemy ships.

The Muslim ships sailed down the Red Sea into the Indian Ocean. When they got to the ocean, they encountered much rougher seas than they had ever known before. The low, narrow, and light galleys were not built for this kind of water, but the Egyptians and Turks continued on to India and put into Diu, an Indian port.

The Portuguese had a much smaller fleet in India under the command of Francisco de Almeida. Almeida, in Cochin, heard that there was a Muslim fleet at Diu and sent his son, Manoel, to scout the area with a few light ships. The Muslim Admiral Husain Kurdi trapped Manoel's flotilla. In the battle that followed, Manoel was killed. Before Almeida could concentrate his ships, the Muslims sailed back to Arabia.

Two years later, in 1509, they returned. Their 200 galleys again stopped at Diu. This time Almeida was ready. His 17 ships were greatly outnumbered by the Muslims, but Almeida's ships were not galleys. They were built for ocean travel. They were unable to ram enemy ships, and they could not be easily boarded. And their sides were lined with guns—heavier guns than any galley carried.

As soon as sails appeared on the horizon, Husain Kurdi led his fleet out. His galleys had trouble keeping a straight line, but they sailed right at the Portuguese. The Muslim sailors had taken down their sails and were using oars for greater maneuverability and short-range speed.

The Portuguese did not charge, as all fighting ships did in galley warfare. Instead, they turned to form a line that was 90 degrees to the approach of the Muslims. Then they fired broadsides. They turned again and fired more broadsides. The galleys never got close enough to ram. Portuguese cannonballs mangled lines of rowers, shattered galley hulls, and sank scores of the long, narrow ships. The few galleys that were not destroyed ran aground and their crews fled into the city. The Portuguese, too, entered Diu and forced the ruler to pay a huge indemnity.

Control of the sea routes to the Indies later passed to the Dutch and then to the English. Almeida demonstrated another major change in history at Diu: the day of the galley was over. Galleys had dominated European naval warfare since prehistoric times, but when 17 sailing ships annihilated a fleet of 200 galleys, the change was obvious. In 1503, Almeida was appointed as the first governor and viceroy of the Portuguese State of India. He died in a surprise attack at the Cape of Good Hope in 1510.

Almeida's fleet carried Portuguese soldiers similar to this man to Indian cities, such as the port of Diu.

22

Hernán Cortés

Conquering the Aztecs

(A.D. 1485–1547)

The Portuguese had established a mercantile empire by sailing east. Their Spanish neighbors, after the first voyage of Christopher Columbus, thought they could do the same by sailing west. The trouble was that the islands Columbus and other explorers found had little world trading for. Then some Spanish sailors landed on the coast of Mexico. They were amazed at what they saw. Here were stone, whitewashed houses with brightly colored wooden shutters, similar to those

The Spanish governor wanted to set up trading posts in the New World, but Hernán Cortés had other ideas.

they had left behind in Spain. The people wore fine cotton clothing and gold jewelry, often containing precious stones. They read books, carved statues, and erected great temples to their gods. What went on in those temples amazed the Spaniards—amazed the horrified them. The Aztec Indians sacrificed people, and then ate them.

Diego Velásquez, the governor of Cuba, appointed Hernán Cortés to lead an expedition. Cortés was a rather surprising choice. His amorous adventures caused him trouble with the governor. After a brief period of imprisonment (during which he escaped twice) Cortés and the government were reconciled, and Velásquez gave him a large tract of land. Cortés became the *alcalde*, or mayor, of the new city of Santiago de Cuba.

Cortes took two priests to convert the local people. His goals were also to rescue some Spaniards who were believed to be alive in that strange land and to establish trading rights. At the last minute, Velásquez had second thoughts and ordered Cortés to cease his preparations for the expedition. Cortés pretended to misunderstand the order and sailed around the Caribbean islands recruiting the best fighting men he could find. Notable among them was Pedro de Alvarado, a giant who may have been the most formidable individual fighting man in the expedition.

Another notable member of the expedition was Juan Garrido, a free, black soldier who became the first black man, free or slave, to land on the North American continent.

Cortés assembled 553 soldiers, including 32 crossbowmen and 13 arquebusiers, and a total of 110 sailors for his 11 ships. He also picked up 14 light and heavy pieces of artillery and 16 horses. Then he sailed to what is now Mexico. His first stop was the island of Cozumel, off the coast of Yucatán, in the land of the Mayas. There he met a man who asked him in broken Spanish "if he were among Christians." The strange man was a Spaniard named Jerónimo de Aguilar, a deacon of the Catholic Church. He and some companions had been shipwrecked. His companions were all dead. He escaped from the Mayans of the coast and fled into the interior, where another Indian king kept him as a slave. He performed his duties so well the king gave him increasing responsibilities. The king wanted Aguilar to take a wife, but the deacon had taken a vow of chastity and refused. That impressed the king even more. Aguilar became a great man in that tribe. When he heard that Spaniards had landed, he begged his master to let him leave. The king did so and accepted a ransom with great regret. Aguilar spoke Mayan and several other Indian languages. Cortés now had an interpreter.

The Spanish rounded the tip of Yucatán and sailed down the coast to Tabasco, where the Indians welcomed them with showers of arrows. After a battle in which a cavalry charge by Alvarado saved the day, the Tabascans made their peace with Cortés and gave him and his troops many gifts. One of them was a beautiful slave girl named Mallinalli (or Malinche). The Spanish called her Marina. They called her Doña Marina after she became Cortés's mistress. As with Aguilar, she spoke Mayan, but she was also an Aztec who spoke Nahuatl, the language of central Mexico. Early in Cortés's expedition, interpreting became a two-person job. Nahuatl-speakers spoke to Marina, who told Aguilar what they said, so he could translate it into Spanish. Marina, however, quickly learned the language of her lover. She and Cortés became so close the Indians gave the Spaniard the name of his mistress. To the Aztecs, Cortés was Malinche or Malintzin (tzin being Nahuatl honorific like Don or Doña in Spanish).

Cortés took his fleet farther up the coast and landed in the country of the Totonacs, vassals of the great king of the Aztecs. They were not happy vassals. While the Spanish were camping in the Totonac city of Cempoala, the Totonac king told Cortés about the tribute the Aztecs demanded. It wasn't gold, or fabric, or food. It was numbers of the best-looking young men and young women who were then sacrificed to the gods. Since the current Aztec emperor began to rule, the demand for victims had grown increasingly heavy. The next time Aztec tribute collectors appeared, Cortés persuaded the Totonacs to imprison them. The Totonacs were impressed with the Spanish cannons and the huge animals they rode, and felt that Cortés and his people could protect them from the Aztecs. Besides, they had seen Spanish soldiers smash the statues of their gods. When the gods did not strike down the Spaniards, they decided to become Christians.

The Aztec Emperor Motecuhzoma II (called Montezuma by the Spanish) was terrified. He had shown his courage in battle many times, but this situation was different. Motecuhzoma was afraid that Cortés was the god Quetzalcoatl, who, legend had it, had brought civilization to the peoples of

Mexico, and then took a boat over the eastern sea after promising that he would return. The return of a god might seem to be an occasion for rejoicing, rather than depression. But Motecuhzoma was the high priest and servant of another god, Huitzilopochtli (the god of war). Huitzilopochtli was a rival of Quetzalcoatl. If Quetzalcoatl got to Tenochtitlan, Motecuhzoma's capital, he and all the Aztecs were doomed. He sent ambassadors to bribe Cortés to go home and magicians to kill him with spells. But the gold only made Cortés more eager to visit the capital, and the spells didn't work.

Montezuma, emperor of the Aztecs, thought Cortes was the god Quetzalcoatl. He was terrified, because he was the high priest of another god, Huitzilopochtli, Quetzalcoatl's rival.

Cortes decided that the only way to get control of the Aztec gold was to conquer the empire. But conquering an empire was contrary to Governor Velásquez's orders. To deal with Velásquez, Cortés founded a city, Vera Cruz. Its population consisted of his soldiers and sailors. The city had all the agencies of Spanish municipal government. The government of Vera Cruz examined Cortés's orders from Velásquez and pronounced them invalid. Then they elected him captain general of an expedition to the Aztec empire.

Cortes asked the Totonacs about the best route to Tenochtitlan. They recommended going through the republic of Tlascala. The Tlascalans had never been conquered by the Aztecs, and they were fierce warriors. Cortés fought three great battles with the Tlascalans before they agreed to an alliance.

Tenochtitlan was built on an island in the middle of a lake. Three causeways connected it to the mainland. There were gaps in the causeways spanned by drawbridges, so canoes could travel to any part of the lake. The Aztecs had no wheeled wagons or carts. Canoes were the vehicle of commerce, and the city was crossed by a grid of canals.

Motecuhzoma welcomed Cortés on the southern causeway. At the time (November 8, 1519), the captain general had 400 Spanish soldiers and 6,000 Indians, mostly Tlascalans, in his army. The Mexican emperor gave Cortés a huge palace near his own and near the great temple of Huitzilopochtli.

Cortés's army was surrounded by the Aztecs. To increase his security, he and a handful of knights kidnapped Motecuhzoma and brought him to their palace. They continued to treat the emperor as royalty, but they didn't let him leave. The Aztec emperor agreed to become a vassal of Cortés's sovereign, Emperor Charles V, but the Aztec people were growing restless. Cortés said he'd like to go home, but he had no ships. Then one day, Motecuhzoma showed him a note he had received from a city on the east coast. Pictures showed European ships and European soldiers. Cortés now had transportation, Motecuhzoma said. Cortés noted that the leader of the soldiers was a very tall, heavy redhead. It could only be Pánfilo de Narváez, Governor Velásquez's right-hand man. Narváez was an enemy of Cortés.

Because he had left garrisons between Cempoala and Tenochtitlan, Cortés had only 210 Spaniards in the Mexican capital. He took 70 soldiers and left Alvarado in command of the 140 Spaniards in Tenochtitlan and headed east, adding soldiers from the garrisons as he went along. While moving east, he sent a messenger to the Chinantla, a tribe that had allied itself to the Spanish, asking for 2,000 warriors armed with long, copper-tipped pikes. Cortés knew how infantry pikemen could stop cavalry. But even with the Indians and the Spaniards from the garrisons, Cortés's force was far inferior to that of Narváez.

Narváez had 900 Spanish soldiers, 80 of whom were cavalry, 80 arquebusiers, and 150 crossbowmen. He also had thousands of Indians from the islands. He felt he had no reason to fear Cortés and his puny force, so he relaxed at Cempoala.

The King of Cempoala said to Narváez "Why are you so heedless? Do you think Malintzin is so? Depend on it, he knows your situation exactly, and, when you least dream of it, he will be upon you."

Cortés moved in the middle of the night during a drenching rainstorm when Narváez's sentries were taking shelter from the storm. During the attack, Gonzalo de Sandoval, Cortés's best lieutenant, led 60 picked men up the great pyramid of Cempoala and captured Narváez in his headquarters. Narváez's men joined Cortés's army. The captain-general returned to Tenochtitlan with a far larger army than he had ever had.

But in the city, the streets were deserted and there was a deathly silence. When he reached the palace, Cortés learned what had happened. The Tlascalans, who hated the Aztecs, told Alvarado that the Aztec nobles were planning to revolt during the festivities honoring the war god. Alvarado remembered that Cortés massacred the leading men of Chohula when he discovered that they were conspiring against him. But he had solid evidence, including the unforced confession of one of the conspirators. Alvarado had only the accusation by the Aztec's mortal enemies, the Tlascalans. So while the Aztec nobles were dancing before the image of Huitzilopochtli, Alvarado and his men drew their swords and cut them all down. Then the people of Tenochtitlan revolted. They besieged the Spanish in their palace. When Cortés approached, the Aztecs retired to their homes. They wanted all the Spanish in the city so they could wipe them all out. Once Cortés's army was inside the palace, the attack resumed. Cortés brought Motecuhzoma up on the battlements to speak to his people. He was greeted by a cloud of stones and arrows. One sling stone killed the emperor.

The Spanish attempted to sneak out of the city in the dead of the night. They brought a portable wooden bridge to span the canals and the gaps in the western causeway, the shortest way to the mainland. A woman drawing water from a canal saw the marching troops and gave the alarm. Aztec warriors appeared all around them. The portable bridge became wedged in the first gap in the causeway and could not be moved. Aztec war canoes paddled up to the sides of the causeways and shot at the troops trying to reach the mainland. Soldiers tried to swim the gaps in the causeway, but many could not bear to leave so much gold, and the weight of it took them to the bottom. The Aztecs snatched many of them from the water. Cortés's unarmored Indian allies suffered the greatest losses in this operation. Cortés took some men and rode back along the causeway to help the rear guard. There was no rear guard—only Pedro de Alvarado, unhorsed, holding off the Aztec forces with his lance. As Cortés and the others watched, Alvarado turned, planted the point of his lance in the lake bottom, and vaulted across the gap.

The Aztecs were too busy securing captives to follow. Cortés counted his losses. Of 1,100 Spaniards, 450 were dead or missing. Of 6,000 Indians, 4,000 had been killed or captured. All of the artillery and all of the arquebuses were lost. Only a few crossbows could be found. Of the 69 cavalrymen, only 23 horsemen remained.

For a while, Cortés and his men met with only a few skirmishers as they circled the north shore of the lake on the way to Tlascala. Then, a week after *la noche triste*, they faced a huge Aztec army in a narrow valley. Cortés told his cavalry to aim their lances at the faces of their opponents and instructed his infantry to rely on the points, not the edges of their swords. He formed the troops in a long line that could not be flanked and advanced. The Spanish fought desperately, especially Alvarado, Sandoval, and Cortés, but the odds against them seemed hopeless. Then Cortés identified the Aztec who seemed to be the leader. He and his knights attacked and killed the leader; the Aztec army fled.

The Tlascalans welcomed Cortés and his troops. The last battle had proved that the Spanish couldn't be destroyed. Indian tribes from far and near sent delegates offering to join these strangers who could free them from the domination of the Aztecs. At the same time, more Spanish soldiers arrived. Some came from Velásquez, who sent them to

reinforce Narváez; others came from the governor of Jamaica.

Cortés built warships and put them on the lake to wipe out the Aztec war canoes. He and his Indian allies slowly advanced up the causeways. When they finally broke into Tenochtitlan, the Indian allies went wild. They massacred 150,000 people. "I have never known a race to be so pitiless, nor human beings so deprived of pity," Cortés wrote.

Under Cortés, the Spanish conquered their first overseas empire. They also opened a new route to the Indies. Alvarado, in fact, was about to take a ship across the Pacific when he stopped in what is now the state of Jalisco to help some Spaniards in trouble with Indians. He was killed, but a generation later the Manila galleons were regularly plying the Pacific between Mexico and the Philippines.

Charles V made Cortés captain-general of New Spain. Cortés lived in Mexico like a king—an Oriental king with a harem, which included Malinche. His legal wife came to Mexico, but she was murdered soon afterwards. Accused of that crime (and many others), Cortés returned to Spain to defend himself. He left his enemies in disgrace, and soon married again. Finally replaced as the viceroy of Spain, Cortés returned to his homeland, where he remained close to the emperor. He died on his Spanish estate in 1547.

An Aztec drawing depicting the European soldiers with their superior arms.

23

Francisco Pizarro
The Incredible Conquest
(A.D. 1475–1541)

Hernán Cortés was a knight with a college education and who was—at one time—a favorite of the governor of Cuba. He was the mayor of a city, a rich landowner, and had social position before he set out for Mexico. The man who followed in his footsteps had neither money nor position. His name was Francisco Pizarro, and he was a bastard whose mother left him as an infant on the steps of a church. He first became a swineherd, then a common soldier. To better himself, he took a job (at the age of 40) as a seaman on a ship bound for the New World, where he joined the expedition led by Vasco Nuñez de Balboa. He became a friend of the explorer and waded into the Pacific Ocean with him. Later, to curry favor with the governor of Panama (Pedro Arias de Avila, the infamous "Pedrarias Davila"), he arrested Balboa and turned him over to his executioner.

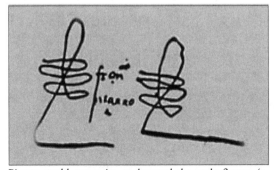

Pizarro could not write, so he used the curly figures (a rubrica) to sign, and then a scribe set his name between.

Pizarro joined a partnership with another illiterate old soldier, Diego de Almagro, and a priest named Fernando de Luque to seek a rumored empire somewhere to the south in the Pacific Coast. Pizarro would be field commander; Almagro would find men and supplies; and Luque, the only partner who could read, would take care of paperwork. They got Pedrarias's permission to explore the coast, but when they spoke to him, they made no mention of gold. They raised money for the trip, but found nothing. Two years later, they tried again. Pedrarias demanded to know why they were wasting so much time and money. He suspected they were on the trail of gold. They persuaded him to renounce claim to any lands they might find for the immediate payment of 1,000 pesos. They continued exploring. A new governor, Pedro de los Rios, also worried about the waste of time and manpower.

At one point, Pizarro and his crew were waiting on an island for Almagro to come with supplies. They were half-starved—a frequent condition for them. Instead of Almagro, a ship from the governor showed up with orders for Pizarro to release any men who wished to return to Panama. Pizarro drew a line on the sand with his dagger. Pointing south, he said: "Comrades, on that side are toil, hunger, nakedness, the drenching storm, desertion, and death. On this side, ease and pleasure." Pointing south again, he said: "There lies Peru and its riches; here Panama and its poverty. For my own part, I go to the south." He jumped over the line; 13 men followed him. Then the supply ship left, and the exploration continued. After seven months of starving, swatting mosquitoes, battling predators, and hiding from vampire bats, they found little, although they heard of a powerful kingdom to the south. Del Rios, the new governor, ordered them to return to Panama in six months.

With a handful of followers and fantastic luck, Pizarro conquered the largest empire in the New World.

When Pizarro returned to Panama, his backers said they were bankrupt. When he asked the governor for money, del Rios laughed at him. Pizarro went to Spain and tried to see King Charles I of Spain (who was also Charles V, the Holy Roman Emperor). Hernán Cortés was visiting Spain at the time. Cortes interceded for Pizarro with the emperor. Pizarro got an imperial commission and enough money to make him independent of del Rios.

Pizarro and Almagro sailed from Panama in 1531. They had three ships, 183 men, and 37 horses. While they were moving south, two ships and 100 men under Hernando de Soto came down from Nicaragua to join them. This was still a ridiculously small force with which to conquer the largest empire in the Western Hemisphere.

But Pizarro had some advantages he wasn't even aware of. One was smallpox. The disease had been introduced by Europeans on the eastern coast of South America and had moved across the continent before the Europeans ever appeared on the west coast. In Peru, it is estimated to have killed a third of the population in a few years. The smallpox epidemics were followed by a succession of epidemics of other European and African diseases. The death rate among Native Americans from these epidemics is mind-boggling. In some places, the population was only a fraction of its pre-Columbian number a century after the white men appeared. Smallpox prepared the way for Pizarro. The Spanish, having been exposed to smallpox for centuries, had a greater immunity.

Civil war was also an advantage for Francisco Pizarro. The Inca emperor had divided his empire between his two sons. Each son led a faction that believed its leader was the only true emperor; war followed. The winner,

Atahualpa, had just defeated and captured his half-brother, Huascar, when Pizarro marched into the Andes.

The third Spanish advantage was the nature of the Inca monarchy. The Inca emperor was considered to be a god. Nothing could happen unless he or one of his ancestors had ordered it. Every citizen of the empire knew his or her place, which was fixed within society. "The mountains and the mines, the pastures, the game, the wood, and all kinds of resources were controlled and shared so that each knew and possessed his own, without anyone else being able to take it," wrote one of Pizarro's soldiers. But the Inca owned everything.

Pizarro learned of the political situation in Peru when he was approached by partisans of the deposed Inca, Huascar. It was a great opportunity to divide and conquer. At the moment, he was more interested in the winner of the Peruvian power struggle than the loser. He sent couriers to Atahualpa, saying he had come from a friendly monarch to aid him in battle. Atahualpa was camped with his army outside Cajamarca, a town near the Peruvian capital, Cuzco. The Inca emperor ordered all the inhabitants of Cajamarca to leave their homes so Pizarro and his men would have a place to stay.

When they arrived in the town, Pizarro sent de Soto to the emperor's camp. The Peruvians were greatly interested with de Soto's horse, although Atahualpa himself showed no emotion during the meeting. To entertain the emperor and his soldiers, de Soto put on a display of horsemanship, at one point riding his charger at full speed toward the emperor, then stopping him suddenly inches from the emperor's chest. Atahualpa didn't move a muscle, although the men around him dashed back in panic.

The emperor had his frightened men put to death for showing fear.

Atahualpa agreed to meet Pizarro the next day in Cajamarca. Both sides prepared for the meeting. Pizarro hid his cavalry, commanded by his brother (Hernando Pizarro) and by Hernando de Soto, in buildings around the central plaza. He hid the infantry in other buildings. The artillery went into a stone building from which it could cover the whole plaza. Pizarro kept a few soldiers and a priest with him. Atahualpa had not been idle, either. He sent his men, who outnumbered the Spanish 100 or 200 to 1, to cover all exits from the valley in which Cajamarca was built. The rest moved over hidden trails to surround the town. Atahualpa arrived, carried in an enormous litter by the highest nobles of his nation, behind a line of other nobles sweeping the dust from the road. The emperor had an escort of unarmed (but richly dressed) nobles. Outside the town, his general, Ruminagui, waited for the signal to rush in and kill the strangers.

The first person to approach the Peruvian emperor was a priest, Vicente de Valverde. Speaking through an interpreter, Valverde said he had come to tell the Inca about the true God. "I am a priest of God, and I teach Christians the things of God, and in like manner, I come to teach you," he said. "What I teach is what God says to us in this book. Therefore, on the part of God and of the Christians, I beseech you to be their friend, for such is God's will, and it will be for your good." Atahualpa asked to see the book. Valverde handed him the Bible.

The Peruvians, unlike the Aztecs and the Mayas, had no books. Instead of writing, they stored information in a code using knotted cords. Atahualpa appeared to expect the book to talk to him. Valverde tried to open the

Bible for him, but the emperor, outraged by this stranger touching his sacred person, struck the priest's arm away. He opened the Bible himself, but as he could make no sense of the strange marks on its pages, threw it on the ground. It was Valverde's turn to be outranged. He screamed for the Spanish to attack.

Pizarro gave the signal to attack. The guns went off, and the Spanish charged. Atahualpa's unarmed escort tried to block the attackers with their bodies. They were all cut down, and Pizarro seized the emperor and dragged him away.

Atahualpa never gave the signal to attack. His army, stunned that these strange people had captured their living god, fled back to Quito, more than 700 miles away. The Spanish soldiers looted the abandoned Indian camp. Atahualpa, seeing how gold delighted his captors, told Pizarro he would give him enough to fill one room with gold and two rooms with silver up to the height of a man. The rooms were 21 feet long and 15 feet wide. Pizarro agreed to the bargain.

In his prison in Cuzco, Huascar (the emperor's defeated brother) heard of the bargain. He told the Spanish that if they would free him and return him to the throne, he

The Battle of Cajamarca between the Spanish and the Incans, November 16, 1532.

would fill the same rooms with gold and silver right up to the ceiling. Atahualpa heard of that bid from some of his Indian attendants. He issued an order; a few days later, Huascar was murdered. Atahualpa's people filled the room with gold and silver as he had offered. But he wasn't released. Pizarro had him tried for conspiring against the Spanish, usurping the throne, killing his brother, practicing polygamy, and sacrificing to false gods. Because he agreed to be baptized, he was strangled to death instead of being burned alive.

Most modern historians say that without his Indian allies, Hernán Cortés and his "handful of Spaniards" could not have conquered Mexico by themselves. That's probably true, although it's seldom mentioned that without those allies there would not have been the horrible massacre that followed the fall of Tenochtitlan. But Pizarro didn't have half as many Spaniards as Cortés, and he had no Indian allies at all. He triumphed because, without their emperor, the vast majority of Peruvians could do nothing at all. Ruminagui tried to fight back, but his troops were disheartened and demoralized. They outnumbered the Spanish, but they had no horses, cannons, guns, armor, steel swords, or trained discipline. Ruminagui was easily defeated by a much smaller force under Sebastian de Belacazar. Later, Manco (a member of the royal family Pizarro had appointed to be a puppet Inca emperor) rebelled. He laid seige to Cuzco, which his troops burned down with a rain of fire arrows. But the Spanish garrison held out, and as the planting season started, the Incan army began to melt away. Manco raised the seige and retired to the mountains, from which he waged a guerilla war for several years.

Pizarro's most dangerous enemies were not Indians, but Spaniards. One of the first was Cortés's companion, Pedro de Alvarado, who (after conquering Guatemala) landed in Peru. Alvarado lost many men crossing the Andes, and then he was confronted by an army commanded by Diego de Almagro. But battered as it was, Alvarado's army was larger and better equipped than Almagro's. Even if it were not, Pedro de Alvarado was no commander to sneer at. On the other hand, the impetuous Alvarado began to realize that trespassing on territory the crown had given to Pizarro was not good policy. In the end, Almagro bought Alvarado off for 100,000 pesos. Alvarado returned to Mexico, where he died after a horse rolled over him. Many of his men joined Pizarro.

One enemy who did not leave was Diego de Almagro. There was tension between Pizarro and Almagro, originating in petty disputes from years earlier. Finally, Almagro led his faction in a civil war against the Pizarro brothers. By this time, he and Francisco Pizarro were both in their 60s. Hernando Pizarro led the Pizarro people against Almagro's forces at a place called Las Salinas. Almagro was captured, convicted of high treason, and executed with the garrote. But Almagro's followers were offended by Pizarro's arrogance, and conspired to assassinate him. Pizarro died at his palace in Lima on June 26, 1541. Francisco Pizarro conquered Peru with a combination of recklessness, ruthlessness, and luck. Although his methods have been questioned, none can deny that he changed history.

24

Ivan IV
The Terrible
(A.D. 1530–1584)

For more than 300 years, Russia was isolated from the rest of Europe. It was conquered by the Mongols early in the 13th century and incorporated into the Golden Horde, a division of the Mongol Empire founded by Batu Khan (the grandson of Genghis Khan). Russia before the conquest had been a conglomeration of independent principalities. The Mongols gave the princes a certain amount of independence, but they did not hesitate to replace a prince who displeased them. Prince Alexander Nevsky of Vladimir, for example, became a Russian hero by defeating the Swedes, but he still had to touch the ground with his forehead before the khan.

In the late 14th century, it looked as if Russia might throw off the Mongol yoke. Civil war weakened the Golden Horde, and some of the Russian princes neglected to send their annual tribute. In 1373, the khan sent an army against Moscow. Prince Dimitrii Donskoi repulsed the Mongols. Then he actually invaded their territory and twice defeated the Mongol general Mamai.

In retaliation, Toqtamish Khan destroyed Moscow and sacked a number Russian cities. The Lithuanians tried to help the Russians, but Toqtamish annihilated their army. Toqtamish's Russian expedition was so successful he decided to conquer the territory of another Central Asian potentate, Tamerlane, a Turkish conqueror often compared with Genghis Khan. Strangely, Tamerlane, famed for building towers with the skulls of his enemies, did not kill Toqtamish after crushing his army. He left the Mongols to rebuild their shattered domain and rode back to Samarkand. The Golden Horde split into two rival khanates, the Crimea and Kazan. Moscow was subject to the Khan of Kazan.

Ivan the Terrible took advantage of the weakness of the Mongols's and broke the hold of Central Asia on Russia.

War broke out between the khans of Crimea and Kazan. Kazan was defeated and the Mongols in Russia divided into three khanates—Kazan, Crimea, and Astrakhan. Meanwhile, Moscow and the other Russian principalities began adopting two Western devices—cannons and muskets. The balance of power in Russia was changing.

The Mongols were still raiding Russian villages to capture slaves, who would either be kept or sold to the Venetians and Ottomans for profit. The khan of Crimea tried to bluff the teenage prince of Moscow into sending him tribute. The prince, Ivan IV (later known as Ivan the Terrible), was a hard man to bluff. He was cruel, deceitful, and, in his later years, insane. Ivan broke the power of

the Russian nobility and had himself crowned as tsar (or caesar). The ruler of Moscow, he proclaimed, was now the successor of the emperor in Constantinople.

The Russians captured a courier from Kazan. He carried a message to the Khan of Crimea asking for military aid. Ivan decided to strike first. His forces marched against Kazan, because it was the weaker of the two khanates (and because a pretender to the throne of Kazan, Shah Ali, asked for his help). Ivan besieged Kazan in November of 1549. The siege dragged on until February, when a premature warm spell turned the ground into a sea of mud. Fearing that his artillery would be hopelessly bogged down, Ivan lifted the siege. Before he left, though, he built a fortress

This painting, commonly referred to as "Ivan the Terrible Killing his Son," was painted by Ilya Repin.

20 miles from the city, where troops could keep an eye on Kazan. He also allied himself with nomad tribes in the area. The khan of Kazan, decided the situation was hopeless and tried to flee. The Russians caught him and cut off his head. Ivan installed Shah Ali as the new khan.

Shah Ali was not properly respectful toward the tsar of all the Russians, so Ivan besieged Kazan again. He brought his artillery, of course, but it wasn't much help. The walls of Kazan were 25 feet thick. Nomads in the surrounding forest helped Kazan by attacking the Russian rear while the defenders were sallying out against the Russian front. The nomad attacks were hit-and-run raids. When Russian resistance hardened after the initial shock, the nomads would ride back to a hidden camp in the forest. The forest was too vast to allow the Russians to search for their base. So Ivan hid part of his cavalry, and when the nomads retreated, the Russian horsemen followed them and destroyed their camp. The Russians emerged from the forest with a huge amount of loot, including grain and cattle, and hundreds of Russians who had been enslaved by the nomads.

Meanwhile, the Russians around Kazan had been undermining its walls and towers.

The explosion of hundreds of barrels of gunpowder knocked down two towers and tore wide gaps in the wall. All the Mongols who did not surrender were killed.

Two years later, Ivan marched against Astrakhan. Again, he installed a puppet khan. And when the puppet tried to break his strings, Ivan annexed Astrakhan. Crimea survived, greatly reduced in territory, only by becoming part of the Ottoman Empire. The Mongol grip on Europe was broken forever.

In 1581, Ivan beat his daughter-in-law for wearing immodest clothing. She was pregnant at the time, and beating caused her to miscarry the child. Reportedly, Ivan's son (also named Ivan) was so enraged at this father's actions that the two men fought, resulting in the son's death. This ended the Rurik Dynasty and began the Time of Troubles.

Ivan IV ruled for many years, and he earned his nickname of Ivan the Terrible many times over. He died while playing chess with Bogdan Belsky on March 18, 1584. It is believed that Belsky and another advisor (Boris Gudonov) decided to poison Ivan with mercury after discovering Ivan in the process of raping Gudonov's sister. The two men probably felt that they had to murder the tsar or risk their own deaths.

25

Yi Sun-sin
The First Ironclads
(A.D. 1545–1598)

Toyotomi Hideyoshi was nothing if not confident. He had reason to be. Born a peasant, he became involved in the seemingly endless series of civil wars that racked Japan during the 16th century. Through talent, not birth, he rose to become the henchman of Oda Nobunaga, the general who deposed the shogun Ashikaga Yashiaki. Hideyoshi succeeded Oda Nobunaga after the latter died. He managed to unify Japan for the first time in more than a century. No other man in all Japanese history has ever risen from the peasant class to leadership of the country.

Hideyoshi knew that one way to keep the country unified was to conduct a foreign war. And, he thought, he had the means to do so successfully. Japan had thousands of experienced, battle-hardened soldiers. And since Japan had adopted the matchlock handgun, it had armed thousands of men with this weapon. "At least in absolute numbers, guns were almost certainly more common in Japan in the late 16th century than in any other country in the world," Noel Perrin wrote in his book *Giving Up the Gun*. Hideyoshi planned to first conquer Korea, then China, and then the Philippines.

Hideyoshi's plans were known in Korea. There, an officer named Yi Sun-sin made plans to counter them. Yi became a military officer in 1576. The Korean military at the time, similar to many others, did not have a separate army and navy. Yi commanded frontier posts on the Yalu River and fought the Jurchen nomads before being appointed an admiral. He knew that the greatest threat to Korea was a sea-borne invasion from Japan. He immediately began modifying the Korean fleet.

Admiral Yi Sun-shin is almost unknown in the West, but he was the inventor of the ironclad ship, and perhaps the most successful admiral in history.
Korean Cultural Center

The mainstay of the Korean Navy for more than a century was the *kobukson,* or turtle ship. These ships had two or three decks, with the top deck covered by a curved wooden roof (about 10 inches thick). That roof made the Korean warships look like floating turtles. They were propelled by both sails and oars, and carried almost 40 cannons. Spear points and sword blades fringed the decks to discourage boarders. Yi's modification was adding iron plates to the roof and sides. There were gun ports in the armor, and openings through which flaming arrows could be shot or grenades thrown.

Hideyoshi struck in May of 1592 and took Pusan. A few days later, Yi Sun-sin's ironclad turtle ships attacked a Japanese fleet of 800 ships. After 26 Japanese ships were burned, the invading fleet fled. On land, the Japanese had little trouble. They pushed up the peninsula and reached Seoul in 19 days. The invading army, however, had to be supplied. Yi and his turtle ships kept busy. During May and June, the Korean Navy routed several Japanese flotillas, sinking 72 enemy ships in the process.

Toyotomi Hideyoshi did not achieve his rank by being stupid. He mounted heavy cannons to guard the entrances to Japanese harbors. Until then, while Japan had an abundance of handguns, it had few cannons. Hideyoshi also put heavier guns on his ships

A restored turtle ship (*kobukson* in Korean). This is one of the ironclad ships Admiral Yi used to destroy the Japanese fleet of Toyotomi Hideyoshi.
Korean Cultural Center

and protected the ships with iron plates. Yi's success, though, was based on more than armored ships. He invented new tactical formations, such as the one called the "fishnet formation," an inverted V that surrounded Japanese formations and concentrated fire on them from two sides. Another time, he attacked a Japanese fleet of 800 ships with only 180 of his own. But by the clever use of fire ships, he destroyed 400 Japanese ships. In 1593, the Japanese withdrew.

But Hideyoshi would not give up. He planned another invasion, but first he had to get rid of Yi Sun-sin. A Japanese man (posing as a Korean spy) reported that a huge Japanese fleet was coming and proposed sending Yi Sun-sin and his ships to a location where he could ambush the enemy. In 1597, King Seonjo of Korea ordered Yi to take his ships to that location. Yi refused. He knew that the area was studded with sunken rocks, and he might lose all his turtle ships. He was tortured, but still refused. The king ordered his execution, but relented after most of his officials pointed to Yi's record in defending the country. Instead of killing him, the king demoted Yi to a common soldier. A new admiral, Won Kyun, dismissed all Yi's friends from the navy and took his ships to the proposed ambush area; he lost all his ships. The king quickly reappointed Yi.

Yi immediately began construction of a new fleet of turtle ships. He had only 12 completed when a new Japanese fleet of 133 ships appeared. Yi attacked with his 12 ships

and destroyed 31 enemy ships. The rest fled. The Japanese tried again, but in November of 1598, at the Battle of Chinhae Bay, Yi sank 200 of the 400 Japanese ships. He was killed before the battle ended.

But that battle ended the war. The Japanese sailors brought news of the disaster back to the ailing Hideyoshi, who died soon afterwards. Without the dynamic Hideyoshi to push them, the Japanese gave up their dreams of conquest.

If it were not for Yi Sun-sin, who won every one of his 22 naval battles and never lost a ship, Japan would certainly have conquered Korea. Some experts believe it could also have overcome China. And if Japan had wrested control of the eastern seas from Korea, nothing could have stopped it from annexing the Philippines, where Spain's forces would have been vastly outnumbered and outgunned by the Japanese.

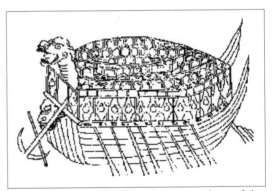

Drawing of a turtle ship from the court archives of the medieval Korean kingdom of Chosun Silrok-Chosun. *Korean Cultural Center*

26

Tokugawa Ieyasu
The Shogun
(A.D. 1543–1616)

In 1582, Oda Nobunaga seemed about to end the long and bloody period the Japanese called the Age of Battles by unifying Japan and suppressing its scores of rival *daimos* (lords). He was bringing up reinforcements for his general (Toyotomi Hideyoshi) when he stopped at Kyoto. Oda never reached Hideyoshi. Another general, Aketchi Misuhide, assassinated him. Hideyoshi, usually considered the best general in Japanese history, succeeded him. Because of his low birth, he was never named *shogun*. "Shogun" simply means *commanding general*, but the shogun was actually the real ruler of Japan. The emperor was venerated as a god, but his functions were purely ceremonial. In the year 1331, Emperor Go-Daigo had decided to get rid of the shogun, an action which initiated the Age of Battles.

Hideyoshi's death, following the last defeat of his navy by Yi Sun-sin, destroyed the unity of the empire. He had divided rule among five regents for his infant son. The regents immediately began fighting each other. One of them was Tokugawa Ieyasu, who eventually seized power.

Tokugawa Ieyasu founded the Tokugawa shogunate of Japan, which ruled from 1600 until 1868. Ieyasu seized power in 1600, was appointed shogun in 1603, and abdicated in 1605. However, he remained a powerful voice in the government until his death in 1616.

Japanese soldiers fencing with wooden swords. To the samurai, swordsmanship was the supreme military art, but Tokugawa unified Japan with the power of guns.
London Illustrated News

When Ieyasu seized power, the daimos recognized Ieyasu as the ruler of Japan, but others said that he was usurping the place of Hideyoshi's son, Toyotomi Hideyori, and claimed to be fighting for him. The two factions met at Sekigahara, where one contingent of the Toyotomi army defected and joined the Tokugawa army and turned the tide of the battle. Tokugawa Ieyasu was sufficiently noble for the emperor to name him shogun (and thus commander of all samurai). Ieyasu knew, though, that many samurai thought that Toyotomi Hideyori was the rightful ruler. Ieyasu had his granddaughter marry

Hideyori, but he named his own son, Tokugawa Hidetada, as his heir to the shogunate. Tension between the Toyotomis and the Tokugawas increased, and Tokugawa Ieyasu besieged Osaka Castle, Hideyori's stronghold.

The siege dragged on. Unable to take the castle, Ieyasu offered peace terms, which included dismantling the castle's defenses. Hideyori's mother was terrified by Ieyasu's cannons, and she begged her son to accept the terms. Against the advice of his officers, he did. When the defenses had been dismantled, Ieyasu renewed the war. He led 150,000 troops against Hideyori's 55,000. The numbers made the outcome inevitable. Hideyori and his mother committed suicide. Ieyasu murdered Hideyori's infant son and burned the castle.

Tokugawa Ieyasu, at the age of 57, became the undisputed ruler of Japan and founded the Tokugawa Dynasty of shoguns, who ruled Japan from 1603 to 1867. Under the Tokugawas, Japan became increasingly isolated. Some of the trends were begun by Hideyoshi (who expelled Christian missionaries, limited foreign trade, banned anyone who was not a samurai from owning weaponry, and forbade anyone from moving or changing his profession). The manufacture of guns practically ceased. In 1616, Ieyasu fell ill and died in his bed at the age of 74.

Medieval Japanese armor of the type worn by Tokugawa's samurai warriors.
Natural History

The Tokugawas limited foreign ships only to Dutch ships visiting Nagasaki. In 1825, antiforeign policies reached the point where the shogun ordered his samurai to fire on any foreign ships. Considering the state of Japan's military, that was not a very bright idea, as the Japanese government learned 23 years later when Commodore Matthew Perry sailed into Hiraga.

27

Maurice of Nassau
The Importance of Firepower
(A.D. 1567–1625)

Europe's wars of religion in the 16th and 17th century were unmitigated horrors—a continuous round of robbery, rape, and murder. But they resulted in many military innovations and ultimately led to the creation of modern armies. The foremost innovator was Maurice, Prince of Orange and Count of Nassau.

A portrait of Maurice of Nassau, painted by Michiel Jansz van Mierevelt.

Maurice was the son of William the Silent, Prince of Orange, who was known in his own country as Willem der Schluw—William the Prudent. (Somehow, English writers confused prudence with silence.) William actually talked enough to organize a serious revolt in what were then called the Spanish Netherlands, which included modern Netherlands, Belgium, and Luxembourg.

The revolt was caused by the effort of Holy Roman Emperor Charles V to make the Netherlands universally Catholic. William the Prudent became the leader of the revolt, although he had been a close friend of Charles V. In a comparatively short time, the rebels controlled most of the Netherlands. Philip II (Charles's son and king of Spain) sent Spain's leading soldier, the duke of Alva, to the Netherlands. Alva beat William repeatedly, but his brutality drove the population to side with the rebels. As the war ground on, there were more sieges and fewer land battles. All of the Dutch cities had elaborate water defenses. Alva found sieges in Holland immensely frustrating. Spain ran out of money, and the unpaid troops mutinied in Antwerp and massacred the population.

Philip recalled Alva in disgrace and replaced him with his half-brother Don Juan of Austria. Juan reversed the course of the war, but he died at the age of 39 after a brief illness.

His replacement was Alessandro Farnese, the duke of Parma, one of the greatest soldiers of the era. Parma continued Spain's winning streak until Philip ordered him to suspend his counterinsurgency operations and concentrate on other enemies, first the English, and then the French.

In 1584 William the Prudent was assassinated, and the war took another turn. That turned out to be a lucky break for the Dutch rebels. William was succeeded by his son, Maurice of Nassau. Maurice was only 17 when he stepped into his father's shoes, and until that time, he had been a student, not a soldier. But Maurice took the offensive and recaptured many cities between 1590 and 1594. Even more important, he reorganized the army as he went along.

All major European armies of the time were based on solid masses of pikemen, a formation invented by the Swiss (or reinvented; the Greeks had it first), supported by crosssbowmen and arqebusiers (later musketeers), and a few cannons for sieges.

As a student, young Maurice had devoured accounts of Roman military operations. He divided his army into battalions of 550 men (comparable to Roman cohorts). The battalions were subdivided into companies (something similar to the Roman maniples), and the companies into platoons. The new captain-general established a clear chain of command from the commanding general to the lowest private. Both of these innovations made his army more mobile and more responsive to commands.

Similar to the Romans, Maurice had his men build an entrenched camp wherever they stopped. Every man had to be as skilled with a pick and shovel as with weapons. Other armies hired civilians to dig trenches and other siege works, but Maurice's troops did their own digging.

Maurice also worked with the gun founders of Holland to get lighter cannons, and he greatly increased the proportion of musketeers to pikemen. In other armies, musketeers fought in relatively dense formations. Maurice's musketeers generally fought in a line only five deep, so at any given moment his men could fire more bullets than the same number of soldiers in other armies. They could fire faster, too. The matchlock musket of that day required 42 distinct movements to load, fire, reload, and fire a second shot. Maurice drilled his men to fire "by the numbers" until these movements were done almost subconsciously. None of his men ever "reloaded" a gun that had not been fired (something that happened frequently in the American Civil War).

Musketeers were the backbone of Maurice of Nassau's army. Through incessant drilling, he turned his musketeers into the most potent military force of their time.

Maurice drilled his men in the countermarch. The front rank would fire a volley, then about-face and walk through the ranks of their comrades as they reloaded. While they were marching to the rear, the rank originally behind them would fire and countermarch. This way, his troops could keep up an almost continuous fire on the enemy. Maurice's pikemen were also drilled heavily. When faced with charging cavalry, they could open their ranks to let the musketeers shelter behind the pikes after firing a last volley.

A military scholar, Maurice founded the first military academy in Europe. It accepted foreign students, which helped spread his reforms all over Europe. Many of Maurice's reforms have been credited to a later general, King Gustavus Adolphus of Sweden. One source claims that Gustavus first gave musketeers swords so they could defend themselves when their guns were empty. Jacob de Gheyn's drawings of Maurice's musketeers clearly show these troops wearing swords. (Gustavus did make a number of innovations, but they were mostly simple modifications of Maurice's reforms.)

The duke of Parma returned to the Netherlands in 1591 and stopped Maurice's offensive, but King Philip again sent him to France where he was wounded and died in 1592. The 80 Years' War finally ended with an independent United Provinces of the Netherlands. The independent Netherlands is a small country that has played a large role in world affairs. Much of the credit for that independence belongs to Prince Maurice. The organization of all modern armies can be traced back to his military reforms.

28

Jean Baptiste de Gribreauval
Revolutionizing Artillery
(A.D. 1715–1789)

An old Russian nickname for artillery was "the god of war." Until the 18th century, though, it was a most peculiar god. The earliest artillerymen were not even soldiers. They were civilian contractors, members of one of the medieval guilds of gunners. Soldiers tended to give them a wide berth—some, because they associated anyone involved with guns and gunpowder as being somehow connected with black magic; others, because of the behavior of the gunners themselves. Artillerymen were notorious for abstaining from swearing, whoring, and drunkenness. Working with a device that was liable to explode without warning and blow you to bits had much to do with this eccentricity. As cannons became more common (and safer), gunners lost their aura of the supernatural. They even became regular soldiers.

But artillerymen still didn't quite fit into the military establishment, nor did the artillery quite lose its civilian flavor. This was largely because of the ancient cult of the warrior, as promulgated by senior officers. A warrior fought; he didn't do grunt work such as digging and driving horses. Maurice of Nassau broke new ground by having his regular soldiers break ground for trenches and bastions. Other armies reluctantly began issuing soldiers shovels, although these were usually segregated into special units known as "engineers" or "sappers." Sometimes these engineers didn't even carry weapons.

Fighting, to members of the warrior cult, meant struggling with an enemy hand-to-hand with sword, pike, bayonet, or even bludgeon. The musket was tolerated, but only because it was used at very short range and was merely a preliminary to the decisive bayonet charge. In World War I, French military doctrine was still emphasizing the importance of the bayonet, although American authorities at the end of that war calculated that only .024 percent of their casualties were caused by bayonets. Even in Napoleon's time, his surgeon general said that for every bayonet wound he treated, there were 100 gun wounds. Rifles, which were effective at longer ranges than muskets, were not quite honorable. An English newspaper, the *Middlesex Journal*, on December 31, 1776, quoted a British officer in a piece on the fighting in the American Revolution as saying, "a rifleman is not entitled to any quarter."

So artillerymen, who could kill troops half a mile away, were not accepted as real soldiers. Consequently, little was done to provide artillerymen with uniform equipment, training, or efficient transportation. Then, in 1732, the son of a magistrate in Amiens enlisted in the French artillery. The artillery was a good choice for him. Three years later, he earned his commission. Jean Baptiste Vacquette de Gribreauval would never have become an officer if he had joined the cavalry or infantry. To gain a commission in those arms, a man had to prove he had noble blood. But in the officer corps of the artillery, smart commoners could become officers.

Gribreauval did the best he could with what he had. In truth, the French army was better equipped than most. In 1734, a Swiss engineer named Jean Maritz moved to France and invented a machine for drilling the bore of a cannon from a solid casting. Previously, cannons were cast around a core, so the casting had a bore when it came from the mould. The trouble was that the bore was never straight. The weight of the heavy liquid metal pouring into the mould invariably shifted the core. Drilling the bore from a solid casting ensured that it would be straight. Drilling also meant that the bore could fit the projectile more precisely, which meant that the gun would be both more powerful and more accurate. The drilling process took a lot of development, but Maritz and his son (also named Jean Maritz) worked out the problems. In 1755, the younger Maritz became inspector general of gun foundries.

Some of these new guns began to appear while Gribreauval was commanding troops and studying the art of artillery. Until then though, he (like all other European artillerymen) was working with a weird hodgepodge of cannons. Because each gun was cast in a different mould, no bore sizes were precisely the same. Cannons had been cast to fire projectiles of any weight the gun founder fancied. Some guns were long, some were short, some were heavy, and some were light. The gun carriages had not much improved since the Italian wars of the 15th century.

When the Seven Years' War broke out, Gribreauval was loaned to France's ally, Austria. He became an Austrian lieutenant field marshal, and by the war's end, commanded all of the Austrian artillery. He returned to France in 1764 and became inspector of artillery. The next year, he was promoted to lieutenant general in the French army. But because he was a commoner, it took 10 years before he was promoted to the top artillery position—inspector general. After 40 years as a gunner, Gribreauval had a chance to modernize his favorite weapon. He did more than modernize it; he revolutionized it.

First, he established three branches of artillery—garrison, siege, and field. Garrison guns were the least mobile—mostly heavy pieces. Siege guns were also heavy, but they also had to be somewhat mobile. Field guns were light and mobile. In place of the medley of calibers the artillery once had, Gribreauval limited guns to three sizes: 4, 8, and 12 pounders. (Field guns were four pounders.) He later allowed 6 pounder field guns. Gun weight was limited to 150 times the weight of the iron cannonball it fired. In addition to guns (comparatively high-velocity, flat trajectory weapons) Gribreauval standardized sizes for howitzers (shorter-barreled weapons firing at a higher trajectory), and mortars (very short, high-trajectory weapons).

Gribreauval also introduced the elevation screw. This made adjustments for range far more precise. It also enhanced the value of another Gribreauval improvement: a precise sight for the cannon. The inspector general introduced improvements in the type of ammunition used in the artillery: solid shot (cannonballs), canister (small shot encased in a can), grape (larger shot in a wood-and-canvass container), and explosive shells.

He also improved ammunition by introducing cartridges containing both powder and projectile. Finally, he made his artillery more mobile by improving the gun carriages, by harnessing the horses in pairs, and by eliminating the civilian contractors, who usually took their horses out of harm's way until the fighting was over. Along with the guns, the soldier-teamsters towed separate caissons containing extra ammunition. He trained his artillerymen to use all these improvements by drilling them rigorously.

Gribreauval's reforms were introduced over a long period. It wasn't until the French army introduced the division system in 1788 that all were in place. Gribreauval's reforms were so far-reaching that they remained in place until 1829.

Gribreauval died on May 9, 1789. On July 14, 1789, the citizens of Paris stormed the Bastille, and the French Revolution began. At Valmy in 1792, Gribreauval's artillery drove off the Prussians, Austrians, and Hessians who invaded France to put down the revolution.

Gribreauval's reforms were a big part of another, longer-lasting change—the transition of the "warrior," fighting his enemy hand-to-hand, to the "warfighter," with his rockets, cruise missiles, and satellite-guided bombs. Some think the former was more heroic, but no one denies that the latter is more efficient.

Gribreauval's insistence on standard-pattern guns made the French artillery the best in the world and changed the armaments of all other nations.

29

Peter the Great

The Importance of Sea Power

(A.D. 1672–1725)

Ivan the Terrible wanted to establish trade routes to western Europe. But Russia had no natural outlet to the North Sea. To get one, he invaded Livonia (a Baltic state that included parts of modern Latvia and Estonia). That touched off a long series of wars involving Russia, Poland, Denmark, and Sweden. It ended with Sweden becoming the dominant power in northern Europe. Sweden closed off Russia's gateway to western Europe. That left Russia in limbo—neither part of the Turkish-Mongol culture of the Asian steppes, nor part of modern Europe. Russia languished in this limbo through several Tsars, until the birth of Peter I, who would become known as Peter the Great.

Peter I was proclaimed tsar when he was only 10 years old. There was, of course, some palace intrigue, and the streltsy (a body of musketeers who fancied themselves a Pratorean Guard) revolted. Peter and his older brother Ivan were made co-rulers, although the actual ruler was the regent, Peter's half-sister Sophia.

As a child, Peter showed an interest in affairs of state and the military. He organized his playmates into two companies, drilled them as soldiers, and played war games with them. When, at 19, a *coup d'etat* made him sole ruler, those two companies became the Preobrazensky and Semyonevsky Guard regiments. Peter wanted a counterweight to

the streltsy. The musketeers had been the great Russian advantage in the wars against the Central Asian nomads, but in the century or so since Ivan the Terrible, they had come to think of themselves as indispensable. Peter dedicated himself to modernizing his country, especially its military power. He ended Russia's long feud with Poland, and then formed an alliance. With his western frontier more or less secure, he turned south. The first of his many wars was against the Turks. He took Azov, which did not require an especially sophisticated military machine.

Peter I was a striking figure at 6-feet, 8-inches tall. He had large, green eyes, and was considered especially handsome.

135

Then Peter sent his "Grand Embassy" to all the countries of western Europe. He traveled with the embassy in disguise, posing as a sailor, a shipwright, and other trades to study modern military techniques. He learned about artillery in Prussia and helped build ships in the Netherlands and England.

While he was abroad, the streltsy again revolted. Peter quickly returned to Russia and put down the revolt. He personally decapitated some of the ringleaders and abolished the organization. He then began modernizing Russia, using the techniques he learned while traveling through Europe. He ordered all Russian men to shave their beards—which scandalized Orthodox churchmen. He personally wielded the shears and razor on some of his most important nobles. The nobles lost whatever power Ivan the Terrible had left them, and both they and the peasants were drafted into his military. Thanks to Peter, the Russian military now included a navy. He built roads and canals specifically to speed the mobilization and resupply of the army.

In 1700 (after making peace with Turkey) Peter plunged Russia into what became known as the Great Northern War. It lasted 21 years and involved Sweden, Denmark, Poland, and Saxony. The young king of Sweden, Charles XII, was considered one of the best European generals. Peter was in no way a comparable tactician, but he almost always outnumbered his opponent. In 1714, Peter's brand-new navy defeated the Swedish fleet, making it possible for the Russian army to take Finland. Peter founded St. Petersburg while the war was raging around him. The war ended in 1721, and Russia finally had an outlet on the Baltic Sea and to western Europe.

Peter the Great was a giant by 18th-century standards, standing 6-feet, 8-inches tall and having a muscular frame. He left most of the command decisions of his army and navy to the professional generals and admirals, but he sometimes helped load the guns on his warships, and he marched with his troops, occasionally using his great strength to pull out a cannon mired in the mud.

Peter the Great made Russia a modern nation by modernizing the army, creating the navy, and reforming the Orthodox Church. Peter died on January 25, 1725, while on a visit to the Finnish gulf. He is memorialized throughout Russia.

Peter the Great forced Russia into the modern ages by establishing a navy, revolutionizing the army, and reforming the Russian Orthodox church.
National Archives

30

Robert Clive

The Empire Builder

(A.D. 1725–1774)

His neighbors in the Shropshire village of Market Drayton thought Robert Clive, son of a prominent lawyer and landowner, might well be the first of his distinguished family to end his life on the gallows.

Young Robert was not much of a student; he was expelled from three schools. His fault was not an inability to learn. As he later proved, he was quite bright, but his behavior was most unconventional. For example, he organized a group (which today would be called a youth gang) that extorted money from the shopkeepers of Market Drayton. In addition, he was subject to fits of depression, which were occasionally severe enough for him to consider suicide. He was so much trouble that when he was 17, his father packed him off to India, where he clerked for the British East India Company.

The East India Company, as with similar French, Dutch, and Portuguese companies, was set up to facilitate trade with the East. None of these companies were primarily interested in territory, although the Portuguese established a colony at Goa. The Europeans allied themselves with individual rulers, of which there were many. The old Mughul Empire, established by Mongol Muslims from Central Asia, had fallen on hard times. Shivaji, a Hindu prince, revolted

and establish the Maratha confederacy of Hindu states. The Sikhs then carved out a large chunk of northern India for themselves. The empire itself was divided into several parts, each ruled by a *subadhar* (or viceroy), theoretically subordinate to the emperor. The three greatest of these were the nawabs of the Deccan, Bengal, and Oudh. The nawabs theoretically ruled a host of sultans and sahibs, who may (or may not) have followed their orders.

Robert Clive established a British presence in India, but he couldn't conquer his own depression.
Library of Congress

In 1743, Robert Clive arrived in Madras. It was a long trip. His ship stopped in Brazil, where the Portuguese authorities detained it for nine months. That was long enough for Clive to learn Portuguese, a language that at that time was still widely spoken in India.

In 1746, the War of the Austrian Succession broke out, and France and Britain were on opposite sides. French troops captured Madras, but Clive and several other Englishmen escaped to Fort St. David 20 miles away. Clive immediately joined the East India Company's private army. He was commissioned an ensign in 1747 and led troops in several small engagements until the war ended in 1748.

War broke out again in 1751, when two Indian princes claimed the throne of the nawab of the Carnetic, one of the larger states in the Deccan. The French favored one claimant, the British the other. The French candidate, Chanda Sahib, left his capital of Arcot to besiege Trichinopoly. Clive, now a captain, led 500 soldiers with three field guns against Arcot to draw Chanda Sahib back from Trichinopoly. Chanda's skeleton garrison fled, and Clive and his men occupied the citadel. About 200 of the East India Company troops were British and 300 were Indian *sepoys*, local soldiers who enlisted in the Company army. Chanda sent an army under his son, Raja Sahib, to take back Arcot. Raja besieged the fort for 53 days. As the British force was holding out longer than expected, the Marathas (who had been neutral) decided to join them. Raja knew he'd have to end the siege quickly, so he tried to break down the fort's gate with elephants wearing steel plates on their heads. But as often happened with military elephants, the beasts panicked and stampeded through the rest of Raja's army. Raja lifted the siege, and Clive became a hero.

He then led a small force on raids against the French and their Indian allies, showing himself to be a talented guerrilla leader.

Robert Clive returned to England in 1753 and soon married, and then ran unsuccessfully for Parliament. He was then commissioned a lieutenant colonel in the British army. In 1756 he returned to India. Leading a much larger force of Company troops, he wiped out a pirate base and was drawn into another war.

The nawab of Bengal attacked Calcutta after the British refused to destroy their fortifications there. The French, of course, backed the nawab, Siraj ud Daula. The capture of Calcutta gave rise to the story about the infamous "Black Hole of Calcutta." According to J.Z. Howell, who commanded the British trading post when the nawab of Doula attacked, the Indians confined 146 members of the garrison in a room just 18 feet square. The next day, only 23 were still alive. (Since then, scholars have pointed out that 146 men would not fit into a room that small. Regardless of the details, the story is still horrific.) Howell said the nawab was not personally responsible for the atrocity, that it was instigated by a rich Bengali merchant named Omichand. Howell gives the names of 52 men who died in the "Black Hole," along with two sea captains designated only as "&c., &c." He also mentions 69 non-Europeans whose names he did not know. Together with the 23 survivors, that comes to 146. It seems unlikely that Howell, who was there, made up the story completely, especially as there were 22 other witnesses. Howell probably exaggerated a most trying experience. But it made great propaganda for the East India Company.

Siraj ud Daula went home soon after the battle, leaving a small force in Calcutta. Clive retook the city and rescued the "Black Hole" survivors. The nawab moved against Calcutta again, but Clive repulsed him after a confused battle in which darkness and an unbelievably dense fog left both sides literally blind.

Meanwhile, the French sent some 600 troops to Chandernagore, a few miles north of Calcutta; war resumed between Britain and France. Siraj ud Daula told Clive he favored neither side; but at the same time, he was planning to help the French. Clive attacked and took Chandernagore.

After that, Clive decided that Bengal needed a new nawab. He chose Jafar Ali Khan, one of the top generals of Siraj's army. To contact Jafar, he employed a devious Bengali merchant (the same Omichand may have instigated the Black Hole atrocity). Omichand now professed to favor the British, but he saw a way to do himself some good. After spending a healthy amount of East India Company money in bribes, Clive convinced Jafar Ali Khan to organize a conspiracy. He proposed a treaty with the Indian general, recognizing him as the nawab of Bengal. Then Omichand threatened to tell Siraj unless the treaty included a huge payment to him. Clive produced a phony treaty, with the forged signature of a British official, that contained what Omichand wanted. He kept the real contract hidden, and Omichand got nothing.

Then on June 22, 1757, with 3,200 men (only 650 of them British), Clive marched against the 68,000 men in the army of Siraj ud Daula, drawn up near Plassey. Most of the troops in the nawab's army promptly deserted, fled, or surrendered prematurely. Siraj ud Daula fled before the battle was over and was found and killed by Jafar Ali Khan's followers a short time later. Jafar Ali Khan became the new nawab and rewarded Clive handsomely. Jawaharal Nehru, in his book *Discovery of India* (published in 1946), says Clive won the battle "by promoting treason and forgery," adding that British rule in India had "an unsavory beginning and something of that bitter taste has clung to it ever since."

Robert Clive returned to England in 1767. He defended himself against charges by his enemies of mismanagement in India. Despite his vindication in Parliament, Robert Clive committed suicide by stabbing himself with a penknife at his home in London.

The Battle of Plassey is considered the beginning of British rule in India. Clive, commanding the East India Company army, wiped out French influence in India. The East India Company spread its influence by making treaties with Indian rulers and posting British "residents" in their territories to "advise" them on policy. In the next century, after a massive mutiny by Indian sepoys, the British government took over India from the East India Company. British rule lasted until after World War II. India finally achieved independence on August 15, 1947, under a civil disobedience movement led largely by Mahatma Gandhi.

Robert Clive after the Battle of Plassey.

George Washington

The Old Fox

(A.D. 1732–1799)

The young militia officer, leading 450 men in the wilds of western Pennsylvania, heard that a much larger French force was approaching. He organized his men to construct a trench and a palisade around his camp. Colonel George Washington (a land surveyor in civilian life) was, unfortunately, not a military engineer. The camp was on a poorly drained meadow. It was well within musket range of the surrounding woods, and it was overlooked by hills that would let attackers fire into the stockade from above.

Some 750 French troops and a large body of their Indian allies arrived during a tremendous rainstorm. It rained night and day. The trench filled with water and the camp became a bog. All this time, the French and Indians were firing on the camp. By the end of the day, 13 of Washington's men were dead, 54 were wounded, and another 100 were sick. They had only enough food for three days. They were running out of gunpowder, and most of what they had was wet.

The French commander Captain Coulon de Villiers sent an officer under a flag of truce to request Washington's surrender. Washington curtly refused. Further, he would not let the Frenchman into "Fort Necessity." Washington was a better psychologist than

an engineer. The French didn't know how bad his situation was, and his attitude convinced them he was stronger than they had believed. The next time a Frenchman approached with a white flag, he had a request that Washington discuss terms. In the end, Washington released the few French prisoners he had taken in a previous skirmish, and he and his men marched back to Virginia.

George Washington's moral strength kept the American army in the field, despite many trials and tribulations. *National Archives*

The young Virginian was involved in the first fighting of what came to be called the French and Indian War. The next year, it spread to Europe, where it was called the Seven Years' War. Washington was later engaged in the disastrous Braddock expedition against Fort Duquesne (where downtown Pittsburgh now stands). He helped bring the survivors of the Indian ambush home in good order.

When, 20 years later, colonial settlers in Massachusetts revolted and besieged British forces in Boston, they tried to get help from the other colonies, particularly the largest one, Virginia. The revolutionary Continental Congress, meeting in Philadelphia at the time, sent companies of riflemen from Maryland, Pennsylvania, and Virginia. And congress sent Virginia's most distinguished soldier, George Washington, to command the besiegers.

The besiegers were hundreds of militiamen from dozens of practically independent militia companies. They had no overall commander. Crowds of militia colonels and generals roamed through the rebel camp trying to throw their weight around. Washington brought order out of chaos and selected staff officers to help him. He was a good judge of men. Henry Knox, whom he appointed chief of artillery, led an expedition to Fort Ticonderoga to get guns and bring them back to Boston. Washington then placed the guns on Dorchester Heights and forced the British to evacuate Boston. His strategic sense told him that the British would probably next strike at New York. From there, British forces could proceed up the Hudson Valley and cut off New England (the most radical section of the English colonies) from the rest of the settlements.

Washington calculated correctly. The British decided to attack New York, where Washington was waiting. The British, under William Howe, outmaneuvered him on Long Island. He retreated to New York, but was soon forced out of the city.

Because Washington is correctly hailed as the "father of his country," few Americans realize that in the whole Revolutionary War—from 1776 to 1783— he won (as historian Thomas Fleming points out) only three clear victories: Trenton, Princeton, and Yorktown. The first two occurred close together, Trenton at the end of 1776 and Princeton at the beginning of 1777. Yorktown, of course, was the battle that ended the war. One of Washington's great gifts as a military commander was his ability to evade battle until he was ready to fight. It was not for nothing that the British general Charles Cornwallis referred to him as the "old fox."

Cornwallis was nipped by the "old fox" when he tried to catch Washington after the American's tactical masterwork at Trenton. Washington had crossed the Delaware River from Pennsylvania on Christmas Day and fallen on the hung-over Hessian troops in Trenton. Washington evaded him and attacked a British force coming up to reinforce Cornwallis. His raw recruits panicked, but Washington rode to the front and restored order so his experienced New England contingents and the Pennsylvania riflemen were able to get in position and rout the British. Washington's bravery, coolness under fire, and inspirational presence were important assets of his success.

Washington's grasp of strategy, though, was his most important military gift. The British were 3,000 miles from home, and reinforcements and supplies had to come across the Atlantic Ocean, a trip that could take as long as three months. They were trying to subdue a country 1,000 miles long and 1,000 miles wide. The roads were few and poor, and there was no central city like London (although Philadelphia at the time was the second-largest English-speaking city in the world). The colonies were thinly peopled as a whole, but the population of that huge area was about a quarter of the combined population of Britain and Ireland. To win, Washington knew that all he had to do was keep the army together and stay in the field. By doing so, he forced the British to stay concentrated. If they split up their forces, Washington's army could overwhelm the British piece by piece. Keeping the army in the field was no easy task. The first Continental soldiers enlisted for periods as short as three months. When their enlistments were up, many soldiers simply went home. Washington had to recruit replacements, and he had to persuade new recruits to sign up for at least a year. The colonial governments did not help. The support of their own army was so meager, the troops were half starved, wearing rags, and mostly without medical attention. For most of the war, Washington's army was usually outnumbered by his opponents.

Ironically, Washington was greatly aided by a force he thoroughly despised: the militia. Every free man in the colonies (usually up to the age of 60) was a member of the militia. Today, some historians contend that only 30 percent of the colonists were Whigs (who favored revolution), and that 30 percent were Tories (or loyalists to the British crown), and the rest were indifferent. The militia, however, overwhelmingly favored independence. When the war shifted to the Carolinas, British officers Patrick Ferguson and Banastre Tarleton were able to enlist a substantial number of Tories, but these men were losers in a civil conflict called the War of Regulation. (Small farmers in the back country believed they were being oppressed by dwellers in the eastern cities, and formed a revolutionary group called the Regulators. Their revolt was put down by the colonial militia in 1771. When the American Revolution began, many of the former Regulators became Tories merely because the militia establishment was primarily Whig.) Therefore, the men who joined Ferguson and Tarleton were not true loyalists, they were merely exercising the old adage, "the enemy of my enemy is my friend."

The war in the South was a disaster until Congress let Washington appoint the commanding general there. He named Nathaniel Greene, who, similar to Henry Knox, was one of the staff officers Washington appointed when he was outside Boston. Before Greene arrived, Lord Charles Cornwallis routed every Continental force he met. He still beat Greene, but he lost far more men than the American. His Tory contingents were wiped out—Ferguson's troops at King's Mountain and Tarleton's at the Cowpens. Cornwallis's main army was so battered he had to camp at Yorktown to await supplies from the Royal Navy. A militia force was the victor at King's Mountain, and militia were a great help to Daniel Morgan at the Cowpens.

The surrender of Lord Cornwallis's army at Yorktown.

Washington despised the militia because they lacked the military virtues he tried to inspire in the Continental Army. The militia did good work at Concord (where they mostly used guerrilla tactics), and at Bunker Hill (where they were entrenched), but they were hopeless in a formal 18th-century battle. They wouldn't stand shoulder-to-shoulder and trade volleys with the enemy, and they had no desire to use bayonets. They frequently panicked. They would defend their homes, but they didn't want to fight in strange places. What the militia did, though, was make it impossible for the British to occupy the country. The British could easily occupy cities such as New York and Philadelphia, but they couldn't control the small towns.

Cornwallis had to hole up in Yorktown because he had to get supplies from England. He couldn't even leave his wounded in the countryside. When the French fleet, not the British fleet, arrived at Yorktown, Cornwallis (afflicted by a severe case of bruised ego) sent a subordinate named Brigadier General Charles O'Hara to surrender. In London, Lord North (the British prime minister) threw up his hands and exclaimed, "Oh God! It is all over!"

After retiring from the presidency in March of 1797, George Washington settled at his Virginia home, Mount Vernon. In December of 1799, he died of pneumonia. According to his personal secretary, his last words were: "Tis well."

32

Benedict Arnold
General Jekyll and Mr. Hyde
(A.D. 1741–1801)

As soon as they heard the news from Concord, the Second Company of the Governor's Foot Guard, a New Haven militia outfit, put on their new red uniforms (the company had only recently been organized) and prepared to march to Massachusetts. But they had only a little ammunition. Most of it was locked up in the powder house, and the town selectmen had the key. The company commander, Captain Benedict Arnold (a prominent merchant who had experience in the French and Indian War), demanded the key. The selectmen hesitated. Connecticut people liked to think of their colony as the "land of steady habits." What those people in Massachusetts did was treason.

Arnold gave an order, and the militiamen trundled up the company's cannon and trained it on the town hall. Arnold told the selectmen they had a choice: either give him the key, or he would use the powder he had to blow them and the town hall to pieces. He got the key. This 1775 incident is still reenacted every year on the New Haven Green. It celebrates the day the Connecticut city joined the American Revolution. It also marks the appearance of one of the strangest actors in the great drama of the American nation.

Benedict Arnold was an apprentice in an apothecary shop run by his cousins in Norwich, Connecticut, during the French and Indian War, but he twice ran away and joined the army, probably lying about his age. He narrowly escaped being caught in the massacre at Fort William Henry, which might have contributed to his abiding hatred of the French, which would impact his later actions. When his company joined the siege of Boston, Arnold convinced the Massachusetts Committee of Safety to let him lead an expedition to capture Fort Ticonderoga. The Committee made him a colonel in the Massachusetts militia and sent him to Ticonderoga. Unknown to Arnold, Ethan Allen had the same idea and got an identical assignment from the Connecticut Committee of Safety. Allen led the Green Mountain Boys, who came from what most colonists called the Hampshire Grants (a wild frontier territory claimed by both New Hampshire and New York but which, to its inhabitants, was the independent republic of Vermont). Arnold and Allen, about as incompatible as two officers on the same side could be, met en route and captured the fort jointly and bloodlessly. In their report to Massachusetts, the Green Mountain Boys downplayed Arnold's role in the capture. Arnold challenged the messenger, a man named Colonel Easton, to a duel. Easton refused the challenge, and Arnold sent his own report to the Continental Congress. Feeling slighted by Massachusetts, Arnold resigned his militia commission.

Congress was planning an invasion of Canada to limit the ability of the British to attack from the north, and George Washington nominated Arnold for a Continental colonel's commission. General Philip Schuyler was commander of the northern theater, but he gave Arnold and General Richard Montgomery, who would lead the two invading forces, almost total autonomy. Montgomery took Montreal, but Arnold was wounded in the leg trying to storm the fort at Quebec. Montgomery, who brought up reinforcements, was killed. A combination of bad weather, smallpox, and British reinforcements eventually forced Arnold to retreat. He stopped a British attempt to retake Montreal, but later was

Benedict Arnold went from being one of America's greatest heroes to one of our worst villains.

forced to leave Canada entirely. Still, Congress considered his performance good enough to promote him to brigadier general.

The British commander in Canada, Guy Carleton, began a counter-invasion. He pushed south along Lake Champlain to the Hudson River Valley. To foil Carleton, Arnold patched together a "navy" of small gunboats. Carleton managed to get a much larger fleet on the lake. When the two fleets finally met, Arnold lost all his boats, but Carleton had spent so much time preparing for the battle it was too close to winter for him to push on to Ticonderoga.

Arnold seems to have had the knack of making enemies in his own army. Although Washington praised him, Congress passed him over for promotion. After he routed the British raiders who burned Danbury, Congress did promote him, but without his seniority. In a huff, Arnold resigned his commission.

Washington persuaded him to stay in the army and go north to help Schuyler. A new British invasion, led by "Gentleman Johnny" Burgoyne, was about to begin. Burgoyne's plan was elaborate: he would march down the Champlain-Hudson route while Sir William Howe would march up the Hudson from New York and Lieutenant Colonel Barry St. Leger (leading a force of regulars, Tories, and Indians) would march along the Mohawk River. All three armies would meet at Albany.

But there were problems Burgoyne had not foreseen. One was that while he had a plan the government approved, Sir William had another plan; he decided that a seaborne attack on Philadelphia (which he considered the rebel capital) would end the revolution with one stroke. He took the bulk of his army to Philadelphia, which, although a big city, was not a nerve center in the same way as

London or Paris. The 13 colonies were really 13 independent countries, and highly decentralized ones at that. Sir Henry Clinton, Howe's second-in-command, took a small force a few miles up the Hudson. Washington, having failed to save Philadelphia, was back in the area, and Clinton was afraid the "Old Fox" would snatch New York while his back was turned.

St. Leger wasn't going to make the rendezvous either. His Tory officers had assured him that the Mohawk Valley was full of loyalists who would flock to his army. But most of the loyalists in the valley had left long ago to join John Butler's Tory Rangers or John Johnson's Royal Greens. Instead of Tories, St. Leger met the Whig militia who fortified Fort Stanwix. St. Leger besieged the fort and, at Oriskany, stopped a militia force that tried to break the siege. Arnold volunteered to relieve Fort Stanwix. Schuyler gave him orders to go to Tyron County and take command of all the Continental and militia troops in the area and relieve the fort.

Arnold didn't find many troops, but he found a madman named Hon Yost Schuyler, who was given to raving in unknown tongues and had acquired a reputation among the Indians of being a shaman. Hon Yost was a Tory and had been imprisoned by the rebel militia. Arnold told the prisoner he would release him if he would go to the besiegers and tell them that the rebel General Arnold was coming to relieve the fort with a huge army. Hon Yost agreed, and even shot some holes in his coat so it would look as if he had a narrow escape from the rebels. When the Indians heard his story, they broke camp. Without the Mohawk Indians, the British decided they weren't strong enough to continue, so they retreated, too.

When Arnold rejoined the main force, he learned that it had a new commander, Horatio Gates, a former British officer who proved to be overcautious and slow moving. Burgoyne was still moving, but his grand plan was rapidly unraveling. A few days after St. Leger left Fort Stanwix, 1,400 German mercenaries (traveling in two parties and looking for supplies and nonexistent Tories) ran into 2,500 New Hampshire, Vermont, and Massachusetts militia and were wiped out a little west of Bennington, Vermont. The woods were now full of rebel militia. They had been aroused by the murder of Jenny McCrae, a young woman of Tory sympathies who was killed and scalped by Burgoyne's Indian allies. Militiamen were flocking to Gates's army. At the same time, the British and Brunswickers were deserting Burgoyne's force. Most of the Indians had deserted after the Battle of Bennington. When Schuyler first faced Burgoyne, he had only half the men the British general had; now Gates outnumbered Burgoyne two to one. Washington, sensing a crisis in the north, sent Daniel Morgan and 1,000 riflemen to reinforce Gates.

Arnold, commanding the left wing of the army, wanted Gates to move quickly and overwhelm the enemy. But Gates just dug in near the town of Saratoga. He said he was afraid his new recruits (almost all frontiersmen and used to Indian fighting) wouldn't be able to cope with Burgoyne's Indians.

Odds of two to one didn't bother Gentleman Johnny, even though the enemy was entrenched. To lead the attack, he chose Simon Fraser, a Scottish nobleman who was a cousin to the murdered Jenny McCrae. Fraser took 2,000 light infantry on a wide sweep around the American left flank. Burgoyne led 1,100 regular British infantry against the center of the American line, while

Baron Adolph von Riedesel (commander of Burgoyne's Brunswick mercenaries) circled around the American right flank. Burgoyne was trying to encircle an entrenched army twice the size of his own. Arnold raged at Gates to attack while the enemy troops were on the move, but Gates ordered all his men to stay in the trenches. Finally, he allowed Arnold to send out Morgan's troops to protect the left flank. Morgan proceeded to outflank the outflankers. His riflemen scattered the Canadian militia, who made up Fraser's right flank. But when they reached the Scotsman's light infantry, the situation changed. The light infantry had bayonets; the riflemen did not. Without orders, Arnold led two regiments of Continental infantry out to support Morgan. After a bitter fight, those troops were also pushed back. Burgoyne ordered a general advance.

Arnold noticed a gap between Fraser's corps and the British center. He led a brigade into the gap. The fighting was ferocious. Arnold and Burgoyne each led charge after charge; Morgan's riflemen cut down officers and gun crews. Gates stayed behind his trenches. Arnold rode back to headquarters to demand reinforcements. Gates reluctantly sent up another brigade, but he confined Arnold to headquarters. Meanwhile, Riedesel, hearing the guns on his right, brought up his Brunswickers and hit Arnold's men on their right flank. The Americans withdrew as night was falling, and the fighting at Freeman's Farm ended. The British lost 600 men killed, wounded, or captured; the Americans, 316.

So far, nothing had been decided. Gentleman Johnny rolled the dice again. Once again, Fraser opened the action. Once again, Arnold and Morgan urged a strong counterattack. Gates allowed Morgan's and one other brigade to counterattack Fraser.

Arnold exploded. He berated Gates so vigorously the commanding general put him under arrest.

The counterattack appeared to be succeeding, and Fraser rallied his men. Gates sent in another brigade, but Burgoyne threw in all his troops. Vastly outnumbered, Fraser led charge after charge. Morgan called his best marksman, Tim Murphy. "Kill that officer," he said, pointing to Fraser. Murphy fired. The bullet passed through the mane of Fraser's horse. Murphy rotated the barrel of his double-barreled rifle and fired again. A chip flew off Fraser's saddle. Aides begged Fraser to make himself less conspicuous. Fraser told them a general's job was to make himself conspicuous. Murphy reloaded and fired again. Fraser slumped in his saddle. The aides supported him on the horse and led the animal off the battlefield. Fraser's wound proved mortal. His men fell back as he was taken to shelter.

But Burgoyne's army was far from finished. Riedesel's Brunswickers, standing firm, pushed back the Americans. Then a little man on a bay horse rallied the Americans and led them against the Germans. The noise of battle had been too much for Benedict Arnold. He broke arrest, mounted his horse, and led a mass charge. The Brunswickers dashed back to a British redoubt, and Arnold rode right into the fort after them. A wounded German fired at him and hit him in the same leg that had been wounded outside Quebec. Arnold saw an American about to bayonet the Brunswicker. "Don't hurt him!" the general yelled. "He's a fine fellow. He just did his duty."

Burgoyne tried to retreat, but he was surrounded; 10 days after the fall of the redoubt, he surrendered. The surrender of an entire British army in the wilds of America shook Europe. The Netherlands, Spain, and France all saw a chance to recover territory they had lost. They declared war on Britain. Britain's chances of putting down the rebellion while Washington was alive were slim. Now they were nonexistent.

Arnold's leg wound was so serious the doctors recommended amputation. Arnold wouldn't allow that. He recovered, but he was a cripple, with one leg 2 inches shorter than the other. That increased the bitterness he felt about being passed over for promotion, about being deprived credit for Ticonderoga, and about Gates being hailed as the victor of Saratoga. He recuperated in Philadelphia, which the British had evacuated. Arnold, a widower, then met 18-year-old Peggy Shippen, who became his second wife. Benedict Arnold began to throw elaborate

parties and social events; the Arnolds were soon living well beyond their means. During the British occupation, Peggy Shippen had been frequently seen with Major John Andre, a young officer who was a British intelligence agent.

Arnold eventually returned to active duty as commandant of West Point, a key fortress on the Hudson. While he sat in his fortress, he brooded about the slights and snubs he had suffered. He had won the decisive battle of the war, but he got no credit for it. Unfortunately, what made Saratoga decisive was that it brought the French to the American side. Arnold began corresponding with Sir Henry Clinton. (The intermediary was John Andre.) Arnold offered to turn over West Point to the British in return for money and a commission in the British army. His treason

Benedict Arnold takes the German redoubt at the Battle of Saratoga. Because of his leadership, the colonialists won that decisive battle.

was discovered when bandits captured Andre and found a letter from Arnold in his shoe. The bandits sold Andre to the Americans, who hanged him. Arnold fled to British-held territory and, as a British general, led two raids, one against Richmond and another against New London. The latter ended with the massacre of the garrison of Fort Griswold.

The British did not trust Arnold and would not give him command of a force in Virginia, which was supposed to support Lord Cornwallis, who was moving up from the Carolinas. This was in spite of the comments of a British admiral who, after visiting British headquarters in New York, wrote back that Benedict Arnold was "worth more than all the British generals put together." After the war, Arnold and his wife left the United States. They settled in England and Arnold died there in 1801.

Although Benedict Arnold is considered a traitor to the American Revolution, it is important not to forget his contributions to the cause before West Point. He was a hero in the Battle of Saratoga, which persuaded the French to support the Americans; this alliance tipped the balance and ensured a victory to the colonists.

A monument at Saratoga stands in memory of Benedict Arnold, although he is not mentioned by name. The statue of a wounded leg stands with no marker, except for a plaque that reads:

In memory of the most brilliant soldier of the Continental Army, who was desperately wounded on this spot, winning for his countrymen the decisive battle of the American Revolution, and for himself the rank of Major General.

33

Napoleon I
The Emperor
(A.D. 1769–1821)

In his book titled *The Story of Mankind*, Hendrik Willem van Loon describes Napoleon as a war-mongering military dictator. But, he writes, when Napoleon entered the Netherlands, his own great-grandfather eagerly joined the conqueror's army. So did young men from all over Europe. They did so not just in expectation of adventure, but because they saw Napoleon and the French army as a force liberating the world from the oppressions of the Middle Ages and substituting science for superstition. Many years later, at the extreme ends of Europe, young men rose up spontaneously to fight Napoleon and the French army. Similar to Loon's great-grandfather, they did that because they, too, had adopted an idea Napoleon was spreading.

To understand how these things could happen, we have to go back to 1789, when a 20-year-old artillery officer named Napoleone Buonoparte was an active revolutionary. Soon Napoleon changed his Corsican name to sound more French, then later dropped the Bonaparte entirely. When Corsica declared its independence from France, Napoleon took his family to France and remained loyal to the Republic. The Republic was being attacked by enemies on all sides, and the young officer had plenty of opportunity to display his courage and intelligence.

Reactionary French elements allowed the British to establish a naval base at Toulon. Republican troops then laid siege to Toulon. Napoleon suffered a bayonet wound at the siege, but when the commander of the Republican artillery was seriously wounded, Napoleon took his place and directed the artillery so skillfully he was promoted to brigadier general at the age of 26.

Napoleon Bonaparte was an autocrat who proclaimed the doctrine of "Liberty, Equality, and Brotherhood" during the French Revolution.
Library of Congress

Two years later, Napoleon delivered his famous "whiff of grapeshot" to put down a royalist uprising in Paris. That led to his being given command of the "Army of Italy," fighting both the Austrians and the Piedmontese. He won battle after battle and gained a nickname—the "Little Corporal." The "little" came from his size, a towering 5-feet, 2-inches tall. The "corporal" from his actions when the enemy was blocking a French column from crossing a bridge: Napoleon seized a flag and dashed over the bridge himself, with his men following. The army was not used to commanding generals leading them that way.

Napoleon inherited a superior military machine, one with the best artillery in the world and organized into divisions, which allowed it to operate with more mobility and flexibility. It also had the kind of morale that was seldom seen.

French revolutionaries prepare to storm the Bastille.

For most countries in the 18th century, war was the "sport of kings." And to the kings, armies were animated toy soldiers. The French army was an army of the people. It was far bigger than any other army because it was composed of draftees and volunteers from all walks of life. It was, of course, not as well trained as the uniformed automatons in royal armies, but its tactics were more flexible. It employed clouds of skirmishers who fired from any cover they could find. It often attacked in columns instead of the perfectly straight lines of traditional armies, and it often did so at double time instead of at the stately pace of 80 steps per minute. Most important, the French army had the kind of fervor not seen since the religious wars of a century or two earlier. French soldiers were fighting for their liberty, to avoid the "slavery" imposed by the *ancien regime*. And they wanted to spread the benefits of liberty, equality, and brotherhood to the oppressed people of Europe.

Napoleon didn't confine himself to Europe. He took an army to Egypt and beat both the Mameluke rulers of that country and the soldiers of the Mamelukes's overlord, the Ottoman Empire. The object was to interfere with Britain's trade with India, a good portion of which was carried by caravan from the Mediterranean to the Red Sea. But Napoleon also brought along a corps of scientists and scholars. The Rosetta Stone (the key to ancient Egyptian hieroglyphs) was discovered during this expedition. Napoleon encouraged scientific progress because it was another way to make France a great nation.

But the advancement of science was never as important to him as the advancement of Napoleon. When the British fleet under Horatio Nelson destroyed the squadron that brought the French troops to Egypt,

Napoleon abandoned them and returned to France alone. He participated in the coup that overthrew the corrupt Directory government and replaced it with three consuls. He became first consul, which gave him dictatorial powers. In the year 1802, he revised the constitution, making himself first consul for life. Two years later, Napoleon crowned himself emperor.

Looting at the Bastille during the French Revolution.

Napoleon continued making war and winning battles. He improved the army organization by inventing the corps, a group of divisions incorporating all combat branches of the service. He made conscription more efficient and greatly improved the training of the army. He selected his marshals for their aggressiveness and intelligence, and then gave them a great deal of autonomy in conducting operations. In the field, he often scattered his corps and divisions over a wide area to confuse the enemy as to his intentions. But his basic intention was always to destroy the enemy's army, not merely seize territory or strong points. Speed, surprise, and the ability to concentrate quickly on an enemy's weak spots were hallmarks of his operations. So was the masterful handling of artillery. Britain, protected by the English Channel and the Royal Navy, was the only country in Europe able to defy Napoleon: it organized alliance after

alliance against him. Its allies, though, always succumbed to Napoleon. The French emperor put his brothers and close friends on thrones all over Europe.

But Napoleon kept the form of republican government. He abolished feudalism and serfdom, guaranteed freedom of religion, and established free public education. He revised the old Code of Justinian, and the resulting Napoleonic Code became the basis of law in most European countries (and strongly influences the law in the State of Louisiana). Loon's great-grandfather was not befuddled when he thought he was fighting for freedom.

The bywords of "Liberty, Equality, and Fraternity" were products of the French Revolution, ideas Napoleon spread all over the continent. So were nationalism and its military version—the nation in arms. Before Napoleon, war was the sport of kings. After him it was an expression of the national will. After France, nationalism and the popular war first appeared in Spain, then in Russia. It appeared in the form we still call by its original Spanish name—guerrilla warfare. The Peninsular War in Spain began in 1807, a bloody, indecisive war that didn't end until Napoleon abdicated in 1814. Although that war was going on, Napoleon took his Grand Army in the other direction. He went into Russia. He won all his battles, but the Russians scorched the earth in front of him and cut all his supply lines. When he got to Moscow, they set the great city on fire. Thousands of miles from home, across vast, empty spaces and with no supplies (and the Russians still unconquered); the only option was to retreat. Napoleon eventually abandoned his army. The leaderless Grand Army, beset by the Russian weather, starvation, and Russian guerrillas, was almost annihilated. Of the 600,000 men who entered Russia, only about 20,000 escaped.

The Russian disaster encouraged all of Napoleon's enemies, who had also caught the nationalism fever and introduced conscription and other French innovations. They defeated Napoleon at Leipzig and pushed his outnumbered men back into France, where the French marshals mutinied and forced the emperor to abdicate on April 11, 1814. He went into exile as ruler of the Mediterranean island of Elba. But on March 1, 1815, Napoleon returned to France and was welcomed by the marshals who had forced his abdication. He ruled for 100 days. After a final defeat at Waterloo, Napoleon was exiled to the lonely island of St. Helena. He died there May 5, 1821, reportedly of a stomach ailment. (It was possibly cancer, although some experts believe he was poisoned. Recent scholarship has even suggested that Napoleon's wallpaper was glued to the walls using an arsenic-based glue, which, over time, poisoned the former emperor.)

The powers of Europe redrew the old boundary lines and restored the old ruling dynasties and believed they had eliminated all traces of the Corsican adventurer. But they hadn't. The restored absolute monarchs soon found that if they were going to rule, they would have to do it with parliaments. Serfdom was abolished everywhere but in Russia. Freedom of religion, free public education, and the Napoleonic Code were found almost everywhere. So were nationalism and its corollary, the nation in arms. All continental nations established conscription with various types of reserve obligations. The changes that Napoleon introduced could not be eliminated.

Napoleon is defeated at the Battle of Waterloo.

34

Horatio Nelson
The Triumph of England
(A.D. 1758–1805)

British supremacy on the water was born during the wars with revolutionary and imperial France. Horatio Nelson's victories showed that while Britain, even with the help of many allies, could not defeat Napoleon on land, Napoleon's invincible army could not conquer Britain. The situation was later described as the "conflict of the lion and the whale." If the lion had succeeded in landing on Britain, the history of the world would have been quite different. Britain's success in the Napoleonic wars led it to adopt a grand strategy of maintaining—at all costs—a navy so strong no other power could match it. The navy allowed England to keep the home islands safe from Napoleon III, Bismarck, Kaiser Wilhelm, and Adolf Hitler, while transporting an army to the ends of the earth and establishing the largest empire in the history of the world.

Horatio Nelson, the man whose victories inspired this grand strategy, was the son of a country parson. Instead of following his father into the ministry, he went to sea in 1770 at the age of 12. He did not go, however, as a cabin boy or a powder monkey. He reported for duty as an ordinary seaman, but was soon promoted to midshipman. Nelson went on the ship of his uncle, a man named Captain Maurice Suckling, who later became controller of the navy. Thanks to his uncle, Nelson became a lieutenant in 1777, a commander in 1778, and a captain in 1779. Three years later, while Nelson was campaigning in the West Indies, Pierre Andre de Suffren defeated a British fleet off Trincomalee in Ceylon. Deprived of naval support, the British lost their fort at Cuddalore to Hyder Ali Sultan, ruler of Mysore. A British expedition that had been prepared to go to America was diverted to India. The next year, the Treaty of Paris ended the American Revolution.

Lord Admiral Horatio Nelson had only one eye and one arm, but that didn't stop him from defeating his enemies. *Library of Congress*

155

Nelson married a young widow, Frances Nisbet, and returned to England in 1797, where he was put on inactive status and half-pay. In 1793, Britain joined the coalition against republican France, and Nelson was given command of the 64-gun *Agamemnon* in the Mediterranean squadron. The next year, he received a wound that blinded him in one eye. In most modern navies that would have automatically retired him; but in 1795, he was given a bigger ship, promoted to commodore, and placed in command of a squadron in the Gulf of Genoa. The next year, General Napoleon Bonaparte defeated the Austrians, conquered all northern Italy, and forced Naples to declare its neutrality. The Royal Navy withdrew from the Mediterranean. In 1797, Nelson's initiative was an important factor in the victory of 15 British ships over 27 Spanish ships at Cape St. Vincent. He was promoted to rear admiral and knighted. In 1797, he made a daring attempt to seize the Spanish city of Santa Cruz de Tenerife in the Canary Islands. He didn't take the town, and he lost his right arm. A year later, the one-armed, one-eyed admiral was back in action, leading a small squadron to investigate French naval action at Toulon.

A storm dismasted his flagship, and he had to return to his base for repairs. When he got back to Toulon, he learned that Napoleon and a French army had recently embarked for Egypt. He searched the Mediterranean for a month before he found the French fleet anchored at Abukir Bay at the mouth of the Nile. Nelson did not form a line of battle. He ordered his ships to attack immediately. Each captain picked out a French ship and anchored beside it. Night was falling as they approached the line of anchored French ships from both the seaward and landward sides. Some British ships sailed through gaps in the line of anchored vessels to get on the landward side of the column. The shore batteries, which were expected to protect the French ships, were useless in the dark. When the fighting was over, two of the 15 French ships had burned and nine had been captured. The rest fled.

Nelson was wounded again, but less seriously than in his earlier fights. Before the battle, he predicted he would either get a peerage or a grave in Westminster Abbey. He became Baron Nelson of the Nile. Luckily, he didn't get what the government gave the last naval flag officer who failed to form a proper line of battle: Admiral Sir John Byng was shot by a firing squad on the quarterdeck of his own flagship in 1757. The Battle of the Nile decisively defeated Napoleon's Egyptian enterprise. There was no way to supply his army on the other end of the Mediterranean. Napoleon abandoned the troops and returned to France on a Venetian ship.

Lady Emma Hamilton engaged in a scandalous *ménàge a trois* with her husband and Lord Nelson.

The British were now back in the Mediterranean, and Nelson based his squadron at Naples. He became friendly with British ambassador Sir William Hamilton and his gorgeous wife Emma. Emma Hamilton (once called Amy Lyon) had an interesting life. She had been a prostitute and the paramour of some of the most powerful men in London before marrying the much older Sir William. Nelson was dazzled by Lady Hamilton. She apparently found the naval hero more interesting than her aged husband. She and Nelson began an affair that scandalized all of England. When Napoleon's troops overran the Kingdom of Naples, Nelson evacuated the Hamiltons to Sicily and later took them back to England, where he abandoned his wife and moved in with the Hamiltons.

In 1801, Nelson was second in command of the British fleet that attacked the Danish navy to break up the "Armed Neutrality" of the Baltic nations. The Danes fought so well that Nelson's commander signaled him to break off the action. According to legend, Nelson put his telescope to his blind eye and later claimed he didn't see the signal. At any rate, he did not break off the action and won the victory.

In 1805, Napoleon decided to settle the British problem once and for all. He now had control over (besides the French navy) the Spanish, Dutch, and Genoese navies. But the British were blockading all the ports of Europe. Napoleon's plan was to concentrate as many ships as possible in the West Indies, where a number of French ships already were, have them come back across the Atlantic, and then release other French and allied ships that were blockaded.

Nelson, who was responsible for keeping watch over the French fleet at Toulon, did not establish a tight blockade. He wanted the French, under Pierre de Villeneuve, to come out so he could destroy them in battle. The French did come out, when Napoleon ordered Villeneuve to go to Martinique, but Nelson missed them. When he heard that Villeneuve had left Toulon, he decided he must have gone to Egypt again, even though everyone else in Britain knew that Napoleon was preparing to invade England. He was searching the Mediterranean while Villeneuve arrived at Cádiz, on the Atlantic side of Gibraltar, picked up a Spanish squadron and proceeded to the West Indies. When Nelson finally learned that Villeneuve had gone to the West Indies, he crossed the Atlantic after him. The British plan for the conduct of the blockade was that if any blockaded ships escaped, the British blockading fleet they had escaped from was to join Admiral William Cornwallis at the western end of the English Channel, thus blocking the most probable invasion route. Nelson chose to ignore the plan, as he had ignored plans for battle tactics in the past. But while Nelson was the greatest of all British naval tacticians, he was far from the greatest strategist. His trip across the Atlantic and back was a wild goose chase.

Other British units sighted Villeneuve as he approached Europe. The movements of the French fleet were confusing, because the overcautious Villeneuve couldn't decide what to do. He ended up back in Cádiz, having accomplished nothing. A British squadron under Cuthbert Collingwood then blockaded Cádiz.

Before that, Nelson finally joined Cornwallis, something he should have done months before, and was ordered to take the HMS *Victory* to Portsmouth. He was soon enjoying the pleasures of domestic life with Emma Hamilton; he had about a month to enjoy them. On September 2, 1805, he got word that Villeneuve was blockaded at Cádiz. He rode to Portsmouth and took the HMS *Victory* out to join the blockade.

Meanwhile, the political situation in Europe had changed. William Pitt was again prime minister and had negotiated a new alliance against Napoleon. Napoleon, seeing that his plan for a naval concentration had failed, dropped his plans for a cross-channel invasion and shifted his army to central Europe. In October, he surrounded an Austrian army at Ulm and forced its surrender. In November, he occupied Vienna. At Austerlitz, on December 2, 1805, he trounced a Russian-Austrian army and destroyed the Holy Roman Empire. Prussia, which had been on the point of joining the Third Alliance, signed a peace treaty with Napoleon. Before that, on October 21, 1805, as part of his push to the east, Napoleon ordered

Villeneuve to Italy to restore French dominance in the Mediterranean.

Nelson, now in command of the blockaders outside Cádiz, had 27 ships of the line; Villeneuve had 33 (18 French and 15 Spanish). Nelson planned another innovative attack on the Franco-Spanish fleet after it emerged from the harbor and was passing Cape Trafalgar. Instead of forming a line of battle and running parallel to the enemy fleet, he formed his ships into two columns and broke into the Franco-Spanish line at two points. Naval orthodoxy has long put great store on "crossing the T" so your ships could deliver broadsides against enemies who could not reply. Nelson was sending his two columns right into a T-crossing. T-crossing, however, was a much more potent form of attack later when ships had rifled guns that were effective at long range. Further, Nelson was facing opponents who had been in a harbor

Denis Dighton's painting depicting Lord Nelson's death.

so long they were out of practice in both gun-handling and seamanship. Nelson's tactics let him concentrate several ships against individual enemy ships. When the fighting was over, the British had sunk one enemy ship and captured 17. (In the days of "wooden ships and iron men," when warships slugged it out at pistol range and boarding was a frequent method of attack, ships were more often captured than sunk.) A total of 10 French and Spanish ships left the battle and sailed back to Cádiz. The British lost no ships.

But they did lose one admiral. Nelson was hit by a musket ball and died before the battle ended. Nelson was a great fighting admiral and a brilliant naval tactician, but not a great strategist. His victories however, demonstrated to his countrymen that their national survival depended on control of the sea. That prompted the British grand strategy for all conflicts.

After Nelson's death, the British spared no effort or expense to maintain naval supremacy. In the early 20th century, Britain engaged in a naval arms race with Germany that was almost ruinous to the economies of both countries. The British won, though, and the only decisive action by the German High Seas Fleet was its mutiny at the end of 1918 that brought about the end of World War I.

After that war, a naval race was too expensive for any European country. The British navy fell behind that of the United States and probably that of Japan. But by that time it—and Lord Nelson—had changed history.

Nelson's strategies for battle at sea established the strength of the British Navy.

Carl von Clausewitz

The Philosopher of War

(A.D. 1780–1831)

Carl von Clausewitz fought in the Prussian army against the French. He was captured and imprisoned. When he was released two years later, he helped Gerhard von Scharnhorst reform the Prussian army after its defeat by Napoleon. When Napoleon forced Prussia to contribute a corps to his Grand Army for the invasion of Russia, Clausewitz resigned from the Prussian army and joined the Russian. In Russian service (with some 30 other Prussian generals) he helped persuade a Prussian corps to join the Russians. When Napoleon was driven out of Russia, he tried to rejoin the Prussian army, but King Wilhelm, irked by his role in the Russian campaign (and, no doubt, still afraid of Napoleon) would not have him until after the French emperor's first abdication. Clausewitz returned to the war as a private observer, and then as chief of staff in a small multinational force in the Baltic area.

Clausewitz, in other words, saw a great deal of war, and did so from several different perspectives. His fame though, rests not on what he did, but on what he wrote. Starting with Sun Tzu in 500 B.C., hundreds of writers have written about war and military theory, but none have been as influential as Clausewitz. In his book *Seven Pillars of Wisdom*, T.E. Lawrence tells of his reading of military theorists such as Napoleon, Caemmerer, Moltke, Jomini, Willisen, Saxe, and Guibert:

"However, Clausewitz was intellectually so much the master of them, and his book so logical and fascinating that unconsciously I accepted his finality." In fact, however, Lawrence rejected Clausewitz's ideas in the conduct of his own guerrilla war against the Turks. Clausewitz said that the aim of every general should be the destruction of the enemy's army. Lawrence knew he was not strong enough to do that, so he aimed to keep the Turkish garrison in Medina in existence, where they would be a drain on Turkish resources, but too weak to do any harm.

Clausewitz, however, recognized that the principles he presented were an ideal theory of war and that, in practice, there would be many variations, often because of what he called *friction*. He believed that friction could include everything from weather and minor errors to good luck. He was the first military theorist to include friction as an element that must be considered. His rules aimed to reduce friction to a minimum, but he acknowledged that it cannot be eliminated. A belligerent, he said, might also modify his ideal principles for several reasons; for example, it knew the enemy was so weak it was not necessary to exert maximum force or if it could achieve its objectives with less than maximum force. The latter case is an example of how politics plays a part in war. Clausewitz held that politics, as with physical violence, is one of the two basic components of war. Clausewitz realized that weapons and tactics change. He sought to expose the basic principles of war. He also sought to present what he called an objective analysis of war, so he had absolutely nothing to say about the morality of war.

Carl von Clausewitz saw war from many points of view—as a Prussian, Russian, prisoner, and conqueror.
Library of Congress

Clausewitz began writing about war when he was in his early 20s, and many of his early thoughts were incorporated in his greatest work *Vom Krieg*, or *On War*. His writing was strongly influenced by the German philosophers Emmanuel Kant and Georg Hegel, especially in the first chapter. The book is organized to go from the general to the particular, and is divided into eight sections:

1. On the Nature of War
2. On the Theory of War
3. On Strategy in General
4. Engagement
5. Military Forces
6. Defense
7. Attack
8. War Plans

Although Clausewitz wanted to present underlying principles, he couldn't completely ignore current technology. As a result, some of his ideas have become obsolete. Clausewitz died before he had completed *On War*, but his widow, Marie, gathered up his unpublished writings and had them published. *On War* is still considered the definitive work of military theory.

36

Simón Bolívar
Liberator of the North
(A.D. 1734–1830)

The struggle for independence in Spanish South America was one of the longest and most confused of the many wars that made up the Age of Revolution. The American Revolution inspired the French Revolution, which began in 1789. One of the early leaders of that revolution was the Marquis de Lafayette, who played a prominent part in the American fighting. The French Declaration of the Rights of Man was largely copied from the American Declaration of Independence. In addition to the French revolutionary wars and the Napoleonic wars that followed them, there was the Haitian Revolution, Spanish America's wars of liberation, the First Mexican Revolution, the uprisings of 1848 in Europe, the American Civil War, and the rising of the Paris Commune.

Similar to the Americans, the French revolutionists turned a blind eye to slavery. But in their colony of Haiti, the slaves saw the situation all too well (slavery was only prohibited in metropolitan France). In 1791, they revolted and established the second independent nation in the Western Hemisphere. In 1808, Napoleon put his brother Joseph on the throne of Spain, thereby ousting one of the most corrupt royal families in Spanish history. King Charles IV abdicated, making his (equally corrupt) son, Ferdinand, king.

Ferdinand previously tried to murder his father in order to gain the throne, but he willingly accepted Napoleon's offer of a life of luxury in France. But because Ferdinand was a victim (of sorts) of Napoleon, he became a national hero. The Spanish people revolted against Napoleon and gave a generic name to the type of irregular fighting they engaged in—guerrilla warfare.

On his deathbed, Bolívar asked is aide-de-camp to burn his extensive collection of correspondence. Luckily, his aide did not follow orders, leaving historians with a wealth of knowledge about Bolívar.

In 1810, the Spanish rebels established the Cortes (or parliament) of Cadiz. The Cortes was a medieval institution that flourished before the age of absolute monarchy that came with the Renaissance. The Cortes of Cádiz declared that all of the colonial population were citizens, and invited the colonies to send representatives. The trouble was that there were only 10 million people in Spain, and 14 to 16 million in the colonies. So the Cortes allowed the colonies only 30 of 107 delegates. That did not endear Spain to the colonies.

The French occupation of Spain and the guerrilla war raging there led to the rapid decline of Spanish military power in South America. The South American colonies established governments of their own. In 1810, juntas (the governing councils) were organized in every colonial headquarters except Lima. At first these juntas declared that their aim was to protect the rights of the depraved King Ferdinand VII. The juntas were really aiming for complete independence, but they were hoping for help from Britain, which was allied to King Ferdinand. Also, there was a huge conservative element in most South American colonies. The lower classes (Indians, mestizos, and blacks) saw the monarch as their only protection from oppression by the Creoles.

There were big differences between the revolutions in North and South America. The North Americans had been largely governing themselves for centuries; all authority in South America was exercised by *peninsulares*, Spaniards from the peninsula who came to America as governors and then returned to Spain. Further, the class system in the Spanish colonies made aristocratic Virginia and New York look purely egalitarian. Only the Creoles (people of pure Spanish blood) were educated and held large estates and good jobs. The rest of the population was severely repressed.

Simón Bolívar, born to a wealthy Creole family in the same year as the treaty that ended the American Revolution, quickly became a leader in the revolutionary movement in Venezuela.

Bolívar had been orphaned at the age of 9, but his guardian ensured that he received an excellent education. He devoured the writings of Jean Jacques Rousseau. He went to Spain at the age of 16 and married a noble Spanish girl three years later. The newlyweds returned to the Bolívar estate, but Bolívar's bride fell ill and died after less than a year of marriage. To distract himself from his grief, he returned to the study of the Enlightenment philosophers and traveled to France, where he imbibed more revolutionary ideas. He visited Italy and returned to Venezuela via the United States. Back home, he joined the movement that set up the Supreme Junta of Venezuela. The Junta said it was established "to safeguard the rights of Ferdinand VII." However, it also nullified Spanish taxes, abolished slavery, and removed the tariffs on many foreign products. It appointed Bolívar to a committee sent to England to request aid in what it saw as a future struggle with Spain and to request a pioneer revolutionary, Francisco Miranda, to return to Venezuela from his exile in London. The Supreme Junta, entirely Creole, declared Venezuela to be independent of Spain.

The move was not universally popular. The lower classes preferred the monarchy. The Creoles had always been their oppressors; the monarchy was the only restraint on Creole oppression. A tremendous earthquake in Caracas convinced the lower classes that God was punishing them for abandoning the king.

They joined the small Spanish military force and defeated Bolívar, Miranda, and their forces. Miranda was imprisoned, but Bolívar escaped to New Grenada, the rich colony that is now modern Colombia. The revolutionary movement was thriving in New Grenada, but the revolutionists were split. One side favored a federalized government, similar to the United States under the Articles of Confederation. The other (the Unitarians) favored a strong central government. Bolívar joined the New Grenada Unitarian army as a colonel. After several victories over the Spanish, he was promoted to general.

Simón Bolívar was born in what is now Venezuela, and led the forces of freedom in the northern parts of South America. *Library of Congress*

Bolívar led an army into Venezuela. His object was to free Venezuela and unite it with New Grenada in a new republic called Colombia. The war in Venezuela turned into a bloody affair, with both sides torturing and killing prisoners. Bolívar's new campaign made progress until the *llaneros*, Venezuelan cowboys, turned against him. Bolívar was again driven out and fled to New Grenada, where he found himself in another civil war.

Meanwhile, Napoleon had been defeated and the Spanish monarchy reestablished. Ferdinand sent a large army to South America to deal with the rebels. Once again, Bolívar went into exile, this time to Jamaica. Unable to get support in Jamaica, he went to Haiti. There he got money and ships from the president of Haiti and an English merchant. Attempts to invade Venezuela met with little success; but in 1817, the United States recognized the belligerent status of the Venezuelan revolutionaries, and American privateers joined Bolívar and began to sweep the seas of Spanish shipping. Even better, some 5,000 English and Irish veterans of the Napoleonic wars joined him.

Bolívar returned to the Venezuelan plains, and this time the *llaneros* flocked to his banner. He defeated the Spanish in Venezuela, then crossed the mountains and drove them out of Colombia. He was elected president of Colombia (modern Colombia and Venezuela). He then led his army against the Spanish forces in Quito, in what is now Ecuador.

Bolívar resigned the presidency in 1830, and intended to retire to Europe. Unfortunately, he contracted tuberculosis and died before his ship set sail, on December 17, 1830.

José de San Martín
Liberator of the South
(A.D. 1778–1850)

José de San Martín was the son of a rich Spanish family. He was a seasoned soldier before he became involved in the revolutionary politics of his native Argentina. Actually, he was more of a Spaniard than a South American when he became involved with the revolutionary movement in Argentina. His family moved to Spain when he was 8 years old. He joined the Spanish army and fought the French, rising to the rank of lieutenant colonel. He resigned in 1812 and returned to Argentina when he was 34. "I heard of the revolution in South America," he later wrote, "and—forsaking my fortune and my hopes—I desired only to sacrifice everything to promote the liberty of my native land."

San Martín found a revolution lacking an effective leader or a coherent policy. The viceroyalty of Buenos Aires at that time consisted of modern Argentina, Paraguay, Bolivia, and part of Uruguay (which was disputed by the Portuguese of Brazil). The first leader of the movement in Argentina was Mariano Moreno, who was in Buenos Aires when a largely citizen army of Argentineans drove the British invaders out of the city. That showed him and many others that the Argentine people had the power to make themselves independent of Spain. In 1809, Moreno published a book, the *Memorial*, pointing out the economic advantages of free trade (which was not possible under Spanish rule). Moreno, similar to most of the leading citizens of Argentina, favored finding a member of European royalty, who would rule a constitutional monarchy in South America. The next year, a junta was established in Buenos Aires. The junta sent invitations to the people of Uruguay and Paraguay to join them. The invitations were refused, but revolution came to those areas anyway.

In Uruguay, the revolution was led by José Artigas, a rancher and former Spanish officer. He was also a smuggler and cattle rustler. Artigas raised an army of gauchos and declared his allegiance to Buenos Aires. While he got reinforcements from Argentina, the Uruguayan royalists still outnumbered his army. But even though some of his gaucho lancers had no weapons except knives fastened to long poles, Artigas defeated the loyalists, captured 500 prisoners, and converted most of them to revolutionists. He established a revolutionary government and sent five delegates to represent Uruguay at the junta in Buenos Aires. But the Argentineans would not let them be seated. Artigas then ignored the junta and took control of all of Uruguay and part of Argentina.

In Paraguay, the revolutionary leader was Dr. José Gaspar Rodriguez Francia, who got his doctorate in theology and went from revolutionary firebrand to the first of South America's *caudillos barbaros* (brutal dictators), something of which Paraguay was destined to have more than its fair share.

Across the Andes, Chile was ruled by the viceroy in Lima, who was also the paramount viceroy in all of South America. There, the revolutionary leader was Bernardo O'Higgins, bastard son of the viceroy. As soon as the news of Argentina's revolution crossed the mountains, the leading citizens of Chile organized a junta and elected the younger O'Higgins president.

The elder O'Higgins (Ambrose, or Ambrosio, as the Peruvians called him) had been an Irish sea captain who settled in Lima. He became wealthy and a leading citizen of the South American capital. In 1762, the Viceroy sent him to southern Chile to improve the fortifications on the frontier with the fierce and formidable Aurcanian Indians. He did the job so well the king of Spain made him governor of Chile. While in Chile, the 55-year-old governor fell in love with and seduced an 18-year-old girl. She bore him a son, Bernardo. O'Higgins tried to keep the affair secret (what was permissible in the Spanish court was not acceptable for royal officials), but he sent the boy to the best schools in Chile, Peru, and England. In England, Bernardo met the Venezuelan patriot Francisco Miranda and became an advocate of independence.

Shortly after Bernardo's conversion, news of his father's affair leaked out, and the king deposed him as viceroy. The old man died before he got the news, though, and Bernardo inherited his extensive estate in Chile. When fighting broke out, Bernardo O'Higgins proved to be a brave and competent general, but the Spanish forces coming from Peru were too strong. O'Higgins and what was left of his army went into exile in Argentina.

Meanwhile, the junta in Buenos Aires established a Congress and declared the independence of what had been the viceroyalty of Buenos Aires. The delegates aimed to liberate the rest of South America (except the parts of the north, which Bolívar was in the process of liberating). There were still royalists among them. San Martín, for example, wanted to find an heir of the last Inca emperor and make him a constitutional monarch. The national congress made San Martín, the most experienced soldier among them, commander of the army of the Andes, which was to liberate Chile and Peru. San Martín established a base near Mendoza (in western Argentina, below the Andes) and began training an army.

San Martín combined his army with that of O'Higgins and crossed the Andes. They had about 6,000 men and 21 guns. They met and defeated the small Spanish force then in Chile and occupied Santiago. The Chileans acclaimed San Martín as a conquering hero and wanted to make him ruler of Chile. San Martín declined the honor and appointed O'Higgins as director of Chile. San Martín wanted to go on and conquer Peru, the seat of Spanish power.

A Spanish army under Mariano Osorio struck first, however. It narrowly defeated San Martín at Cancha-Rayada on March 16, 1818. Less than a month later, on April 5, 1818, San Martín routed Osorio's forces and ended Spanish power in Chile forever. Between San Martín and Peru, however, were some of the highest mountains in the world, and one of the world's driest deserts. San Martín decided to go by sea. He began gathering ships and converting some of them to warships. To command his fleet, he hired a genuine English sea-dog named Admiral

Thomas Cochrane. Cochrane had a brilliant record in the Napoleonic wars, but he was so outspoken criticizing naval blunders and malfeasance after the war that he was convicted of a trumped-up charge of stock exchange fraud, imprisoned, and discharged from the service. Cochrane defeated the Spanish navy off Peru and made it possible for San Martín to land his army. In the course of his operations, Cochrane led a party in rowboats across the harbor at Callao, climbed aboard the Spanish line-of-battle-ship *Esmeralda*, overpowered the crew, and captured her.

San Martín landed his army—half of them veterans of his Army of the Andes and the other half Chileans—at the little port of Huacho on September 8, 1820. San Martín slowly made his way to Lima, all the time telling Peruvians that he came not to conquer them but to allow them to establish their own government. He took Lima on July 6, 1821, and proclaimed Peru independent. But in spite of his repeated statements that the Peruvians would establish their own government, he tried to get them to make that government a monarchy. When the population apparently wanted a republic, San Martín appointed himself the "protector" of the country. He thought he knew what was best.

Bolívar, a better politician (but an inferior general) was still mopping up in what is now Colombia and Venezuela. When San Martín was preparing his invasion of Peru, Bolívar wrote to San Martín's friend O'Higgins: "A Colombian army is marching on Quito under order to cooperate actively with the armies of Chile and Buenos Aires against Lima."

José de San Martín proclaims Peru's independence on July 6, 1821.

With the defeat of the powerful Spanish force in Peru, the small Spanish army in Ecuador was all that was left of Spanish power in South America.

All was not well for San Martín. His high-handed rule alienated both the Peruvians and Admiral Cochrane, who resigned and took command of the navy of Brazil, which, inspired by the revolutions in neighboring countries, had declared its independence from Portugal. San Martín secretly sent envoys to Europe to find a prince who would be willing to take a throne in South America, but he failed to convince his old friend O'Higgins that Chile should have a king.

Meanwhile, Bolívar's general (Antonio José de Sucre) defeated the last Spanish force (excepting guerrillas holed up in the Peruvian Andes) on the continent at Quito. San Martín, who had promised Bolívar support, went to Guayaquil. The Liberators of the North and the South embraced warmly, but San Martín was disappointed. He had hoped to add Ecuador to Peru, but Bolívar had gotten there first. The reason for the conference was to decide who would lead the army that would mop up the Spanish hold-outs in the mountains. San Martín thought he should have the command on the basis of his much superior military record. He had been narrowly defeated only once and responded by annihilating his opponent's army less than a month later. Bolívar, in contrast, had been defeated repeatedly and frequently driven into exile. The conference was a battle of egos. Seeing that Bolívar would not yield, San Martín offered to be second in command. Bolívar would not hear of it. He feared that San Martín's Argentinean and Chilean troops would regard that as an insult. In the end, San Martín resigned from the government of Peru, moved to Europe, and died in exile.

38

Sam Houston

Retreat to Victory

(A.D. 1793–1863)

In 1818, relations between the United States government and the Native American nations were handled by the War Department. When the Cherokees Indian tribe felt they were being cheated, they thought they had the ideal delegate to present their case to the secretary of war (the very formal John C. Calhoun). Their delegate was a white boy who had run away from home and had been adopted by a Cherokee chief; he was a Cherokee, but he was also white. Best of all, he was an officer in the U.S. Army. His name was Samuel Houston.

Houston was as offended as his Cherokee friends by the cheating government agents, and said he would be proud to present their case. He would denounce the agents both as an army officer and as a Cherokee. But since he would be speaking primarily as a Cherokee, he decided to appear as a Cherokee. First Lieutenant Houston appeared before the secretary of war wearing only a loin cloth and blanket. He presented the Cherokee case eloquently, but Calhoun hardly heard him. He was too busy being outraged at the sight of Sam Houston. Soon after that, Houston found it expedient to resign from the army.

Young Sam was not without resources, though. He had served with Andrew Jackson in the Creek War and had fought in the Battle of Horseshoe Bend in 1814. He had been involved in the removal of the Cherokee Indians to Oklahoma, which resulted in the infamous "trail of tears." Houston had tried (with little success) to mitigate the suffering of his fellow Cherokees. Jackson was no friend of the Cherokees, but the brash young Houston had caught his eye. After Houston left the army, Jackson encouraged him to study law and to go into Tennessee politics.

Sam Houston was both of European descent and a member of the Cherokee Indian Nation.
Library of Congress

Because of his natural eloquence, his common sense, and because of Jackson's powerful patronage, Houston did well. In 1821, he was appointed a major general in the Tennessee militia. In 1823, he was elected to Congress. He served in Washington until 1827, when he was elected governor of Tennessee at the age of 30. He was reelected in 1829, but then his rise in the world came to a screeching halt. His wife of three months deserted him, and Sam Houston was crushed. He resigned as governor and concentrated on drinking. He went back to live with the Cherokees and was formally adopted into the tribe. Several times he roused himself from an alcoholic stupor to go to Washington and plead for the causes of his tribesmen.

Andrew Jackson (now president of the United States) tried to help Houston by giving him an assignment. He was to go to Texas, a territory of Mexico that was populated mainly by immigrants from the United States, and negotiate with several of the tribes there for safe passage for American traders traveling the old Santa Fe Trail. The responsibility seemed to bring Sam Houston back to the real world. He became involved in Texas politics. In 1833, he attended the San Felipe Convention that drew up a constitution for Texas and a petition to the Mexican government to give the territory statehood.

Stephen Austin took the petition to Antonio López de Santa Anna, who had just been elected president of Mexico. After a struggle that began in 1800, Mexico had secured its independence in 1821. The leader of the rebels, Augustin de Iturbide, a former Spanish army officer, crowned himself Emperor Augustin I. A few years later, the Mexican army (including another former Spanish officer, Santa Anna) ousted the emperor, and Mexico became a republic and adopted a liberal constitution. In 1829, Spain attempted to reclaim Mexico. The Spanish expedition was outmaneuvered and crushed near Tampico by Santa Anna. The Mexican government was seized by an extreme conservative named Anastacio Bustamante, who ended all immigration and clamped down on Texas, where immigrants from the United States outnumbered the Mexicans 10 to one. Santa Anna, the "Hero of Tampico," overthrew Bustamante and was elected President. The Texans were delighted with Santa Anna's victory. In addition to the proposed constitution and the request for statehood, Austin gave the new president the congratulations of the Texas Provisional Council.

To his astonishment, Austin was arrested and imprisoned as a rebel. Santa Anna made himself dictator and eliminated all the liberties of the Mexican states, especially the northern ones. He led an army against the states of Coahuila and Zacatecas, and ordered his brother-in-law, Martin Perfecto de Cos, to subdue Texas. At the same time (by pure coincidence) Austin was released under a general amnesty. Back home, he told the Texans that Santa Anna was "a base, unprincipled, bloody monster." He added that "War is our only recourse. No halfway measures, but war in the full."

The Texans declared their independence and appointed Sam Houston commander of the army. He was the only prominent citizen with significant military experience. The army at this time consisted only of militia who supplied their own guns. After preliminary skirmishing (in which the Texans were generally successful), Santa Anna decided to personally lead an army against the Texas rebels. After his victories over the Spanish and Bustamante, Santa Anna considered himself the "Napoleon of the West." In truth, he was an excellent tactician, but he was an abominable leader.

Santa Anna gathered an army from all over central and southern Mexico and set out for Texas in the middle of winter. There was no march discipline. *El Presidente* plunged boldly into the mountains and the desert plateau of northern Mexico, and proceeded by forced marches, leaving his men to follow as best they could. There was no grass for the horses. Scores of men from tropical regions froze to death in ferocious blizzards. Santa Anna's route was marked by the bodies of dead men and dead horses. Most of the army could not keep up with its leader.

He arrived at his first objective, the city of San Antonio de Bexar, on February 23, 1836, a week before Texas declared its independence, after a march most Texans believed to be impossible. Most of Santa Anna's army was still struggling through the desert when he besieged 182 Texas militiamen and some civilians in an old mission-turned-fort called the Alamo. Some of the army hadn't arrived by the time Santa Anna took the fort and massacred its garrison.

Sam Houston knew it was madness to try to hold a fort with a quarter-mile of walls with such a tiny garrison. He ordered the commandant of the fort to blow down its walls and retreat. But the garrison, and especially its fiery, young commander, William Travis, refused to retreat.

Meanwhile, Houston rounded up all the militia he could and advanced on San Antonio. He would have agreed with what George S. Patton said more than a century later: "Fixed fortifications are a monument to the stupidity of man." Houston had seen

The defense of the Alamo was heroic, but Sam Houston preferred strategy to heroics.
Library of Congress

what happened to Santa Anna's army during the march to San Antonio. He resolved to use Texas's greatest natural resource—empty space.

Outnumbered more than six to one, Houston and his men retreated before Santa Anna's army. The farther Houston retreated, the more favorable to the Texans the odds became. Santa Anna had to peel off detachments to hold territory and protect his supply lines. And some Mexican soldiers— hundreds, even thousands, of miles from home in a strange, barren land—simply left the army and tried to make their way home. Santa Anna, plundering and burning settlements, saw none of this. All he knew was that the Texas rebels were being routed. The Texans, however, were gaining strength. Word of Santa Anna's depredations— especially the massacre at the Alamo and another at Goliad—had traveled ahead of him. All along Houston's retreat, settlers grabbed their rifles and joined his army. It was a long retreat, ending at San Jacinto, near the modern city of Houston—some 200 miles.

On April 20, Santa Anna believed the war was about to end. He had the Texans bottled up in a maze of bayous along the San Jacinto River. He had started the march with some 5,000 men. Now he had only 750, but he was not worried. The Texans must have suffered proportionate attrition, and the long retreat had surely sapped their morale. And that morning, General Cos, his brother-in-law, had arrived with 500 more men. At noon, the Mexicans pitched their tents and took a siesta. They expected to finish the campaign that afternoon.

Sam Houston, too, planned to end the campaign that day. He had led Santa Anna to an island with only one exit. While the Mexicans were sleeping, he sent his chief scout, Deaf Smith, to destroy that bridge.

He gathered his army, more than 800 men armed with muskets, percussion rifles, and two six-pounder cannons, and moved through the woods. The cannons, the Twin Sisters, were loaded with double charges of grapeshot. At 3:30 p.m., the Texans saw Santa Anna's camp. The Mexicans were all sleeping, their muskets stacked. Suddenly, the Texas band— three fifes and a drum—broke into *Come to My Bower*, a slightly bawdy popular song. The Twin Sisters belched grapeshot into the Mexican tents, and Houston's men charged. They cut down the Mexicans with rifle and musket fire, bayonets and swords. The Mexicans fled into the water, and the Texans lined up and shot them down like ducks in a shooting gallery. The Texans killed 600 and captured 650. They annihilated Santa Anna's army.

But when the victors looked over the bodies and inspected the prisoners, they couldn't find Santa Anna. Two days after the battle, Houston was taking siesta when he felt someone grab his hand. He opened his eyes and saw Santa Anna. A Texas patrol had found him hiding in the woods. He wore a rough work suit, but he still had his fine linen shirt and jeweled cuffs. According to David Nevin's book (*The Texans*), when Houston's soldiers brought him back to camp, some of the prisoners yelled, "El Presidente!"

"The man may consider himself born to no common destiny who has conquered the Napoleon of the West," Santa Anna told Houston. "And now it remains for him to be generous to the vanquished."

"You should have remembered that at the Alamo," Houston replied.

The Texans wanted to execute Santa Anna, but Houston had a better idea. He made the dictator order all his troops back to Mexico; then Houston had him sign a paper recognizing the independence of Texas.

39

Winfield Scott
Old Fuss and Feathers
(A.D. 1786–1866)

You can't keep a bad man down, and Antonio Lopez de Santa Anna proved it. As soon as he returned from his defeat at San Jacinto, the Mexican Congress rejected the treaty with Texas he signed and removed him from office. Skirmishing, including a naval battle, went on between the forces of Texas and Mexico. Eventually, the United States agreed to annex Texas. That was considered a highly unfriendly act in Mexico. To compound the trouble, Texas claimed that its southern border was the Rio Grande, while Mexico said the traditional boundary of Texas was the Rio Nueces, considerably farther north. President James Polk sent an army under Zachary Taylor to the Rio Grande.

In 1838, a French army invaded Mexico, and the "Hero of Tampico" was recalled to service. He defeated the French as he had the Spanish a decade before, although he lost a leg in the process. And, as he had after defeating the Spanish, he seized control of the government. Three years later, the Mexicans threw him out of office and banished him from the country. From his exile in Cuba, Santa Anna approached (of all people) President James Polk of the United States. The American politician was most intent on taking territory from Mexico. If the Americans could smuggle him back into Mexico, Santa Anna told Polk, he would

regain power and sign the sort of treaty the United States wanted. But as soon as he landed, Santa Anna issued a statement calling for all-out war on the United States:

Mexicans! There once was a day, and my heart dilates with the remembrance, when…you saluted me with the enviable title of Soldier of the People. Allow me again to take it, never more to be given up, and to devote myself, until death, to the defense of the liberty and independence of the republic.

In a very short time, Santa Anna was back in Mexico City preparing to drive the *yanquis* out of Mexico and out of Texas.

In the meantime, Mexican troops in the Rio Grande area fired on American troops, so Polk told Congress that a state of war existed between the United States and Mexico. Zachary Taylor, "Old Rough and Ready," won a series of victories against the Mexicans under Mariano Arista and pushed on to Monterrey, the capital of the state of Nuevo Leon. He was there when Santa Anna led a new army against him. Old Rough and Ready won the Battle of Buena Vista, thanks to the superb American light artillery.

Soon after the war began, the U.S. Navy, with the aid of the somewhat bogus "Bear

Flag Republic," claimed to have captured the sparsely settled Mexican state of Alta California. General Philip Kearney came down the Santa Fe Trail to New Mexico, secured Santa Fe, and continued on through what is now Arizona to southern California. The California cavalry checked Kearney at first contact—the only defeat Americans suffered in the whole Mexican War—but Kearney rallied his troops and completed the conquest.

Winfield Scott tried to win the battle with a minimum loss of life. That endeared him to the troops, but not to the politicians.
National Archives

But the main American effort, Taylor's push into Mexico, seemed to be stalled. Buena Vista Ranch was a long way from Mexico City, and the territory between the two points was no more inviting than it had been during Santa Anna's march to San Antonio.

The best route to the Mexican capital was the one Hernán Cortés took in 1519. But who would lead an army along it? It was possible to recall General Taylor and assign him command of the amphibious expedition that would land at Vera Cruz. But Taylor had criticized the Polk administration, and the Whigs were talking about nominating him for president. The president looked at the files of Democratic generals, but military talent seemed to be lacking in the party. There was one exception, Major General Winfield Scott, one of the few American officers who had demonstrated real ability during the War of 1812. Winfield Scott was a Whig, but his outspokenness had offended so many people that he had no future in politics.

Scott's words had almost ended his military career. He called his superior officer, General James Wilkinson, a crook, and had been suspended from the army during 1809 and 1810. As a matter of fact, Wilkinson was a crook. He has been called "America's greatest rascal—an honor to be treasured, since the competition is severe." Among other things (while commanding general of the United States Army), he secretly renounced his citizenship, swore allegiance to the king of Spain, and was a secret Spanish agent. Repeatedly court-martialed, but always found not guilty, he was known as "the general who never won a battle and never lost a court-martial." His infamy did not become public until after he died and was buried in Mexico.

Scott, at the time of the Mexican War, was commanding general of the army. In that position, he was so formal and so fond of plans and calculations that field commanders nicknamed him "Old Fuss and Feathers." Although he supported Taylor's work in northern Mexico, he was the one who pointed out the advantages of the Cortés invasion route. Polk agreed, and after considering possible leaders, appointed Winfield Scott to command the invasion. Scott's devotion to plans and calculations was to bear early fruit.

Vera Cruz was protected by a powerful fort. Scott personally scouted the harbor, coming well within cannon range of the fort before the Mexicans spotted him and opened fire on his boat. The general then landed his troops some distance from the fort (without losing a man) and laid siege to the city. Scott assigned his engineers to conduct a scientific siege. He had a lot of bright engineers. Among them were Robert E. Lee, Joseph Johnston, P.T.G. Beauregard, and George B. McClellan. The men dug parallel trenches and approach saps, positioned batteries, and did everything following the gospel of Sebastien le Prestre de Vauban, the great French engineer. Vera Cruz and its fort surrendered 20 days after Scott landed. He said he would take the city without losing more than 100 men; he lost only 69.

When Scott's victory was announced in New Orleans, one man asked, "How many men has Scott lost?" "Less than 100," was the reply. "That won't do," the questioner shot back. "Taylor always loses thousands. He's the man for my money."

Scott couldn't spend much time at Vera Cruz. In those days, yellow fever appeared regularly in late spring. Scott and his men started up the national highway that had been built on Cortes's route. Santa Anna had returned to Mexico City and taken an army east to block Scott. He fortified a mountain called Cerro Gordo ("fat hill"). Scott sent Captain Robert E. Lee to find a way around Santa Anna's army. Lee found a way; the Americans dragged their artillery over the mountains; routed the Mexican Army, and captured the money Santa Anna had brought to pay his troops. The United States Army

continued its march, taking the major city of Puebla on the way to the Mexican capital and turning it into a base. On August 7, Scott commenced operations against Mexico City.

Three centuries earlier, Cortés was faced with a city in the middle of a lake, with only three causeways for approaches. Most of the lake was gone now, but smaller lakes and marshes remained, and causeways through the marshes were still the main approaches to Mexico City. Santa Anna skillfully took advantage of these natural defenses. In London, the duke of Wellington (studying reports of the war) opined, "Scott is lost. He cannot capture the city, and he cannot fall back upon his base."

Once again, reconnaissance by the astute Captain Lee helped Scott maneuver through the defenses, but Scott's men had to fight a series of battles to get into the city. Although his men lacked discipline, Santa Anna was an adroit field commander, and the conquest of Mexico City did not occur until September 14, 1847. Santa Anna was forced into exile by his people, a condition in which he spent most of the rest of his life, and the Treaty of Guadalupe Hidalgo on January 1848 forever ended the Mexican War.

The end of the Mexican War greatly enlarged the territory of the United States. Besides Texas (with a southern border on the Rio Grande), Uncle Sam got New Mexico, Arizona, California, Nevada, Utah, and part of Colorado—an area five times the size of France.

Winfield Scott lost the nomination for president on the Whig ticket to Zachary Taylor in 1848, and he lost another presidential nomination in 1852 to Franklin Pierce, who had served under him in Mexico. But he changed history more than either of those presidents.

40

Helmuth von Moltke

The Art of Mobilization

(A.D. 1800–1891)

In the summer of 1914, a young Serb named Gavrilo Princip shot and killed Archduke Franz Ferdinand of Austria-Hungary and his wife. As a result, Austria-Hungary declared war on Serbia. Austria's ally, Germany, assured Austria-Hungary of its support. Russia (Serbia's ally) mobilized its army on the frontiers of both Austria-Hungary and Germany. German Kaiser Wilhelm II ordered his armies to mobilize against both Russia and its ally, France.

Moltke was the first military leader to fully exploit the railroad as a means of transporting troops and materials. *Library of Congress*

The German mobilization followed a plan drawn up many years before by Count Alfred von Schlieffen, which called for a powerful German right wing to cross Belgium and enter northern France, while the weaker German left wing would yield somewhat to the expected French attack farther south. A weaker German army would hold back the slow-mobilizing Russians in the east. After France was defeated, German troops would travel from the western front to the eastern front and knock out the Russians. But there were a couple of problems. The crown prince of Bavaria, who would command the left wing in the west, didn't want to retreat. More important, the British (who had been expected to remain neutral) said they would fight if Belgium were invaded. Germany had been trying to become a naval power to rival Britain, and the British didn't want German warships in Belgium.

The Kaiser began having second thoughts. The French would probably not come to Russia's aid, he reasoned. Further, he had no desire to bring Britain into the war. Britain's enormous navy could cut off all non-European trade with Germany, and it would make it easy for the British to take over all of Germany's colonies. He called the chief of the Great General Staff, Helmuth von Moltke the Younger, and told him to call off the mobilization in the west. Moltke was so shocked he could hardly find the words to protest. According to Barbara Tuchman in her book *The Guns of August*, Moltke replied with outrage: "Your Majesty, it cannot be done," he said. "The deployment of millions cannot be improvised. If Your Majesty insists on leading the whole army to the east, it will not be an army ready for battle, but a disorganized mob of armed men with no arrangements for supply. Those arrangements took a whole year of intricate labor to complete."

The trains were already rolling, carrying troops, equipment, and supplies to points on both the eastern and western frontiers. There were 11,000 trains, each following a precise schedule. If any train failed to reach a checkpoint at the exact hour called for in the mobilization plan, serious confusion would result. To switch to only one frontier would result in utter chaos. Wilhelm would get a two-front war whether he wanted one or not. And Europe—and much of the rest of the world—would get the bloodiest war in history up to that time.

The blame for this belongs to Moltke's great uncle, Helmuth von Moltke (the Elder).

Actually, the elder Moltke was an extraordinary military pioneer. He was the first general to see the strategic importance of railroads and take advantage of this new means of transportation. Railroads had played an important part in the American Civil War, but as with much else in that war, their use was improvised—almost on the spur of the moment—to meet unforeseen developments. For Moltke, chief of the Prussian general staff, railroads were the backbone of his strategic plans—plans developed before a war took place. Moltke's plans enabled the Prussians to win a series of wars with Denmark, France, and Austria. Moltke's work also shifted power

in the Prussian—and later, all European— armies from commanders in the field to general staffs in headquarters.

Moltke the Elder hated military untidiness. Studying reports of the American Civil War, he saw none of the strategic and tactical brilliance displayed by the likes of Grant, Lee, Sherman, Longstreet, Jackson, and Sheridan. He saw the sweeping troop movements in the west, the amphibious campaigns on the Mississippi and its tributaries and the back-and-forth slugging in the east and declared that there was "nothing to be learned from two armed mobs chasing each other around the country."

Moltke was born in the German state of Mecklenburg on October 26, 1800, and was educated in the Royal Cadet Corps in Copenhagen. He served in the Danish army before joining the Prussian army. On leave from the Prussian army, he went to Turkey and served with the Turkish army, fighting against the sultan's supposed vassal Mehmet Ali. He wrote a novel and a study of the Polish insurrection of 1830, as well as a book about his Turkish adventures. Helmuth von Moltke was a cosmopolitan European, but his horizons were the boundaries of Europe.

Moltke was always interested in railroads and wrote an essay on them in 1843. Two years later, he was appointed aide-de-camp to Prince Henry of Prussia. After the ailing Henry died, he was promoted to colonel and made aide-de-camp to another Prussian prince, Friederich Wilhelm, who became King Friederich III. He continued traveling through Europe, going to England, France, and Russia and observing everything closely. He became chief of the Prussian general staff in 1857 and worked closely with Chancellor Otto von Bismarck.

As a young man, Moltke was pledged to the Danish crown as an infantryman.

As chief of staff, Moltke was able to put his ideas into practice. Since the Napoleonic wars, armies (composed of active-duty troops and several classes of trained reservists) had been growing larger and larger. Moltke understood that modern communications and modern transportation made it possible to control much larger armies over much wider areas than was previously possible. He reorganized the Prussian general staff, separating it into four departments. Three were geographical—east, German, and west—handling all supplies and accommodations needed for soldiers in those areas. The fourth department was Railroads.

With the general staff controlling the railroads and telegraph network, it was possible to mobilize troops and put them on an enemy frontier far more quickly than had ever been possible before. Moltke believed that when war occurred, the first nation to complete its mobilization would win. In the 1864 war between Denmark and the combined forces of Prussia and Austria, Moltke was chief of staff of the combined Prussian and Austrian armies. He led the allies to victory in a matter of weeks. King Wilhelm of Prussia was so impressed he made Moltke virtual commander-in-chief of the Prussian army. In 1866, Prussia invaded Austria, with Moltke directing the field generals by telegraph. He won the war in seven weeks.

Moltke continued to refine his use of modern transportation and communications. Although he was in charge of all planning, he refused to rigidly follow a plan. He said that no plan survives the first five minutes of an encounter with the enemy. He trained his subordinates to be flexible and emphasized the importance of flank attacks and envelopment. And in any case, he was always in touch by telegraph.

Moltke's ideas got the acid test when war broke out between Prussia and France (then considered the greatest military power in Europe). The French forces turned out to be totally disorganized, while the armies of Prussia and its allies among the German states followed Moltke's plans precisely. The French field armies were defeated and Emperor Napoleon III was captured in less than two months. Moltke directed the siege of Paris, which began October 19, 1870, and ended January 26, 1871.

When the war ended, King Wilhelm of Prussia became Kaiser (Emperor) Wilhelm I of Germany. And every country on the continent of Europe tried to imitate Moltke's mobilization plans.

Ulysses S. Grant
The War for Survival
(A.D. 1822–1885)

At one time during the American Civil War, someone told President Abraham Lincoln that one of his generals, U.S. Grant, had a drinking problem. "Find out what brand he drinks," the president said, "and send some to the rest of my generals."

In the crucial eastern theater, with fighting raging only a few miles from Washington, D.C. (and from the Confederate capital of Richmond), Lincoln had long been troubled by generals who were either too cautious (McClellan), too bold (Burnside), or simply cowards ("Fighting Joe" Hooker). Grant won battles, and if whiskey fueled his winning streak, then Lincoln would send him barrels of it.

Lincoln finally found a man to win the bloodiest war in American history. (The Civil War killed more Americans than World War II, World War I, the Vietnam War, and the Korean War *combined*. And the population of the United States at that time was not much more than a 10th of what it is today.) But when the war began, Ulysses Simpson Grant looked like anything but a winner. Although he graduated from West Point and had a brilliant record in the Mexican War, Grant, who had resigned his commission, had a hard time getting back in the army. Except for his service under Winfield Scott in Mexico, Grant's whole career looked like a series of missteps.

The boy christened Hiram Ulysses Grant didn't like his initials—H.U.G. He tried to change his name to Ulysses Hiram Grant. But when he got to West Point in 1832, he found that the congressman who sponsored him had listed him as Ulysses Simpson (his mother's maiden name) Grant. He decided that U.S. were pretty good initials, so he kept the name. At the Military Academy, he proved to be an extraordinarily good horseman, but (except for mathematics) an indifferent student. He graduated 21st out of a class of 39. As a second lieutenant he served in Mexico under Zachary Taylor and then under Winfield Scott. He was brevetted a first lieutenant for gallantry at the Battle of Molino del Rey. His performance at the storming of Chapultepec got him brevetted a captain and commissioned a first lieutenant in the regular army.

He married after the war, but was stationed at a series of dismal western outposts where his wife could not join him. He began drinking; he was soon forced to resign his commission or stand trial for drunkenness. As a civilian, he tried a number of business ventures and failed in all of them. He ended up as a clerk in his father's leather business.

The outbreak of the Civil War prompted a huge demand for manpower. Grant, a decorated veteran of the last war, tried to get his commission back. The army wasn't interested. So Grant organized and drilled a volunteer company for the state of Illinois. Then he went to the state adjutant general's office and was appointed colonel of a state volunteer regiment.

This picture of Grant was taken at Cold Harbor in 1864, just before the end of the Civil War.
National Archives

A short note on volunteerism is needed here. "Volunteer" in the Civil War meant something different from what we now call our "all volunteer army." The army took in volunteer units—regiments and divisions organized by the states. These then became part of the "volunteer army," something quite distinct from the regular army. As with the draftees in World War II, Korea, and Vietnam, who were part of the Army of the United States instead of the United States Army (regular army), they served for the duration of the war. Officers from the regular army

were often assigned to volunteer units, usually brevetted at much higher than their regular rank. The volunteer system was used extensively in the Civil War and the Spanish American War to expand the army. It was used on a very small scale in World War I, but has not been used since.

Two months after he got back into the war, Grant was promoted to brigadier general and given command of the district of southeast Missouri. He attracted the attention of Lincoln and the army brass by his brilliant coordination of army and naval units to capture Confederate Forts Henry and Donelson on the Tennessee and Cumberland rivers in February 1862. Surprised by Confederates under Albert Sidney Johnston at Shiloh in April of that year, he defeated the Confederates and drove them back. Johnston was killed in the battle.

Henry W. Halleck, "Old Brains," was in charge of the western theater. Although an excellent administrator, he proved to be a poor field commander, so he was "kicked upstairs" by being appointed general-in-chief of the army. Grant got command of all troops in the west. With the aid of the navy's fleet of riverboats, Grant aimed to control the western rivers and cut the confederacy off from manpower, food, and raw materials. His strategic and tactical masterpiece was the capture of Vicksburg, which he accomplished by confusing the Confederates with his maneuvers and splitting two Confederate armies. The fall of Vicksburg cut the Confederacy in two.

He relieved the siege of Chattanooga, where William Rosecrans's army was cooped up after its defeat at Chickamauga, and routed Braxton Bragg's besieging army. Lincoln promoted him to lieutenant general—then the highest rank in the United States Army—

and put him in charge of all U.S. troops and transferred him to the East. Grant then demonstrated his ability to spot military talent—an ability that had been conspicuously absent in higher headquarters. He left George Thomas, the "Rock of Chickamauga," and William Tecumseh Sherman in charge of the two western Union armies and took the aggressive young Philip Sheridan east.

In the East, Grant brought a major change. Previously, the two armies would meet, fight a battle, and then retire and lick their wounds. The Union maintained a small foothold in northern Virginia, but it was a very small foothold. Robert E. Lee twice invaded the North, but the first time he got no farther than Maryland and the second time barely across the Mason-Dixon Line. Both times, he was beaten back. When Grant came east, there was no more retiring. The wide sweeps Grant was used to in the West were not possible in the densely settled East. Further, Lee, the old engineer, devised field fortifications that could be compared with those on the western front in World War I. Nevertheless, Grant kept his men moving. Stopped in one place, they hit another. There were continuous flanking movements, although narrow ones. Lee blocked the northern approach to Richmond, so Grant moved south to Petersburg. But Lee had just completed field fortifications there, too.

Grant's casualties were enormous. If his foes had repeating rifles and machine guns, the campaign would have been impossible. But the North had more men than the South, and the Army of Northern Virginia was melting away. All the time he was slugging it out with Lee in Virginia, Grant was also directing operations in the whole country using the telegraph.

Lee tried to relieve the pressure by sending Jubal Early up the Shenandoah Valley to threaten Washington, but Grant sent part of his army under Sheridan to take care of Early. Sheridan annihilated the threat, burned out the valley to get rid of Confederate guerrillas, and rejoined Grant as commander of his cavalry. It was Sheridan's cavalry that blocked Lee's last escape route at the Appomattox Courthouse. Lee surrendered. Two weeks later, Joseph Johnston, who had been vainly trying to stop Sherman, also surrendered.

After his presidency, Grant spent two years traveling around the world with his wife.

Ulysses S. Grant later became president of the United States. But the man who had proved to be so expert in the military field was at sea in civilian life. As president, he attracted a strange inner circle. It consisted of good, honest men (mostly soldiers such as Sherman and Sheridan; and one Confederate, Colonel John Singleton Mosby, who, during most of the war, controlled a guerrilla kingdom just northwest of Washington, D.C.). But it also included a motley crew of entrepreneurs and some crooks. Grant himself never profited from their schemes. He was mainly guilty of putting too much trust in his friends. Nevertheless, the people liked Grant enough to elect him for two terms.

After leaving office, he resumed his disastrous career in civilian business. Unwise investments left him penniless. To take care of his family (while dying of throat cancer) he wrote his *Memoirs*, which became a bestseller. He completed the book four days before he died.

42

Alfred Thayer Mahan

The Great Collider

(A.D. 1840–1914)

Alfred Thayer Mahan did not reach the rank of admiral in the U.S. Navy until after he retired, and never reached a rank higher than lieutenant when he was in combat, but he is America's premier naval strategist. In fact, he is the *world's* premier naval strategist. He strongly influenced U.S. naval policy throughout the 20th century. His influence was equally strong in the navies of Britain, Germany. and Japan. Among other things, he was indirectly responsible for the naval arms race between Britain and Germany, which occurred before World War I, and helped set the stage for that conflict. And he accomplished all this with a book about naval grand strategy in the 17th and 18th centuries that he wrote while president of the Naval War College in Newport, Rhode Island.

Mahan's success in military academia may have been genetic. His father, Dennis Hart Mahan, was a professor at the U.S. Military Academy. Dennis Mahan "was instrumental in framing the intellectual conceptions of many army officers who fought in the American Civil War." Over the opposition of his family, Mahan chose to go to Annapolis instead of West Point. He graduated in 1859, second in his class.

Mahan's record in the Civil War was somewhat undistinguished. His courage was indisputable, but his handling of a ship left much to be desired. On November 7, 1861,

while at the helm of the USS *Pocahontas*, he ran his ship into another Union warship during the attack on Fort Walker at Port Royal, South Carolina. For the next 10 months, the navy kept Mahan on blockade duty, and then assigned him to teach at the Naval Academy. Mahan, who never underrated his intellectual gifts, considered the assignment (which consisted of teaching midshipmen how to tie knots and similarly challenging subjects) "humiliating."

Back at sea in 1874, while serving in the U.S. Navy's Brazil Squadron, he rammed a barge with the USS *Wasp* in the harbor of Montevideo, Uruguay. Later that year, he accidentally rammed an Argentine warship off Buenos Aires. Then, once again at Montevideo, he ran *Wasp* into a dry dock caisson, where the ship remained stuck for 10 days. The incident prompted his biographer, Robert Seager III, to note that "Alfred Thayer Mahan may be the only commanding officer in the history of the U.S. Navy rendered hors de combat by a dry dock." In 1883, while commanding the USS *Wachusett*, Mahan ran into a sailing ship, although it was on a smooth sea, in broad daylight, and the civilian bark had the right of way. Mahan is probably the only U.S. naval officer to ever make captain—much less admiral—with such a record of seamanship.

During his tour in South America, Mahan wandered into a library in Lima, Peru, and picked up a copy of Theodore Mommsen's *History of Rome*. What he read convinced him that Rome was able to build its empire because it controlled the Mediterranean. Mahan began writing about naval affairs, which aroused some criticism among traditional sea dogs. Naval officers were not supposed to read books, much less write them. His book about Civil War naval battles earned him the reputation of being an intellectual. So to use his obvious talent (and to reduce the number of naval accidents) the navy assigned him to the newly established Naval War College.

In 1886, the year after he began lecturing at the Naval War College, Mahan was appointed president and commander of the facility. The next year, he met a young politician named Theodore Roosevelt, who was giving a lecture at the college. Mahan and Roosevelt became fast friends. Both were expansionists who believed that since the western frontier had disappeared, the United States should seek colonies overseas, especially in the Pacific.

In 1890, Mahan put together his lectures and published his blockbuster book, *The Influence of Sea Power upon History, 1660-1783*. He followed that in 1892 with *The Influence of Sea Power upon the French Revolution and Empire*. In both books, he argued that in the series of wars between England and France, sea power was the deciding factor, and that control of sea-borne commerce leads to victory in war. Control of the seas, he said, could be achieved only by powerful battleships. He denigrated "cruiser warfare," or naval power based on commerce raiders. (Cruiser warfare had been the keystone of U.S. naval policy since the days of sail, when cruisers were called frigates.)

President William McKinley, another expansionist, was strongly influenced by Mahan, as was Roosevelt, who succeeded McKinley as president. Mahan argued that the United States must have a strong navy and one which was capable of operating worldwide. Under McKinley and Roosevelt, the United States acquired Hawaii, which provided a naval base in the mid-Pacific, and the Philippines, which provided a base in the Far East. The country also acquired Puerto Rico, which allowed the United States to dominate the Caribbean and guard the eastern approach to Panama, where Roosevelt arranged to have an American-owned canal built.

Captain Alfred T. Mahan left much to be desired as a seaman, but very little as a naval strategist. *Library of Congress*

Mahan's influence was equally strong overseas. The leaders of Japan decided that as an island nation, it was imperative that they have a powerful navy that could dominate the waters of the Far East. They began a crash program of modernizing their navy. The program bore fruit in 1905, when their navy trounced a larger Russian fleet in the Strait of Tsushima.

Kaiser Wilhelm II of Germany devoured Mahan's books. He began a program to give Germany a navy second to none. Britain, another island nation that depended entirely on overseas commerce, saw the German campaign as a threat, and began its own battleship building program. This arms race increased the tensions between two nations that had formerly been quite friendly. Novels such as Erskine Childers's *The Riddle of the Sands* (which considered the possibility of war between the two naval powers) were published in both Britain and Germany. These tensions were certainly an important factor in Britain's decision to enter World War I.

World War I, when it broke out, proved that Mahan's theories were partially correct. Britain and Germany had a big battleship battle off Jutland. The British suffered heavier losses, but it was the Germans who broke off the action and fled. The German High Seas Fleet never again attempted to break out into the North Sea. Ordered on October 29, 1918, to sail out and fight the British and American ships blockading Germany, the German sailors mutinied and seized their ships. Only 11 days later, Kaiser Wilhelm abdicated, and two days after that, Germany surrendered.

In dismissing "cruiser warfare," however, Mahan was somewhat off the mark. In World War I, cruiser warfare—commerce raiding— was conducted by German submarines, and it came very close to being decisive. There were submarines at the turn of the century, but neither Mahan nor any other naval strategist at the time dreamed they would become so important.

In World War II, climatic battles such as Midway and the Philippine Sea established American domination of the Pacific and ensured the defeat of Japan. Mahan was again proved correct. As for "cruiser warfare," in the Pacific, thais was carried out solely by U.S. submarines and was more effective than the German submarine effort.

In 1893, Mahan was given command of the new cruiser *Chicago*, which he took to Europe, where he was received with honor. Unfortunately, while on the bridge of *the Chicago*, Mahan collided with a Naval Academy training ship, the USS *Bancroft*, and injured his knee. In his naval career, the great strategist "grounded, collided, or otherwise embarrassed every ship (save the *Iroquois*) he ever commanded," according to an observer quoted by Charles M. Hubbard in *American History*, August 1998. In 1896, Mahan decided that his true calling was writing, and resigned from the navy.

When the Spanish American War broke out, Mahan was recalled to active duty on the Naval War Board. In 1906, he was promoted to rear admiral by an act of Congress promoting all retired captains who had served in the Civil War.

43

Togo Heihachiro

Samurai of the Sea

(A.D. 1848–1934)

The career of Togo Heihachiro spanned two eras. He took part in the last feudal war of Old Japan, fought against the Bakufu (the great lords who governed under the Tokugawa shogunate), and fought and won the first decisive naval battle of the 20th century.

Togo was born in 1848, five years before Commodore Mathew Perry broke Japan's centuries-old, self-imposed isolation. He was born a samurai in a feudal land in which the population was divided into four rigidly defined classes—samurai (warriors), farmers, artisans, and merchants. At the age of 17, the young warrior saw his first combat: he helped defend his hometown, Kagoshima, against a British bombardment. An Englishman named Richardson had been killed in Satsuma *Han* (province) because he hadn't shown proper reverence to a Japanese noble, and the Satsuma lord had refused to pay an indemnity.

The "Anglo-Satsuma War" convinced the Satsuma *daimyo* (lord) that he should have a navy. In 1866, the 20-year-old Heihachiro joined the Satsuma navy. He was an officer on the paddle-wheel steam warship, *Kasuga*, which took part in the battles of Awa, Miyako, and Hakodate against the navy of the shogun. In this conflict, the Boshin War, the shogun and his government, the Bakufu, were overthrown. The emperor, a secluded figure revered as divine but with no real power, became a ruler. The daimyos and their private armies and navies were eliminated. Togo joined the Imperial navy.

Recognizing his talent, Togo's superiors sent him to England to study naval science. His studies were both theoretical and practical, including service aboard British naval ships. He traveled around the world on the training ship HMS *Hampshire*.

As a young man, Togo studied in England for seven years.

Togo attended the Naval Preparatory School in Portsmouth and the Royal Naval College in Greenwich. While he was in England, Japan ordered three warships from British shipyards. Togo got a chance to apply his training by supervising the construction of one of them.

Togo's absence from Japan was most fortunate. While he was away, another Satsuma samurai, Saigo Takamori (who had helped lead the revolt against the shogun), led a rebellion against the emperor. In 1871, the emperor's government abolished the ancient class system. Samurai could no longer wear two swords and lord it over their "inferiors," the farmers, artisans, and merchants. Most of the Satsuma samurai joined Saigo. If he had been in Japan, Togo would probably been among them. The rebellion was crushed in 1877, and Saigo lost his life.

Togo returned to Japan in 1878. He continued to advance in the navy. He was promoted to captain and commanded several ships. Togo was able to observe both naval and ground actions in the war between France and China (1884 to 1885). During this time, friction began to develop between China and Japan. Both were interested in controlling Korea. Togo was captain of the cruiser *Naniwa* when he encountered a British transport ship carrying Chinese soldiers to Korea; he sank the transport. He rescued the British sailors but did nothing to help the Chinese soldiers. He even fired on their lifeboats. The incident caused a diplomatic furor, but British jurists decided that Togo's action was legal under international law. China, however, declared war on Japan. During the war, which Japan won, Togo took part in the Battle of the Yalu and was promoted to rear admiral in 1895. He served in increasingly important posts in the navy, and when war with Russia

threatened, he was appointed commander of the combined fleets.

Togo adapted the ancient customs of the samurai to modern warfare. In the Chinese war, he demonstrated samurai ruthlessness by shooting Chinese soldiers helpless in the sea. In the Russian war, he attacked the Russian Far East Fleet before his government declared war.

The prospect of war with Japan caused considerable amusement in St. Petersburg and Moscow. Russia was a major naval power. The size of its navy was exceeded only by those of Britain and France. It had fleets in the Black Sea, the Baltic Sea, and the Far East. In the Far East alone, it had seven battleships to Japan's six, nine cruisers to Japan's eight, and 25 destroyers to Japan's 19. Its army numbered 4,500,000; Japan's, 283,000. Of course, most of those Russian troops were in Europe or Central Asia. There were only 138,000 Russian troops in the whole area between Lake Baikal and the Pacific Ocean. The only connection between European Russia and the Far East was the single track of the Trans-Siberian Railroad, laid across tundra that turned into a shifting morass every spring.

The Russian naval commanders were as cautious as Togo was aggressive. They let the Japanese land an army in Korea and march to Port Arthur, their naval base in Manchuria. The Japanese encircled Port Arthur and its harbor, which contained the Russian Far East Fleet. The Russian ships tried to break out of Port Arthur on August 10, 1904, but were beaten back by a smaller Japanese fleet.

Treaties prevented Russia from taking the Black Sea fleet through the Dardanelles, so the tsar sent his Baltic Sea fleet to the Pacific. That trip to the Far East, under Admiral Zinovi Petrovitch Rozhestvensky, was one long naval disaster. Before they left the Baltic, the Russians thought they saw Japanese torpedo boats. They opened fire and hit some other Russian ships and sank a British fishing boat. If the tsar's government hadn't hastily apologized to the British government, the Russian fleet would probably have ended up on the bottom of the North Sea.

Born in feudal Japan, Admiral Togo learned 20th-century warfare and skill with modern weapons.
United States Institute Photo Archive

In the Atlantic, the Russians fired on some inoffensive Swedish, French, and German ships they thought were Japanese. Fortunately, all their shots missed. In Tangier, they snagged and broke the submarine cable between Europe and Africa, wiping out communications between the continents for four days. The Russian sailors adopted exotic pets in Africa, and one of them, a poisonous snake, almost killed a sailor. After waiting two weeks for a supply ship in Madagascar, they found that instead of ammunition, the supply ship brought useless winter clothes. At French Indochina, they acquired some reinforcements, many of them the decrepit warships the Russian sailors dubbed "self-sinkers." By that time, the Japanese had taken Port Arthur and decisively defeated the Russian army at Mukden. For all practical purposes, the war was over.

Admiral Rozhestvensky, however, had no orders to turn back. He headed north, along the coast of China, aiming for Tsushima Strait, the narrow body of water between Japan and Korea. He ordered his seven battleships and nine armored cruisers to form a line abreast. With that kind of formation, if they saw the Japanese fleet approaching, they could all turn and perform the classic naval maneuver of "crossing the T." Note: When ships are sailing in a single file and they see the enemy ahead of them, only the first ship in line can fire its main guns, and then only those guns that face the front. An enemy fleet that crosses it at a right angle can fire *all* its main guns and half its secondary guns.

Rozhestvensky's plan would have been a brilliant maneuver but for two things: (1) the Japanese were not approaching him directly: they were coming from the side, because Togo was also dreaming of a T-crossing; and (2) the Russian skippers weren't able to form a line abreast. The best the Russians could do was form two columns.

The Japanese came in a single column, but they cut across the front of the two Russian columns. There were four Japanese battleships and eight armored cruisers, but they were able to use all their main guns. The Russian ships, painted black with yellow funnels were easy to see on that misty day. The faster Japanese ships, painted gray, were not. The Japanese fleet concentrated its fire on two Russian battleships, which could only use half of their main armament.

Rozhestvensky was wounded and knocked unconscious. When he woke up in a Japanese hospital, he learned that five of his seven battleships had been sunk The rest were heavily damaged. Three cruisers got to the Philippines, where their crews were interned. A cruiser and three destroyers reached safety in Vladivostok. The war was over; Russia had lost.

The Russian defeat led to a naval mutiny that became the rebellion of 1905. The Tsar's troops put down the rebellion, but they didn't stamp out all the embers, which flared into a new rebellion in 1917—the Communist Revolution.

At Tsushima, the Russians suffered one of the most complete naval defeats in history. More important, Togo's victory was not just the defeat of one naval power by another. It occurred when colonialism was at its height, when Europeans and descendants of Europeans (the Americans) had conquered non-Europeans all over the globe. In all of Asia and its adjacent islands, besides Japan, only China, Siam, Afghanistan, and Persia remained independent. (Korea, under the heavy thumbs of China, Japan, and Russia,

could hardly be considered independent.) And now an Asian people had defeated—and defeated most thoroughly—the biggest of European nations. Japan had broken the spell of European invincibility. It would take another generation for the idea to bear fruit, but the seed had been planted.

At his death (at the age of 87), the countries of Great Britain, the United States, the Netherlands, France, Italy, and China sent ships to a naval parade in Togo's honor.

Giulio Douhet

The Father of Air Power

(A.D. 1869–1930)

Giulio Douhet was an Italian artilleryman. He had never flown an airplane and he had seen only three airplanes in his life when he first published an article on military air power. He went on to become the first advocate of an independent air force, which (he predicted) would dominate warfare. He became the intellectual father of such pre-World War II theorists as the American General William "Billy" Mitchell and the English Air Marshal Hugh "Boom" Trenchard. Douhet died in 1930, so he never lived to see the application of his theory in World War II.

Douhet was born on May 30, 1869, in Caserta, Italy, to a family with a long tradition of military service. He attended the Genoa Military Academy and was commissioned a lieutenant in the artillery. Soldiering was not his whole life. Douhet was also a poet and a playwright, and he was not averse to writing ideas that offended conservative military authorities. From the beginning, Douhet was fascinated by the technical innovations that were changing warfare—weapons such as Krupp's breech-loading, rifled, steel siege guns; machine guns; and high explosives; as well as weapons carriers such as gasoline-powered armored cars and tractors. In 1909, he met the American airplane pioneer Wilbur Wright and decided that the future of war belonged to the airplane. And, of course, Douhet published his thoughts.

In 1911, Italy went to war with Turkey over Libya. The Ottoman Empire appeared to be crumbling (although it turned out to be remarkably solid a few years later in World War I), and Italy saw a chance to get back part of the long-lost Roman Empire. Douhet, the Italian army's greatest air enthusiast, was given command of Italy's aircraft. The war in Libya saw the world's first use of airplanes for reconnaissance, including photo reconnaissance, and bombing. After winning the war (and Libya), Italy established an aviation battalion commanded by Giulio Douhet. In that position, he wrote a book, *Rules for the Use of Airplanes in War*—one of the first manuals ever written on that subject.

As with other air enthusiasts after him, Douhet became impatient with the inaction of the established military authorities. He commissioned a friend (a young engineer named Gianni Caproni) to build a three-engine bombing plane for Italy. The Caproni bomber was years ahead of its time, but the authorities were not pleased with Douhet's impertinence in authorizing the plane's construction without consulting higher authorities. They transferred him to an infantry division.

When World War I began, Douhet, still an active-duty officer, shifted his gadfly activities into high gear. He called for a vast increase in Italy's armaments, predicting that his country would soon be swept into the European conflagration. He proposed an air force of 500 bombers that could drop 125 tons of bombs a day. Such a force, he said, would quickly knock out an enemy. He continued agitating when Italy entered the war in 1915. He was ignored. Frustrated, he wrote a series of letters to military and civilian officials criticizing the conduct of the war. After one particularly scathing epistle, he was arrested, convicted of spreading false news and agitation, and sentenced to a year in a military prison.

He continued writing in prison, urging the construction of a huge fleet of bombers—"battle planes," he called them, which would take the roles of both bombers and fighters. Shortly after he was released from prison, the Italian army suffered a terrible defeat at Caporetto, which confirmed all that Douhet had written about Italian unpreparedness. He was recalled to the army and made general director of aviation at the General Air Commisariat. But Douhet's new status did not mean that the army had become any more progressive. He became so frustrated he resigned from the army in June 1918. When the war ended in November 1918, Douhet managed to get his court martial conviction overturned, and he was promoted to general.

He was finished with active duty, though. He devoted himself to writing. In 1921, he published *Il Dominio dell' Aria* (*Command of the Air*), which ranks with Clausewitz's *On War* or Mahan's *The Influence of Sea Power upon History, 1660-1783*. Douhet saw an independent air force as the ultimate weapon. The vastness of the sky, he wrote, made

defense almost impossible. Air forces could fly over armies and navies and strike wherever they chose. He identified five basic targets—industry; roads, railroads and canals; communications; government buildings; and population centers. The last class of targets, he wrote, should be hit with explosive and poison gas bombs to terrorize the enemy population. The enemy population would then force their government to end the war. Douhet argued that this sort of air war would guarantee that wars would be short and ultimately less bloody than the conflict that had just ended.

Because *Command of the Air* was published in Italian, rather than French, German, or English, it took a while for the book to influence world military thinking, but influence military thinking it did. In Britain, Hugh Trenchard, a middle-aged major with a ho-hum record, learned to fly. Because he was the most senior officer in the army who knew an aileron from a rudder, when the British formed the Royal Flying Corps (later the Royal Air Force), he was given command of the unit. He became a red-hot advocate of an independent air force before he ever heard of Giulio Douhet. The post-war British military commentators, General J.F.C. Fuller and Captain B. H. Liddell Hart adopted Douhet's idea of strategic bombing. Fuller said cities would not have to be leveled by bombing. According to *The Reader's Companion to Military History*, Fuller said, "It will be sufficient to have the civilian population driven out so they cannot carry on their usual vocations. A few gas bombs will do that."

Hart was much less enthusiastic about gas. Mustard gas had caused him to be invalided out of the army and ended his military career. He did preach the bombing of civilian populations, though. In 1925, he advocated bombing the poorer areas in enemy cities, causing the disruption of the enemy by "the slum districts maddened by the impulse to break loose and maraud."

In the United States, the flamboyant Billy Mitchell, a strong advocate of air power and (unlike Douhet and Trenchard, a combat flyer of great skill and experience) became the darling of a public that really didn't understand the situation. For instance, Mitchell used planes to sink old, captured German battleships. This was taken as proving that ships could easily be sunk by planes. Reports of the action seldom mentioned that the ships were old, decrepit, and unarmed.

Mitchell, as with Douhet, was court-martialed for offending the military establishment, but the United States *did* adopt the doctrine of strategic bombing. It didn't create an independent air force until the end of the war, but it entered the war with the closest thing to Douhet's "battle plane" of any belligerent—the heavily-armed B-17 "Flying Fortress," which was supposed to eliminate the need for fighter escorts.

Although Germany had an independent air force, German military thinking emphasized the land blitzkrieg, with airplanes in a supporting role. When Hitler decided on strategic bombing to pave the way for an invasion of Britain, his Luftwaffe did not have suitable planes for the job. Britain also had an independent air force, and British strategic thinking was thoroughly sold on strategic bombing. But Britain was even less prepared than Germany to carry out a strategic bombing campaign; it wasn't that Britain didn't have suitable bombers. The British didn't have enough bombers of any kind.

The Germans lost the Battle of Britain because the British had more and better fighter planes than they expected, because British fighter production was greater than expected, and because the only German fighter to equal the British "Spitfire" (the Messerschmitt Bf-109) was an interceptor, not an escort. It didn't have enough range to allow it to operate over Britain for a reasonable time. Further, some of the German bombers (such as the famous Junker Ju-87, the Stuka) were flying coffins in aerial combat. But one of the biggest reasons was that Hitler, incensed by an ineffectual British bombing of Berlin, decided to concentrate on bombing London and other population centers.

Spitfires flying in formation.

Hitler learned that Douhet, Trenchard, and Mitchell were all wrong. English civilians did not panic. They did not demand that their government surrender. London slum-dwellers did not "break loose and maraud," as the aristocratic Hart expected.

The failure of the German strategic bombing campaign taught the Allies nothing, however. The British and Americans opened their own strategic bombing campaign over Germany and German-occupied countries. Their effort utterly dwarfed anything Hitler was able to achieve. Huge areas of German cities were leveled. The Allied bombing killed 600,000 Germans, mostly civilian women and children, and seriously injured 800,000 more. The RAF bombed Hamburg four nights in a row and created a "fire storm," perhaps the first such phenomenon since the burning of Magdeburg in 1631. World War II would see many more fire storms. But in no target country did the population panic, agitate for surrender, or "break loose and maraud."

The results of the bombing of German industry were quite unimpressive. In 1942, the British dropped 48,000 tons of bombs, and the Germans produced 38,000 heavy weapons (artillery pieces, tanks, and planes). In 1943, the British and Americans dropped 207,600 tons of bombs, and the Germans produced 71,693 heavy weapons. In 1944, the Allies dropped 915,000 tons of bombs, and the Germans produced 105,258 heavy weapons. Not until 1945, when Allied armies overran Germany, did German weapons production drop.

Douhet's "battle plane" concept failed, too. Unescorted bombing runs by American Flying Fortresses resulted in extremely heavy losses. It was not until long-range fighters such as the P-47 and the P-51 appeared that Fortresses were able to carry out the precision daylight raids they were designed for without taking unacceptable losses.

In spite of the experience of World War II, Douhet's theories have not lost favor with all airmen. They point out that in Kosovo, NATO airpower alone was used, and in Afghanistan, air power aiding the Northern Alliance turned a guerrilla force hanging on by its fingertips into a conquering army.

But they usually forget to mention that in Kosovo, Afghanistan, and now in Iraq (where air power has been far less decisive), there was no enemy air force or any effective air defense.

Nevertheless, Douhet's theories have already changed history, and thanks to him, air forces are an integral part of any major power's military establishment. If they aren't the all-powerful force he predicted, they are a vital part of the military, and seem likely to become even more important in the future.

London children sit outside the ruins of their home, destroyed in World War II's "London Blitz."
National Archives

45

Adolf Hitler
The Monster
(A.D. 1889–1945)

When national leaders are barely muddling through, perhaps even blundering along, their people yearn for leaders with real charisma. But a little charisma can go a long way—perhaps the wrong way. Take the most charismatic leader in modern times: Adolf Hitler.

Hitler started the bloodiest war in history, a war that profoundly changed Europe, Asia, and Africa; that spawned other wars and dictatorships; and completely changed the world balance of power. In addition to the war, Hitler industrialized state-sponsored murder by killing some 14 million people largely because he disagreed with their ethnicity or beliefs.

History is full of royal monsters (though few can compete with Hitler in the magnitude of their evil). Adolf Hitler, though, had no noble birth, no inherited throne. He rose to power from the humblest beginnings. As a soldier in World War I he was severely wounded and gassed. He earned an Iron Cross First Class and three other awards for bravery. But he never achieved a rank higher than lance corporal (the equivalent of a private first class in the U.S. Army). In evaluating him, his military superiors noted that while Lance Corporal Hitler was a brave soldier, he had no leadership qualities.

Hitler was born in Austria-Hungary of a German father and an Austrian mother. He failed secondary school and was rejected by the Academy of Fine Arts in Vienna. For a while he worked at odd jobs and tried to sell uninspired water colors on the street. He blamed his troubles on the multiethnic population. "I was convinced that the State was sure to obstruct every great German," he later wrote. "I hated the motley collection of Czechs, Ruthenians, Poles, Hungarians, Serbs, Croats, and above all that ever-present fungoid growth—Jews."

Hitler gained power in Germany through the use of his charismatic speaking abilities. His propaganda machine was also particularly effective in a country not yet recovered from a post-World War I economic depression.

In 1913, he moved to Germany. Early in 1914, he was called back to Austria for examination for military service but was rejected as unfit. He returned to Germany and joined a Bavarian regiment. After the war, he joined the German Workers Party and helped change its name to the National Socialist German Workers Party. (In German, *Nazionalsozialistische Deutsche Arbeiterpartei*, or Nazi for short.) The loser from Austria discovered that he had strengths he hadn't realized. His oratory could rouse crowds to a screaming frenzy, and he was a master political strategist.

His first attempt to gain power ended ignominiously. In the so-called Beer Hall Putsch, he led a crowd of veterans in an attempt to take over the government of the state of Bavaria. He ended up in prison, but was released in a general amnesty after nine months. While in prison, he wrote *Mein Kampf* (*My Struggle*), which contained the beginning of his Nazi philosophy.

Hitler returned to politics, and the Nazi party grew in strength, especially after the beginning of the Great Depression. Hitler became a major politician after the 1932 Reichstag elections. He copied Mussolini's Fascist party, which had a uniformed band of thugs, the Black Shirts. The Nazis organized the Brown Shirts, or *Sturmabteilung* (Storm Troopers) or SA, then a second uniformed group, the *Schutzstaffel* or SS, which was to be Hitler's personal bodyguard. Hitler cultivated powerful allies, and in January 1933, President Paul von Hindenburg appointed him *Reichskanzler,* or prime minister. A month later, Hitler used a fire at the Reichstag building as an excuse to suppress civil liberties. After taking control of Germany, Hitler began working to expand it. He knew this would ultimately result in war, but he used other means first.

According to Hermann Rauschning in *Hitler Speaks,* Hitler once said: "Our real wars will in fact all be fought before military operations begin," he said. "How to achieve the moral breakdown of the enemy before the war has started—that is the problem that interests me. Whoever has experienced war at the front will want to refrain from all avoidable bloodshed. Our strategy is to destroy the enemy from within, to conquer him through himself."

Hitler's methods of avoiding bloodshed included the cultivation of traitors, such as Vidkun Quisling in Norway and the Nazis of Austria; signing treaties meant to be broken, like his 10-year non-aggression pact with Poland; his later non-aggression pact with the Soviet Union (which included a provision for dividing Poland between Germany and the Soviet Union); supporting Francisco Franco in Spain (to put a Fascist-friendly regime in the rear of France); and a combination of intimidation and mendacious propaganda. Earlier, he used the same combination to convince the World War I allies to ignore his remilitarization of the Rhineland and his rearming of Germany.

During World War II, the Allies liked to portray Hitler as a blunderer who was hamstringing his generals. He did interfere with them, but he was frequently right, while they were wrong. For instance, in preparing for the attack on France, Hitler's general staff resurrected and slightly modified the Schlieffen Plan of World War I. The main thrust would be through Belgium and Holland and down the English Channel coast into northern France. That was also what the French and British were expecting. The Allies concentrated the bulk of their mobile forces near the Channel and expected the Maginot Line to keep back any German forces south of Belgium and Luxembourg. Erich von Manstein, a lower-ranking general, proposed sending troops led by armored divisions through the Ardennes (a hilly, forested area) and piercing the Allied line just north of Sedan, and then swinging north to encircle the Allied troops poised to meet what they expected to be the main German attack.

The general staff officers were not pleased with the upstart Manstein and his new plan. They stuck with the tried-and-not-very-true Schlieffen Plan, which had been German policy for more than half a century. Hitler liked the Manstein plan, but how could he (with his limited military experience) substitute his judgment for that of the army's top generals?

Then a plane carrying the current German plans for the attack was forced down in Belgium. The Germans had to go with Manstein's idea. The result was the incredibly swift victory in what came to be called the Battle of France.

After that, Hitler deferred much less to the generals. As historians John Keegan and Andrew Wheatcroft put it in their *Who's Who in Military History*, "The trenches had taught him, or so he thought, that he understood war in a way his generals did not. There was something to this." All his top military advisers at the beginning of the war had been kept out of the trenches during World War I. "In strict terms, therefore, he knew war with an intimacy which they had been spared."

Adolf Hitler and the Italian Dictator Benito Mussolini ride through the streets of Munich, Germany. Driven by a desire for power and insane racial theories, Hitler caused the death of millions of people. *National Archives*

Hitler never quite lost his respect for flag officers and their opinions, though. Erwin Rommel and Karl von Runstedt had different ideas on how to meet an Allied landing in the west. But neither expected the attack to take place in Normandy. Hitler did. But he refrained from organizing a defense based on his intuition. Fortunately, not all Hitler's insights were good. His decision to divert the German thrust toward the Caucasus oil fields—a desperate effort by a *wehrmacht* that was running out of fuel—to capture Stalingrad was one. Then he compounded the trouble by refusing to allow his troops to retreat when it was apparent that the battle was lost.

One of his biggest diplomatic blunders was declaring war on the United States after Japan attacked Pearl Harbor. He changed the Americans from Allied sympathizers into active belligerents. Imagine the confusion he could have caused if he had declared war on Japan instead of the United States. Germany had no possessions in the Far East, and Japan was too far away to cause him trouble. The Americans, much against their will, would have become co-belligerents with Germany.

Another huge blunder was expecting the British to surrender and become a junior partner with Germany in its invasion of Russia. Still another was believing that the Soviet Union (in which the Red Army high command had been almost obliterated by Stalin's purge) would be a pushover. His biggest, most basic blunder was thinking that Germany had the natural resources and industrial infrastructure to win the enormous war that he had started.

Morally, even the evil of starting the world's biggest war was overshadowed by killing innocent people—6 million Jews and 8 million Slavs, Gypsies, homosexuals, the mentally retarded, and other groups despised because of his theories—simply because they existed.

As his enemies were closing in—the Russians at the gates of Berlin and the Americans and British fast approaching from the west—Hitler took his own life in an underground bunker in downtown Berlin.

Trench warfare in World War II caused the deaths of many soldiers on both sides.

46

Heinz Guderian

Achtung! Panzer

(A.D. 1888–1954)

Germany invaded Poland on September 1, 1939. Except for some tiny, isolated pockets of resistance, the war was over by October 5. The speed of that conquest surprised all observers. On May 12, 1940, Germany invaded France, the nation then believed to have the best army in the world. France surrendered June 21. The world was not merely surprised, it was shocked and stunned. The press named this new German way of war *blitzkrieg,* German for lightning war.

Blitzkrieg relied on motorized troops following *panzer* (armored) divisions, with dive bombers filling in for artillery when the cannons were too far in the rear. The German generals would concentrate their tanks on a weak spot in the enemy line and break through. The tanks, self-propelled artillery, and troops in trucks then poured through the gap and attacked the rear areas, disrupting command and supply centers while infantry and towed artillery established defensive positions to keep the gap open and to surround the enemy forces.

This tank offensive was carried out by an army which, in the last war, had disdained the tank until the very last months of the war, when, on August 8, 1918, a huge force of British and French tanks overwhelmed the Germans near Amiens—what General Erich Ludendorff called "the black day of the German army." The mechanics of the blitzkrieg were developed by a German general who never saw a tank before he went to Sweden on loan to a Swedish tank battalion after World War I.

This panzer tank was first built in 1937.

Heinz Guderian was the son of a Prussian army officer. During World War I, he commanded a wireless station. He became assistant signal officer for the Fourth Army and ended up in the Great General Staff. After the war, he joined the *Freikorps* (Free Corps, a right-wing German veterans' group) and went to the Baltic states to help organize military forces there. Germany was allowed an army no greater than 100,000 men, with 4,000 officers. Guderian was one of the lucky 4,000. Again on the general staff, he was briefly attached to a Swedish armored unit. As a general staff officer and a transportation officer, he closely followed developments in military thinking, especially the theories and experiments in mobile warfare of the British writers J.F.C. Fuller and B.H. Liddell Hart. In 1930, he was appointed commander of a transportation battalion, which he reorganized as a provisional armored reconnaissance battalion. From October 1931 through October 1935, he worked to create Germany's tank forces, after which he was appointed commander of the 2nd Panzer Division while still a colonel.

The appointment recognized the fact that, although a relatively junior officer, Guderian was the main reason the panzer divisions existed. Their equipment, their organization, and their tactics were all inspired by Guderian. He was promoted to major general

in 1936, and the next year he published *Achtung! Panzer*, a book presenting his theories of mechanized warfare. That same year, 1937, he was given command of a panzer corps, composed of three divisions. He commanded another panzer corps in the invasion of Poland, and his troops spearheaded the German breakthrough at Sedan during the invasion of France. Previously, he had strongly supported Erich von Manstein's plan for the invasion in spite of opposition from the general staff.

In these campaigns, Guderian was able to put his theories into practice. He believed that a panzer general should *lead* his troops, because only that way could he see strongholds that should be bypassed and weak spots that should be attacked. Speed was the secret of

Tanks hiding in the woods await the signal to attack in this drawing by a soldier on World War II's eastern front.

effective mobile warfare. Following lines of least resistance and attacking rear areas from all sides disorganized the enemy and led to his collapse with a minimum of bloodshed. Hitler was mightily impressed.

For the invasion of Russia, Guderian commanded a panzer group (an armored army). Stalled outside Moscow by winter weather, he requested permission to withdraw from his exposed position. Hitler hated the idea of withdrawal anywhere. He relieved Guderian of his command December 26, 1941.

In 1943, when things in Russia were looking worse and worse, Guderian was called back to active duty. He did much to repair the damage caused by the results of the disastrous battles of Stalingrad and Kursk, but by that time, nothing could have saved the German army. Hitler fired Guderian again on March 28, 1945. A month later, Hitler killed himself. Guderian surrendered to the Allies after the war, but was never charged or tried for war crimes because it was generally accepted that his actions were of a military professional. He died in West Germany in 1953.

Hitler started World War II, but without Guderian and his blitzkrieg, the German attempt at world conquest would have fizzled out in France, if not before. And the blitzkrieg, with its combination of armored vehicles and close air support, changed the way war was fought.

A World War II-era British tank.

47

Yamamoto Isoroku

There is Only One

(A.D. 1884–1943)

"There was only one Yamamoto, and no one can replace him," said Admiral Koga Mineichi in 1943, when Admiral Yamamoto Isoroku was shot down over the Pacific and Koga was appointed to fill his place as chief of Japan's Combined Fleets.

Apparently his enemies agreed. Yamamoto was the only enemy leader specifically targeted and killed by American forces in World War II. (Or in any other war, for that matter.) Yamamoto was one of the most imaginative naval officers of his time, an inspiring leader, and a man of such immense strength of character, he was able to force the entire Japanese naval establishment to back down. He was also a man whose career was filled with contradictions.

Although one of the world's foremost advocates of naval aviation, he never learned to fly and was killed when the two planes he and his staff were traveling in were shot down. More important, he vigorously fought against the idea of going to war with the United States, but he was also the man who planned the attack on Pearl Harbor.

That attack knocked out all the battleships in the Pacific fleet, the ships that U.S. naval authorities had been relying on to stop any enemy. With no battleships (the most modern battlewagons had been sent to the Atlantic by Admiral Ernest King as part of the country's "Germany first" policy), the

Americans had to reorganize their naval forces. And the model they took was one of Yamamoto's innovations, the "First Air Fleet," a force built around aircraft carriers. In the U.S. Navy, these fleets (there were many of them during the war) were called carrier task forces. When the U.S. Navy, recognizing that battleships were wasted in the Atlantic, sent them back to the Pacific, the battleships were merely escorts for the carriers. Aircraft carriers remained the key component of U.S. naval strength.

Yamamoto, chief of Japan's combined fleets, planned the attack on Pearl Harbor. This caracature was a popular image during World War II.
Library of Congress

Yamamoto was the sixth son of a samurai named Takano Teikichi, who was 56 when the boy was born. Takano was so proud of having a child at that age that he gave his son numbers for a name: *I* (5), *so* (10), and *roku* (6). In 1916, when Lieutenant Commander Takano graduated from the Naval Staff College's senior course, the Yamamoto family, a noble Japanese clan, adopted him. (This was a fairly common procedure for noble families who had no male heir.)

At the time, Yamamoto was already something of a hero. He had served under Togo in the Strait of Tsushima and had been severely wounded. He lost two fingers of his left hand and just missed being invalided out of the navy. Three years after graduating from the senior course, Yamamoto went to the United States to continue his studies at Harvard University. He returned to Japan to teach at the Naval War College. He had more than the usual exposure to foreign military forces, having served as an admiral's aid on a trip through the United States and Europe, and later as a naval attaché in the Japanese embassy in Washington.

Yamamoto was associated with developments on the cutting edge of naval warfare. In 1924, after returning from his observation tour of foreign navies with the admiral, Captain Yamamoto was made deputy commander of the Kasumiga Ura Naval Air Station, and in 1928, after returning from attaché duty in the United States, he was made captain of the aircraft carrier *Akagi*. A year later, he was promoted to rear admiral and made chief of the Technological Division of the Navy Technological Department. Then he commanded the 1st Naval Air Division. Promoted to vice admiral, he headed the Japanese delegation to the London Naval Conference in 1934 and 1935. The Washington

Naval Treaty of 1922 had always rankled him. The treaty covered the construction of battleships and battle cruisers among the world's leading naval powers. It allowed the United States and Britain to have the most. Japan got slightly fewer, with France and Italy still fewer. Yamamoto believed that Japan, an island nation, had the same need for a large navy as Britain, and that the United States got the same number of capital ships as Britain simply because it could afford that many. He refused to agree to extend the treaty's provisions, and led the fight in Japan to abrogate the treaty.

When World War II broke out and Germany overran the Netherlands and France (and left Britain hanging on the ropes), the leaders of Japan saw a golden opportunity. They signed the Tripartite Pact with Germany and Italy. Then, as allies of the Axis powers, they occupied French Indochina. The United States stopped shipping Japan oil and steel. Japan needed both, especially oil, for its long, drawn-out war with China. The Dutch East Indies had oil, and the Netherlands had been an enemy of Japan's "ally," Germany. The United States threatened war if Japan moved into the East Indies. The militarists in the government decided to fight the United States.

Yamamoto was neither pro-American nor anti-American. He was only pro-Japan. He opposed the idea of fighting the United States, because he thought that in a long war, Japan would lose. Edwin T. Layton relates in his book *And I Was There*, that Yamamoto told Japanese Prime Minister Prince Konoye Fumimaro, "If we are ordered to do it, then I can guarantee to put up a tough fight for the first six months, but I have absolutely no confidence as to what would happen if it went on for two or three years. It's too late to do anything about the Tripartite Pact now, but I hope you'll at least make every effort to avoid a war with America." Prince Konoye tried, but in October 1941, the militarists ousted him and replaced him as prime minister with General Tojo Hideki.

Yamamoto knew that Japan was an island nation with few natural resources, while the United States was a vast mainland country with many resources, a larger population, and a huge industrial base. The militarists knew that, but they believed that the American people had lost their "warrior spirit." (A common belief in Japan at the time.)

Naval strategists in both the United States and Japan had long considered the possibility of a war between the two Pacific powers. The Japanese plan was to use their mid-Pacific island possessions as bases for planes and submarines which would whittle down the huge U.S. Navy as it approached Japan. Then the main Japanese fleet would come out and destroy what was left of the Americans in a big, Jutland-style battle.

Yamamoto thought the plan was insane. The American navy was too strong to be whittled down enough. The way to win would be to strike the Pacific Fleet at its home base—surprise it at Pearl Harbor. He mentioned the idea to only a few trusted officers. As chief of the Combined Fleets, Yamamoto had no business-making plans. His job was to execute the plans made by the Naval General Staff.

The obstacles were formidable. Pearl Harbor was the base for U.S. naval patrol bombers, which could cover all the approaches to Hawaii. Hawaii also had the U.S. Army's formidable B-17 "flying fortresses." Pearl Harbor had a restricted entrance. No enemy ships could enter; any attack would have to be from the air, and any aerial attack on armed,

manned battleships was considered extremely risky. Further, the most effective way for a plane to attack a ship was with an aerial torpedo. Pearl Harbor was so shallow any known torpedo would bury itself in the mud on the harbor bottom instead of striking a ship. Besides, Pearl Harbor was so crowded most torpedoes wouldn't have time to arm themselves before they hit a ship. The result would be a dull thud and no explosion. Bombs from dive-bombers probably wouldn't penetrate the heavy deck armor of the battleships. Bombs from high-altitude bombers might, because bombs falling a long distance picked up more velocity than those dropped at a low level from a diving plane. But it was difficult to hit a target as small as a ship from high altitude. And in a test, even high-altitude bombs failed to penetrate enough armor.

Japanese sailors under the command of Yamamoto.

Yamamoto was not discouraged. He planned to approach Hawaii through the North Pacific, an area with such terrible weather in late fall and winter that all navies avoided it. Patrol planes would probably ignore the area. He secured the services of Commander Genda Minoru, Japan's leading expert on aerial torpedo tactics. Genda refined the plan for the Pearl Harbor attack and, with

Yamamoto, got manufacturers to design a new kind of quick-arming, shallow-running torpedo. Genda recruited Lieutenant Commander Fuchida Mitsuo (a flier of legendary skill) to train pilots to drop their torpedoes while barely skimming the water instead of from the standard 250 feet. To get armor-piercing bombs, Yamamoto had fins added to armor-piercing shells for naval guns.

All this preparation was done without the knowledge of the Naval General Staff. The audacity of attacking Pearl Harbor shocked the general staff when Yamamoto revealed his plan, but it didn't try to block him. When the general staff tried to detach some of the carriers in the First Air Fleet to accompany the naval forces aimed at the Philippines, Malaysia, and the East Indies, Yamamoto told them that if they touched his carriers, he and his whole staff would resign. They left his carriers alone.

The man selected to command the First Air Fleet, with its six carriers, was Admiral Nagumo Chuichi, an old battleship admiral who was no airpower enthusiast. The Japanese fliers disabled every one of the American battleships in the harbor. They didn't get the carriers of the Pacific Fleet, because, fortunately, all of them were elsewhere. That fact disappointed Genda. However, Nagumo, the doubter, was elated. Pearl Harbor turned him into a greater airpower enthusiast than Yamamoto.

Just about six months after Pearl Harbor, on June 4, 1942, at the end of the period for which Yamamoto had guaranteed a tough fight, the United States and Japanese navies clashed near Midway. This was the battle to end American opposition once and for all. The Japanese plan was complicated. There was a feint at the Aleutians, and Nagumo commanded the Japanese vanguard, a carrier task force like the First Air Fleet. It included four carriers, including *Akagi,* Yamamoto's first carrier. Nagumo had all the large Japanese carriers fit for service. Yamamoto commanded the main battle fleet some distance to the rear. Everything was going Nagumo's way when dive bombers from the USS *Enterprise* spotted the Japanese carriers and sank two of them. They were joined by other dive bombers from *Yorktown,* which sank a third aircraft carrier. The next day, *Enterprise's* dive bombers wiped out the last Japanese carrier.

When Yamamoto heard what happened, he decided to continue without the carriers. When Nagumo argued against his decision , Yamamoto removed him from command. But on reflection, Yamamoto changed his mind and returned to port.

The Americans had some warning of the attack, because they had broken much of the Japanese naval code. Less than a year later, on April 18, 1943, they intercepted a message that told them Yamamoto planned to visit the defenses of Bougainville. Fighter planes from Guadalcanal shot down the two planes carrying the admiral and his staff, and killed the man they considered their most dangerous foe in the Pacific.

Raymond Spruance

The Fatal Six Minutes

(A.D. 1886–1969)

Nagumo Chiuchi thought he was watching the end of the war against Japan's most dangerous foe on June 4, 1942. Nagumo commanded the fleet that began the war—the fleet that attacked the American base at Pearl Harbor. He was an old battleship admiral who had serious doubts about the advisability of that all-air attack. Pearl Harbor had converted him to an air power enthusiast. Now he was again leading the First Air Fleet. His fleet was part of an elaborate plan by Admiral Yamamoto Isoroku to occupy Midway Island and annihilate what was left of the U.S. Pacific Fleet. Nagumo's fleet included four large carriers (all the large carriers operational in the Japanese Navy), two battleships, and a number of cruisers and destroyers. Approaching from another direction was a fleet of transport ships and naval escorts. The transport ships were carrying soldiers to occupy Midway. About 300 miles behind Nagumo was the chief of the Combined Fleets, Yamamoto himself. Yamamoto had most of the rest of Japan's navy, including the monster battleship *Yamato*. *Yamato* and her sister ship, *Musashi* (still under construction), were the only 18-inch-gun battleships in the world.

According to the plan, the Americans would be drawn to the Aleutians by a feint

attack there. While they were in the north, Nagumo's planes would destroy the American planes and shore installations on Midway Island so troops could land there. The Americans would hurry south, where they would be attacked by 16 submarines Yamamoto had sent to wait between Midway and the Aleutians and by Nagumo's planes. Then Yamamoto and his battleships would arrive and finish off the American fleet.

Because of his quick thinking, Raymond Spruance's nickname was "electric brain."

Nagumo didn't think there would be anything left for Yamamoto to finish off. His fleet had beaten off an attack by Midway-based U.S. bombers. It had virtually annihilated three different navy torpedo bomber squadrons and driven off a lone U.S. submarine that had tried to attack. In all of this fighting, Nagumo's fleet had suffered no damage at all. Nagumo, understandably, felt triumphant.

He had just 100 seconds to enjoy that feeling. Then American dive bombers appeared. All of the Japanese fighters were either on board the carriers being refueled or still at the low altitude they had assumed to shoot down the enemy torpedo planes. The Americans dived at the Japanese carriers. In six minutes, the tide of the Pacific War turned. The war didn't end, but Japan's chance of winning it did. To understand what happened, we have to go back and look at the American situation after Pearl Harbor.

In 1941, the U.S. Navy was the largest in the world. Until it seemed that the United States might enter World War II, the Pacific Fleet was by far the largest part of the U.S. Navy. Then the Navy shifted ships, including the most modern battleships, to the Atlantic. The Pearl Harbor attack sank or crippled every operational battleship in the Pacific Fleet. Fortunately there were no carriers in the harbor. *Saratoga* was being repaired at Bremerton, Washington. *Lexington* was taking planes to Midway, and *Enterprise* was taking planes to Wake Island.

The Navy, bereft of battleships, copied Japan's First Air Fleet on a smaller scale and carried on the fight with carrier task forces—one or two carriers escorted by cruisers and destroyers. For a while, because the country had officially adopted the policy that Germany was the main enemy, Admiral Ernest J. King,

chief of naval operations, continued to hoard battleships on the East Coast. But he rejected the British suggestion that the United States remain on the defensive in the Pacific until Germany was finished. It gradually dawned on King that battleships and big fleet carriers (light carriers or escort carriers were something else) were not terribly useful against German submarines but could do valuable work against the Japanese Navy. King let the Pacific Fleet keep the battleships that had been restored to service after the Pearl Harbor attack and sent some old battle wagons back to the Pacific. Later, he sent all the big, new ships to the Pacific, where they could do the most good. Long before the end of the war, the bulk of the U.S. Navy, including the Marine Corps (and a good part of the Army), were fighting Japan. The Pacific war never became a sideshow, as the British hoped. When the war ended in Europe, American troops were on Okinawa (practically one of the Japanese home islands) and preparing to invade Japan proper.

But in the spring of 1942, American forces in the Pacific were still so weak they had to settle for a psychological blow against Japan. On April 18, 16 army B-25 bombers commanded by Lieutenant Colonel James H. Doolittle took off from the carrier *Hornet* and bombed Tokyo. The army planes were used because they were bigger and had longer range than any carrier-based bombers. *Hornet* was part of Task Force 16, which included another carrier, the USS *Enterprise*, flying the flag of Vice Admiral William F. Halsey. Commanding the cruisers in Task Force 16 was Rear Admiral Raymond A. Spruance. The raid did little damage, but it shook up the Japanese mightily. The Japanese had identified the attackers as U.S. Army planes and decided that they could not have come from an aircraft carrier. They guessed that they had come from Midway Island. That belief led to a new Japanese plan for dealing with the United States.

The Japanese planned to seize Tulagi in the Solomon Islands and Port Moresby in Papua and establish airbases there. That would give them control of the Coral Sea and isolate Australia. Next, they would annihilate the remains of the U.S. Pacific Fleet and establish bases on the Aleutians and Midway. Those bases would add to their chain of fortified islands designed to whittle down the United States Navy.

The United States learned of this plan because it began breaking Japanese codes before Pearl Harbor. Note: Modern code-breaking is not done with a big bang. Nations have many codes, and there are many variations in each. It's a piecemeal process, involving combining bits of deciphered information and making educated guesses. But the United States learned enough to send the carriers *Yorktown* and *Lexington* to the Coral Sea with appropriate escorts. What resulted was the first naval battle in history fought entirely by fleets far out of gun range. It was, in a sense, a tragicomedy of errors, with targets misidentified, with Australian ships firing on American bombers and Japanese planes trying to land on an American carrier. American planes sank the Japanese light carrier *Shoho* and crippled the fleet carrier *Shokaku*. They missed the other Japanese fleet carrier, *Zuikaku*, but that ship lost most of her planes. *Zuikaku* was out of action until they could be replaced. The American losses were heavier. The big fleet carrier USS *Lexington*, one of the biggest in the world, was so heavily damaged she had to be sunk.

U.S. Navy dive bombers prepare to dive on Japanese ships in the decisive Battle of Midway. Smoke at the bottom of the picture comes from a burning ship.
National Archives

Yorktown was also heavily damaged, but she was able to get back to Pearl Harbor for repairs. The Japanese claimed a victory, but battles are not decided by comparing losses. No Japanese warship ever again entered the Coral Sea.

Yorktown, nicknamed Waltzing Matilda, and her crew had little time to recover from the Coral Sea fight. Nagumo was coming. The Americans knew that, and they knew the outlines of the Japanese plan, so they weren't lured to the Aleutians. But they didn't know just where Nagumo, the transports, or Yamamoto were. To oppose Nagumo's four fleet carriers and Yamamoto's battleships, the Americans had three fleet carriers—one of them *Yorktown*. Waltzing Matilda had received jury-rigged repairs—work was completed in two days that normally would have taken 90. But she could never come close to her old speed.

There was no time to waste. Halsey's Task Force 16 came tearing across the Pacific to take part in the expected battle. But when he arrived at Pearl Harbor, Halsey's health was so bad he had to be hospitalized. Admiral Chester W. Nimitz, commander in chief of the Pacific Fleet, appointed Spruance to take his place. Nimitz was disappointed that the colorful flying admiral would not be able to help, but he later said, "It was a great day for the Navy when Bill Halsey had to enter the hospital." Halsey was called "Bull" in the newspapers, because somebody made a typographical error typing "Bill." Nobody called the soft-spoken and affable Halsey "Bull." But at least on one later occasion he acted like one—charging like a mad bull after empty Japanese carriers sent to lure him away during the Battle of Leyte Gulf.

Spruance was not at all like his former boss. Halsey was a pioneer naval aviator and a charismatic leader who sometimes relied on intuition. Spruance had never learned to fly. He was a gunnery expert whose experience was mostly with destroyers. He was taciturn, reserved, and intellectual. He was a man who carefully analyzed a situation before moving—but who could move fast.

To meet Nagumo, Nimitz combined Task Force 16, under Spruance, with Task Force 17, commanded by Rear Admiral Frank Jack Fletcher. Besides *Yorktown*, Task Force 17 included two cruisers and six destroyers. Spruance, from his flagship *Enterprise*, commanded Task Force 16—*Enterprise* and *Hornet*, plus six cruisers and nine destroyers. The American force was greatly outnumbered and outgunned by Nagumo's fleet alone, without even considering Yamamoto's main battle fleet. Fletcher, with his flag aboard *Yorktown*, was not considered the Navy's greatest tactician, but he was senior in rank to Spruance. Because of that, he was to command the combined task forces.

The order of battle of the two fleets shows a stark contrast between Nimitz and his Japanese counterpart, Yamamoto. Yamamoto, who conceived the air attack on Pearl Harbor and fought Japanese Navy and civilian brass to create the First Air Fleet, was at heart still a battleship admiral. He was relying on the guns of *Yamato* and the other battleships to finish off the Americans. Nimitz, an old submariner, had more faith in air power than Yamamoto. He could have called up seven battleships currently stationed in California, but he didn't. Three of the ships, *Pennsylvania*, *Maryland*, and *Tennessee*, were repaired veterans of Pearl Harbor. The others, *Colorado*, *Idaho*, *New Mexico*, and *Mississippi*, were just old. All of them were too old and slow, Nimitz believed, to catch up with Nagumo's fast carriers. Their guns would be useless.

At the time, Nimitz knew Nagumo and the First Air Fleet were coming, and he knew that somewhere in the Pacific a convoy of troop ships was headed for Midway. He soon learned that Japanese troops had occupied the Aleutian islands Kiska and Attu. But he didn't know that Yamamoto and his battle fleet would be following Nagumo. (If he had, he might have called up the U.S. battleships in California.)

Both Nagumo's fleet and the U.S. combined task forces were flying blind, but the Japanese fleet was more blind than the Americans. Nagumo believed the Americans were all on the fringes of the arctic. Fletcher and Spruance knew the Japanese were somewhere in the central Pacific, but they didn't know where. To find out, Nimitz greatly increased patrols by the Navy's big, slow PBY flying boats. He also added Army planes, including B-17 flying fortresses to the planes on Midway.

At 9:25 a.m., June 3, Ensign Jack Reid, pilot of a PBY, radioed that he had sighted the "main body" of Japanese ships 20 miles ahead. What he had actually seen was the Midway invasion force, not Nagumo's or Yamamoto's fleet. American intelligence knew that Nagumo's "strike force" would be coming from a different direction. Fletcher took *Yorktown* to a spot 200 miles north of Midway, which he believed would be a good place to launch planes against Nagumo's ships. Meanwhile, the army B-17s located the invasion fleet and attacked. All their bombs missed.

At 4:30 a.m., June 4, the Japanese carriers *Akagi*, *Kaga*, *Soryu*, and *Hiryu* began launching the planes that were to attack Midway. Nagumo still had no idea that there were any American ships in the area. At just about the same time the Japanese were becoming airborne, Fletcher launched 10 dive bombers from *Yorktown* to look for the Japanese. They didn't find anything, but less than a hour after the American and Japanese planes took off, an American PBY spotted a Japanese carrier heading for Midway. At 5:45, a.m., another PBY reported "many planes heading Midway bearing 320 degrees, distance 150." Seven minutes later, Lieutenant William A. Chase, pilot of that plane, found and reported the location of two of Nagumo's four carriers. A minute later the Midway radar picked up enemy planes. The Marine Corps fighters on Midway—obsolete Brewster Buffalos and obsolescent Grumman Wildcats—scrambled. The bombers also took off and headed for the attacking fleet. The American fighters were horribly outclassed by the Japanese Mitsubishi Zeros; 14 of the 26 pilots were killed, and many others were wounded. Only two fighter planes were fit to fly again. The Japanese lost eight planes out of 108.

The land-based bombers, a mixed bag of Navy torpedo bombers, scout bombers, B-17s, and B26s tried to attack Nagumo's carriers. They had no fighter cover and proved to be clay pigeons for the Zeros. A couple of Japanese sailors were hit by machine-gun fire, but Nagumo's fleet suffered no damage. The American bombers suffered heavy losses, but were not wiped out. Nagumo decided that another raid on Midway was needed to destroy the planes there on the ground while they were refueling. He had kept back some of his planes, armed with torpedoes and armor-piercing bombs, in case he should meet any enemy ships. Now, convinced that there were no enemy ships, he had them rearmed with fragmentation and high-explosive bombs to attack land targets. He also cleared the carriers' decks for the planes returning from Midway.

A Japanese ship under the command of Yamamoto, destroyed during the Battle of Midway.

Aboard *Enterprise*, Spruance and his chief of staff, Captain Miles Browning, checked the reports from Midway and guessed that the Japanese would have to make another attack on the island before they could land. Spruance did a quick mental calculation and decided that if the Americans launched their planes now, they could catch Nagumo's carriers while their planes were being refueled. It was a risky move. The Japanese fleet was almost beyond the operational range of *Enterprise's* and *Hornet's* planes. They would have barely enough gas to get there and come back. On the other hand, catching the Japanese with their planes down would be a golden opportunity. The Japanese Zero was by far the best naval fighter plane in the world. It had proved that several times in the past and would do so again. Attacking the more numerous Japanese carriers, if their superior fighter planes were ready to fight, would be a much graver risk.

No American naval officer had the contempt for the Japanese military that was common in the American White House. Before Pearl Harbor, Henry L. Stimson (the secretary of war) had been lobbying to send all American warships to the Atlantic. After Pearl Harbor, he said, "We know from interceptions and other evidence that Germany had pushed Japan into this." There were no such interceptions or evidence. Some officials even said that the pilots attacking Pearl Harbor were really Germans. No Japanese, they believed, had the skill to carry off the attack.

Spruance informed Fletcher of what he had done. Fletcher waited two hours to launch his planes in case there were other Japanese ships in the area. While Spruance's planes were en route to the spot where Nagumo's carriers had been located, the Japanese admiral got an unpleasant surprise. One of his scout planes had seen American ships. They weren't in the Aleutians. Nagumo again rearmed the planes he was holding back, this time with torpedoes and armor-piercing bombs. That caused some delay in his plans. He also changed course to head for where the American ships were seen.

The American planes had taken off in separate groups—fighters, torpedo bombers, and dive bombers. They got to where Nagumo's ships were supposed to be, but they weren't. They began searching the sea around that spot. *Hornet's* torpedo squadron, Torpedo 8, found the enemy and attacked without fighter protection. Of all the fighting planes of World War II, the torpedo bomber was the most vulnerable. It had to fly a perfectly straight course, barely skimming the waves, before releasing its torpedo. Gunners on the target ship didn't have to take a lead, because for all practical purposes, the torpedo bomber was stationary. They didn't even have to hit it. The plane could be wrecked by the splashes of water caused by shells striking near it. Worst of all, it was a sitting duck for enemy fighter planes. Every plane in Torpedo 8 was destroyed, and only one pilot survived. Next, the torpedo planes from *Enterprise* appeared. They lost 10 of their 14 planes. *Yorktown's* torpedo planes had been launched later, but they arrived right after the destruction of *Enterprise's* torpedo bombers. They, too, lost 10 of their 14 planes. When his planes made contact with the enemy, Spruance informed Fletcher, who turned over command of the combined task forces to him.

The Zeros were still down near the surface or on their carriers refueling when Lieutenant Commander Clarence Wade McClusky, Jr., *Enterprise's* air group commander, leading two dive bomber squadrons, found the Japanese carriers. The torpedo plane attack was still going on, although few American torpedo planes were left. Though practically out of fuel, McClusky led his planes against the Japanese carriers. The Zeros, aboard ship or just above the ocean's surface, were helpless. The attack left *Kaga* ablaze, then an internal explosion sent her to the bottom. One bomb blew all the refueling planes off *Akagi's* flight deck; a second detonated her torpedoes. Nagumo and his men had to abandon the ship, which was later sunk. Once again *Yorktown's* planes, dive-bombers this time, arrived in time for the action. Lieutenant Commander Maxwell Leslie's squadron plunged down on a third carrier, *Soryu*, just as it was trying to launch its Zeros. Three direct hits turned the carrier into an inferno.

Then a submarine, USS *Nautilus*, which had been driven away earlier in the day, shot three torpedoes into her. *Soryu* broke in two and slid beneath the waves. Three quarters of Japan's carrier force was destroyed. McClusky, wounded by a bullet, returned to *Enterprise* with, as Gordon Prange's Miracle at Midway puts it, "barely enough gasoline to clean a necktie."

The fourth Japanese carrier, *Hiryu*, managed to launch its own dive-bombers and torpedo planes. They found *Yorktown* and hit her with three torpedoes and two bombs. Fletcher and his men had to abandon Waltzing Matilda and let her be towed back to Pearl Harbor. On the way, a Japanese submarine torpedoed *Yorktown* and her tow ship. Waltzing Matilda would dance no more.

Shortly before the attack on *Yorktown*, Fletcher sent out 10 more dive bombers to search for other enemy carriers. They found *Hiryu* just about the time her planes were bombing *Yorktown*. They scored four direct hits, and the Japanese carrier slowly sank.

Japan's entire operational fleet carrier force had been wiped out. Yamamoto wanted to continue. Nagumo argued against it. Yamamoto, misunderstanding what had happened, relieved Nagumo of command. Later, when his rage and disappointment abated, he restored Nagumo and turned back. He had an immense superiority in warships, but no carriers except the tiny *Hosho* with eight bombers. The Americans already demonstrated that they had more carriers than he expected, and he didn't know how many more. There were undoubtedly far more enemy planes at Midway and Hawaii. And he had no air cover. If he continued on, he would probably lose not only his fleet carriers, but the whole Japanese Navy.

Yamamoto knew that, ultimately, Japan's fate was sealed. His country's factories and shipyards were hard at work and would produce more planes and aircraft carriers. But they would never come close to what the American factories and shipyards could produce. Yamamoto was killed before he had to witness Japan's long succession of defeats and final surrender.

Raymond Spruance was promoted to vice admiral and made commander of the Fifth Fleet. He directed naval operations against Tarawa, Makin, Eniwetak, and Kwajalein. He was promoted to full admiral and commanded U.S. forces at the Battle of the Philippine Sea—the famous "Mariannas turkey shoot"—that just about wiped out Japanese naval air power. He commanded the naval elements during the invasions of Iwo Jima and Okinawa and directed the first air raids against Japan by naval carrier planes. Spruance helped plan the projected invasion of Japan. He was made commander in chief of the Pacific Fleet, became president of the Naval War College and, after retirement, was appointed ambassador to the Philippines.

Quiet and unassuming, Spruance was never described as "colorful" by war correspondents and is seldom remembered today. But on that moment on June 4, 1942, when he sent the planes from his two aircraft carriers against four distant Japanese carriers with better fighter planes, he changed with world. Spruance died in 1969 in Pebble Beach, California. He is buried next to his friend Nimitz and Admiral Kelly Turner in Golden Gate National Cemetery.

49

Mao Zedong

The Chairman

(A.D. 1893–1976)

Probably no military leader in the last half-century has done more to change the world than a Chinese teacher and librarian who invented a new kind of guerrilla warfare and acquired disciples in places as widely separated as Cuba and Vietnam.

Mao Zedong (also known as Mao Zhedong and Mao Tse-tung) was born in 1893 to a well-to-do family of farmers and landowners in Hunan province. Unlike most Chinese boys at the time, he was able to get a good education and graduated third in his class at a teachers' college in Changsha. In 1911, he interrupted his education to take part in the revolution that overthrew the imperial government that, under one dynasty or another, had ruled China since before the dawn of history. Mao read voraciously, and, after graduation, became an assistant librarian at Peking University. While there, he joined a Marxist study group and became a Marxist.

Mao wanted to create a new China. The China he had grown up in was far from ideal; most of its 400 million people lived on the verge of starvation. Landlords charged exorbitant rents, and the first president of the new republic tried to make himself emperor. He was defeated, but the country was now run by an unsavory crew of corrupt military leaders. The term "warlord" was coined to describe these men. Each warlord ruled a portion of China as he saw fit and taxed the peasants as heavily as his conscience permitted.

Foreign countries added to China's problems. As a result of a series of wars in the 19th and early 20th centuries, Britain, France, Russia, Germany, Japan, and the United States had taken away bits of China's sovereignty. At the "treaty ports," foreigners were exempt from Chinese law and kept their own military and police units. Russia owned railroads in China, Germany owned a port, American and other foreign gunboats patrolled the Yangtze River. Mao said China at this time was "semi-colonial and feudal."

To change things, Mao returned to Hunan and became a teacher at his alma mater in Changsha. In 1921, he became Hunan's chief delegate to the congress that founded the Chinese Communist Party. Two years later, he and the rest of the Communist Party joined a nationalist movement, the Kuomintang, or KMT.

The same year, a general named Chiang Kai-shek (who was intent on putting down the warlords) joined the KMT. Chiang had an interesting career. He attended the Paoting Military Academy in northern China. Then he studied at the Japanese Military Academy. In 1911, when the revolution broke out, he deserted from the Japanese Army and returned to China. He later took part in an uprising against the dictatorial rule of the new president, General Yuan Shi-k'ai. He joined the Third Revolution, which frustrated Yuan's attempt to make himself emperor. For a while, he belonged to the Green Gang of Shanghai, one of the world's oldest criminal organizations, which specialized in financial manipulation. After joining the KMT, he studied in the USSR and then, with Russian help, organized the KMT army and led it to the north against the warlords and the national government.

Meanwhile, Mao and the KMT were working together closely, with the former librarian forming worker and peasant unions aimed at overthrowing the warlords and the corrupt government in Peking. In 1924, Mao became an alternate member of the KMT's Shanghai Executive Committee. He became the Kuomintang's propaganda chief. The KMT went from success to success. As it grew, two strongmen appeared—Mao and Chiang. The inevitable happened: the Kuomintang wasn't big enough to contain both of them. Mao led an uprising against the KMT when Chiang turned on the Communists. The uprising had not been approved by the Communist Party politburo. When the uprising was crushed, the Communist Politburo criticized Mao for "military adventurism" and ousted him from the party. An underlying cause of this action was Mao's reliance on the peasantry rather than the urban proletariat, who (according to Marxist-Leninist doctrine) would lead the revolution. The politburo's decision was not especially smart. A short time later, Chiang killed all the urban Communists he could catch.

Mao and his followers retreated to the mountains, where they tried to establish a rural base. That was, as the politburo action showed, a radical idea. Marx believed that

only a highly industrialized country such as his native Germany was ripe for Communism. Lenin proved him wrong, but Lenin relied on the urban masses in cities such as Petrograd and Moscow, not the peasants of the countryside. Mao's emphasis on peasant support resulted in a break with Moscow, which held that Communism could only thrive among the urban proletariat.

Mao Zedong organized the strategy and tactics of the post-war Communist insurgencies.
Library of Congress

Chiang launched his army against the Communist "Kiangsi Soviet" in the mountains. He listened to his German advisors and proceeded against the Communists the way the British had fought the Boers. Peasant villages were evacuated; hundreds of mutually supporting blockhouses for KMT soldiers dotted the mountains, and miles of barbed wire were strung to impede guerrilla movement. The Communists were deprived of the support of the peasants. Another reason for the defeat, Mao later said, was that the Communists tried to hold a fortified position.

Mao led his people on the "Long March," a 6,000-mile retreat that took them west through the desert province of Xinjiang and then northeast to northern China. Of the 86,000 men and women who began the march, 4,000 reached the end. During the march, Mao, who had been ousted from the Communist Party by urban Communists, gained complete control of all the Communists in China. Faced with a Japanese invasion, Mao and Chiang agreed to make peace and unite against the Japanese.

Mao established a base in Yenan, an out-of-the-way spot in northern China. He began proselytizing the peasants and organizing military forces—the home guard, a reserve armed with surplus weapons (including spears and swords) and the mobile army. The home guard collected information, extorted "contributions" from rich merchants, and executed collaborators with the enemy. The mobile army, with rifles, machine guns, and mortars, ambushed enemy parties, attacked enemy outposts, and captured enemy weapons. In spite of Mao's emphasis on mobile warfare, the Communist-controlled area was honeycombed with tunnels under houses to allow wanted persons to hide or escape.

Mao's organization and its operations against the Japanese provided areas secure enough to shelter many of the Americans who participated in the Doolittle raid on Tokyo. (The Army planes on that raid were too big to land on the carrier that had launched them.)

Mao said his revolutionary war had three phases. The first was organizing the peasants and establishing a base area. The second was progressive expansion of the area controlled by revolutionists. The third was defeating the enemy. By the third phase, the revolutionists would have acquired enough heavy weapons, such as artillery, tanks, and aircraft. These weapons could be acquired from outside sources, but the most reliable source of supply would be the enemy. If the revolution truly represented the masses, and if it was able to grow stronger, enemy troops and whole units would desert the enemy and join the revolutionists. What began as a group of guerrillas would turn into a regular force. Victory would not come easily or quickly. Mao himself called this kind of fighting "protracted war."

When World War II ended with the Japanese surrender, Mao's army was at the end of Phase Two (or at the beginning of Phase Three). The conflict with Chiang resumed. As Mao predicted, Chiang's Nationalist troops began deserting and joining Mao. Chiang's leadership offered nothing but another dictatorship, although one free of warlords. Communist propaganda promised an earthly paradise with equality for all. (It did not, of course, promise what it delivered—a dictatorship far more oppressive than Chiang's.) Besides, the Communists were winning. The Communists advanced steadily and Chiang and his most steadfast followers fled to Taiwan. Mao become the sole authority in China and consolidated his hold on the country with a series of bloody purges. Under Mao, China was involved in only one major external affair: the war in Korea.

Mao Zedong's greatest impact on history was not a regime change in China. It was the development of a new kind of warfare. What was new in Mao's war was that a guerrilla army not cooperating with any regular force turned itself into a regular army and defeated an established regular army.

It had long been military doctrine that guerrillas were mainly useful fighting behind the enemy's lines while a regular army confronted the enemy in the front. Russian guerrillas, cooperating with Kutusov's army, destroyed Napoleon's *Grand Armee*. Spanish guerrillas, cooperating with Wellington's army and Spanish regulars, defeated the French at the other end of Europe. In the American Revolution (when New England militiamen penned the British up in Boston) the Continental Congress hastily created a regular army, and appointed George Washington as commander-in-chief. In the French Revolution, the regular army went over to the rebels, and the government vastly expanded the regular army to defeat armies approaching from all over Europe.

What Mao had demonstrated was that a guerrilla force could grow into a regular army and defeat another regular army if it could convince the population that the other army was a tool of oppressors. One of the things that made this possible was the nature of modern armies. Another thing is modern communications that facilitate propaganda. Mao Zedong's doctrines of protracted revolutionary war are a major factor in the world today, and they will be for years to come.

In 1972, President Richard Nixon made history by making an official state visit to China.

50

Matthew B. Ridgway

Old Iron Tits

(A.D. 1895–1993)

Australian historian and war correspondent Russell Spurr called him "America's most underrated military genius." He rescued an American army that was disintegrating under the misadministration of America's greatest war hero. He may even have prevented World War III. He certainly saved his country and the world a vast amount of grief. But today, few (except military historians) remember Matthew Bunker Ridgway.

Ridgway reorganized and reinspired U.S. troops in Korea, drove back the Chinese and North Koreans, and prevented the conquest of South Korea.
National Archives

Ridgway is forgotten because he won the "forgotten war." The Korean War, which culminated in a (so far) half-century truce, ended after the Communist side put out peace feelers through a friendly neutral (the USSR) and the United Nations, and the Chinese and Korean Communists concluded peace talks. It was not a lost war for the United States. It was not even a draw. It was, by any rational measure, a win—and it changed the history of the world.

While it was raging, it was not a popular war, and it made President Harry Truman increasingly unpopular. The Truman Administration tried to downplay the fighting. Truman's opponents (the Republicans) were happy to keep it out of mind once Douglas MacArthur "faded away." That helped sell their favorite myth—that Dwight D. Eisenhower ended the war.

Another reason for downplaying a war that killed more than a million people (more than 50,000 of them American), may have been that if what happened in Korea were remembered, it would have left the reputation of MacArthur in shreds. Douglas MacArthur had powerful connections with the national media and with national politicians. That was shown by what happened after Pearl Harbor; when the Japanese sprang their lethal surprise, all the Army planes in Hawaii were caught

223

on the ground—all lined up and irresistible targets. General Walter C. Short, commander of Army forces in Hawaii, was charged with dereliction of duty and immediately retired, with hints of a court-martial to follow. *Eight hours later*—real time, not figuring in the International Date Line—the Japanese caught the Army planes in the Philippines on the ground and destroyed almost all of them. But the commander of U.S. forces in the Philippines, Douglas MacArthur, did not get the Short treatment. He was made supreme commander of all Allied forces in the Southwest Pacific and awarded the Medal of Honor, the nation's highest award.

MacArthur was perhaps the American military's greatest self-promoter, a supreme egotist, and an astute office politician. But he was also a genuine hero. He won 13 awards for personal bravery. (That is probably a record.) He was a general in three big wars, and in the biggest one, World War II, he commanded a theater, the Southwest Pacific, which was about half of the whole Allied effort against Japan. After the war, he was made supreme commander of the Allied forces in Japan. In reality, he was viceroy for the United States. In that position, he was able to use his extraordinary talents as a politician, an orator, and a writer, as well as a general.

MacArthur's domain included South Korea, as well as Japan. The Allied treatment of Korea was most peculiar. The country had been conquered by Japan in 1910 and, as a result, Korean hatred of Japan and the Japanese could not have been surpassed by any European ethnic hatreds, including those of the Balkans. The Allies did not consider Korea a liberated country, however. To them, it seemed, Korea was just formerly enemy territory. They divided it into spheres of influence—Russian in the north, and American in the south. As supreme commander, MacArthur issued a hasty "occupation" decree and left administration of South Korea to Lieutenant General John Hodge. Then, faced with many problems in the large and complex society he now ruled, he shoved Korea to the back of his mind.

Hodge administered South Korea through the old Japanese colonial government, including its Gestapo-like secret police. Eventually, Washington abolished the colonial government and ordered Hodge to organize a democratic government. Hodge's previous administration, however, had outraged all the progressive elements in Korea. Their denunciations of his government led Hodges to align himself with the most conservative elements in Korea, including the man who became president, Syngman Rhee.

Rhee was a despot, but the government of North Korea was even less democratic. The Russians got into Korea literally in the last days of World War II, when Japan had collapsed but had not yet surrendered. On October 14, 1945, the Russians staged a mass rally in Pyongyang. Under a banner with the words "Welcome General Kim Il Sung," they introduced a 36-year-old native of the Soviet Union. Born to Korean parents exiled in the USSR, "General" Kim was supposed to have been a guerrilla leader who fought the Japanese colonialists during the late 1930s. (No Koreans had heard of that fighting. Nor had they ever heard of "General" Kim.) But Kim was to lead North Korea because Josef Stalin said so.

Stalin gave Kim more than his blessing. His military occupiers organized and trained a modern army and equipped them with Russian small arms, artillery, and tanks, including the superb T-34 (the best tank of World War II). By 1950, Kim Il Sung had a motorized army of 135,000 men in 10 divisions, including an armored division, completely equipped with artillery (some of it self-propelled), and supported by an air force.

The Americans, in contrast, feared that Syngman Rhee would launch a preemptive war to unite the peninsula, so they tried to limit him to a 25,000 man constabulary with no weapons heavier than the 81mm mortar. When the U.S. forces evacuated Korea in 1948, Rhee upgraded the constabulary to a 100,000 man army. The United States, however, gave him only some obsolete antitank guns, obsolete bazookas, and 100 obsolete howitzers. The South Korean army had no tanks and no effective antitank weapons. South Korea had no air force. Rhee believed that he could depend on the U.S. Air Force in Japan for support. The disparity of the North Korean and South Korean military forces didn't worry many in Washington, D.C., where it was firmly believed that any future war would begin and end with an exchange of atomic bombs.

When the U.S. forces left Korea, responsibility for dealing with Rhee's domain was shifted from MacArthur to the U.S. State Department. In January 1950, U.S. Secretary of State Dean Acheson announced that the United States would hold a Pacific defense perimeter stretching from the Aleutians through Japan, Okinawa, and the Philippines. Korea was excluded. Acheson was later accused of signaling to the Communists that South Korea was available for the taking. Acheson protested that he never meant that, but Kim Il Sung and Josef Stalin may have gotten that message.

At any rate, six months later, on June 25, 1950, the North Korean Army rolled across the border. The South Korean Army could not stop, or even slow, it. The United Nations Security Council, which (fortunately) the Russians were boycotting, ordered North Korea to withdraw its army behind the 38th Parallel, the border between North and South Korea. U.S. President Harry S. Truman ordered American naval and air forces to help the South Koreans. The next day, the U.N. Security Council voted to intervene militarily and appointed MacArthur commander of U.N. forces.

In World War II, MacArthur used U.S. command of the sea and the air to isolate Japanese outposts on New Guinea and smaller islands. Korea was a peninsula, not an island, and its transportation facilities, although primitive, were not nonexistent (as on New Guinea). MacArthur learned that only land forces could stop the North Koreans.

The only land forces available were the four under-strength divisions of the U.S. Army occupying Japan. This was the post WWII all-volunteer Army, when men joined the Army to learn a trade, not to fight a war. They were poorly trained for combat, and much of their equipment was poorly maintained.

Getting troops to Korea became a race against the clock. North Korea had almost overrun the South in a few days. American troops arrived piecemeal. The first units had no tanks, no self-propelled artillery, and almost no antitank rounds. There were not enough troops to form a continuous line. North Korean troops repeatedly flanked or enveloped U.S. and South Korean units. Eventually, Lieutenant General Walton "Johnnie" Walker was able to form a perimeter around Pusan, Korea's largest port.

The North Korean Army was concentrated in the extreme south of the peninsula, trying to break through Walker's perimeter and take Pusan. To MacArthur, with total command of both sea and air, the solution looked obvious—an amphibious landing farther up the peninsula. Strangely, it did not seem obvious to the U.S. Joint Chiefs of Staff. During World War II, the United States had successfully carried out amphibious landings all over the Pacific. They made one on Morocco, another on Sicily, and a short hop from Sicily to the foot of the Italian boot. Then there was the big one—the landing in Normandy. None of these landings were on a peninsula. But the Japanese in World War II had repeatedly used amphibious landings to outflank the British defenders of the Malayan Peninsula. The one peninsular landing the Joint Chiefs were most familiar with was the landing at Anzio, Italy.

Note: The Allied forces landing at Anzio had done everything wrong. The landing was not far enough behind the German front lines, and it was too close to Rome, a major German base. The commander, Major General John Lucas, took too seriously the instructions of his superior, General Mark W. Clark, "Don't stick your neck out." While Lucas was protecting his neck, the Germans besieged the beach head. Anzio just missed being a disaster, and was a vast waste of manpower and time.

The chairman of the Joint Chiefs, General Omar Bradley, was a veteran of the European campaigns, and he remembered Anzio well. He may also have had a personal dislike for MacArthur (a feeling not uncommon among higher ranks in the military). "He was awesomely brilliant," Bradley wrote of MacArthur; "but as a leader he had several flaws: an obsession for self-glorification, almost no consideration for other men with whom he served, and a contempt for the judgment of his superiors."

The Navy brass had no objection to an amphibious landing, but they didn't like MacArthur's choice of a landing site, Inch'on. MacArthur picked Inch'on because it is the second largest port in Korea, because it was

far enough behind the front line, and because it was close to Seoul, which (although a transportation and communications center) was not heavily guarded. The Navy objected that Inch'on harbor had a narrow entrance and some of the most extreme tides in the world, as much as 35 feet. When the tide was out, the harbor was a mile-long expanse of mud—too thin to walk on and too thick to sail on.

MacArthur, though, had an answer to the tide. He put a Navy lieutenant, Eugene Clark, on an island in the entrance to Inch'on Harbor. Clark spent two weeks on the island. He recorded the tides and waged a mini naval war of his own. He captured 30 North Korean boats and several North Korean soldiers and policemen. He learned all about military conditions in Inch'on and Seoul. When the landing began, he turned on the long-dead navigational light in the channel. Eugene Clark was the hero of the Inch'on landing. He got the Navy Cross, but should have received the Medal of Honor. And he has been largely forgotten. William Manchester, in his acclaimed biography of MacArthur, *American Caesar*, does not even mention this "Prince of Tides" in his account of the Inch'on landing.

The landing was a runaway success. As soon as they heard that the enemy was in their rear, the North Koreans ran away. Their retreat was practically a stampede. One result of this success, achieved over such strong opposition in Washington, was that the Joint Chiefs now believed that MacArthur could do no wrong. That belief made disaster possible.

The original United Nations objective was to push the North Koreans back behind the 38th Parallel. But with the enemy in headlong flight, MacArthur could not resist the urge to push right up the Yalu River, North Korea's border with China. Nobody in Washington tried to restrain him. The Chinese had warned against U.N. troops pushing up to the border, but MacArthur, convinced that he was an expert on the "Oriental mind," did not believe they would intervene. Even after Chinese prisoners were captured, he was promising to "have the boys home by Christmas."

Korea is shaped like funnel. Its border with China is more than four times longer than the width of the peninsula at midpoint. Troops that could maintain a solid line through most of the country could not possibly cover the border with Manchuria. But they weren't even trying to maintain a solid line. The Eighth Army under Johnnie Walker was pushing up the west coast, while X Corps under Ned Almond (who was also MacArthur's chief of staff) drove up the east coast. There was no unified command in the field. Walker and Almond both reported to MacArthur, who never spent one night in Korea during the entire course of the war.

The Chinese sent four complete armies into Korea. Although the command structure of each of these armies was intact (from generals to privates), although each had all its artillery and support units, and although all four armies were commanded by one general (Peng Dehuai), the Chinese government maintained that they were all volunteers. The official party line was that these men were not acting for the Chinese government; they merely wanted to help their Communist brothers in North Korea.

"I've been up and down this peninsula like a yo-yo," old hands in the Eighth Army would tell replacements. The Eighth Army and X Corps started their second trip down. The Chinese "volunteers" moved mostly at night to avoid observation and attack by American planes. U.S. Air Force and Navy planes had a monopoly of the skies over Korea. On the ground, the United States and South Korea supplied the bulk of the U.N. Army. The British Commonwealth eventually sent a division; Turkey, a brigade; France, Belgium, the Netherlands, Greece, Thailand, Ethiopia, and the Philippines sent a battalion each.

Dispatches from the Pentagon would lead you to think the enemy consisted of the Chinese alone. Chinese were credited with attacks that were conducted by North Koreans. The implication was that the North Korean Army had been wiped out by MacArthur's offensive. But in 1951, 1952, and even at the end of the war, North Korean troops were holding the mountainous eastern section of Korea. And troops who faced them both agreed that the North Koreans were a tougher enemy than the Chinese.

During the winter of 1950 to 1951, Communist forces greatly outnumbered those of the U.N. They would push the U.N. forces back until they outran their supplies. Then they would pause, distribute supplies, evacuate the seriously wounded, and push forward again.

The Chinese caught the MacArthur/ Truman fever. The American leaders had entered the war to push the North Koreans out of South Korea, but the Inch'on landing proved to be such a success they decided to drive on to the Yalu and unify Korea. The Chinese became involved to help the North Koreans (to protect their border). Their counterattack, however, proved so successful they also decided to unify Korea. Kim Il Sung, a Soviet citizen by birth, was obviously a Soviet puppet. But China now had the main military clout in Korea. The Chinese leaders aimed for a unified Korea that would be a Chinese, not a Soviet, puppet. China announced that it was going to wipe out the U.N. Army.

MacArthur hit the panic button. On November 28, 1950, he told the Joint Chiefs that his forces "were not sufficient to meet this undeclared war by the Chinese. This command has done everything humanly possible within its capabilities but is now faced with conditions beyond its control and strength." On December 3, he added that unless he quickly got heavy reinforcements, he would be driven to a tiny beach head, and there, "facing the entire Chinese nation" his army would be destroyed by "steady attrition." On December 30, he proposed blockading Chinese ports, bombing its factories and railroads, (with atomic bombs, if necessary), and reinforcing the Eighth Army with Chinese Nationalists.

He apparently did not consider that China's enormous border with the USSR could not be blockaded. China got most of its war-making potential from the Soviet Union; its factories in 1950 were few and primitive. China had a very rural economy. As such, it was not likely to be seriously disrupted by air raids. Even the tremendous tonnage of bombs dropped on highly-industrialized Germany in World War II did not slow its weapons production. As for Chinese Nationalists, Syngman Rhee threatened to pull his South Korean troops out of line and use them to drive the Chinese into the sea. Chinese—Communist or Nationalist—were not much more popular in Korea than Japanese.

At this dark moment in the Korean War, December 23, 1950, Johnnie Walker was killed in a jeep accident. MacArthur recommended Walker's replacement, Matthew B. Ridgway, and the Joint Chiefs agreed. Matt Ridgway was in many ways similar to MacArthur. He was a good administrator: he had supervised the transition of the 82nd Infantry Division to the 82nd Airborne Division. He was brave: he had led the 82nd Airborne in combat in

Sicily and jumped with them into combat in Normandy. He proved to be a skilled tactician and strategist. He was not, however, as colorful or charismatic as MacArthur. He tried to be. He adopted a trade mark similar to MacArthur's corncob pipe, Patton's ivory handled sixgun, and Montgomery's two regimental badges on a black beret. Ridgway wore his paratrooper's jump harness with a hand grenade on one strap and a first aid kit on the other. But that merely earned him the nickname "Old Iron Tits."

Ridgway had more important qualities than charisma. One was attention to detail. His skills ranged from what GIs described as "chicken shit"—requiring the proper kind of silverware at the general's mess, to making sure that all units in his command were in constant touch—using smoke signals, if necessary, he told his subordinates.

The first thing Ridgway did in Korea was reassure the South Korean government and military that the United States was *not* going to pull out. Then he inspected the troops under his command.

What Ridgway saw in Korea appalled him. The troops had been retreating for weeks from an enemy who sometimes appeared in their rear when they had no idea it was near. American morale could not have been lower. "Even their gripes had to be dragged out of them," Ridgway wrote later of the soldiers he talked to. Food was in short supply and often late in arriving. Their clothing was not adapted to the ferocious Korean winter. Field hospitals were far to the rear. The GIs had lost all confidence in the high command.

Ridgway raised hell. He ordered winter uniforms to be delivered as soon as possible, or even quicker. He moved field kitchens up close to the front lines so most soldiers could have hot meals. He moved up the field hospitals, too, and instituted helicopter evacuation of the wounded. He told officers of the Eighth Army and X Corps, as well as the Republic of Korea (ROK) Army and the allied units that the U.N. force had become too road bound. From now on, all units would be in touch so no Chinese or North Korean troops could infiltrate through gaps in the line. Communications were of the utmost importance, he told his subordinates. If radios didn't work, if telephone lines are cut, use runners. Stay in touch with the rest of the army, even if it means using smoke signals.

Ridgway reviewed the performance of his officers and replaced a number of them. One minor problem was Major General Edward M. "Ned" Almond, commander of X Corps. Almond, who was also MacArthur's chief of staff, managed to be both obsequious and arrogant—obsequious with MacArthur and arrogant toward everyone else. He had been a problem for Johnnie Walker, because he ran X Corps as if it were an independent command instead of part of the Eighth Army. Ridgway told Almond in no uncertain terms that his corps was part Ridgway's command and that no part of that command would operate independently from now on. "Almond came out of that meeting a very sober guy," said Colonel William McCaffrey, X Corps' deputy chief of staff.

Colonel John A. Dabney, assistant chief of staff (and Walker's right-hand man all through the war) gave Ridgway a plan for retreating to a new Pusan Perimeter come spring. Ridgway dismissed him on the spot. Ridgway knew he would have to retreat a few times until he got everything in shape, but he was not going to be defending Pusan in the spring. He planned to be moving in the opposite direction.

In the past, the ROK units had been a problem. Most of their higher officers were political appointees, and most of them had no military talent. Ridgway prepared a defensive line where retreating troops could stop, and he posted MPs behind the ROK divisions to halt their retreating. He reorganized the ROKs so they could go on fighting.

As expected, the Chinese and North Koreans renewed their attack. It began on New Year's Eve. Also as expected, the ROK line broke. But American MPs stopped the retreating troops. Americans fed them, rearmed them, and got them back to the fighting lines. The whole U.N. line fell back, but the troops fell back in good order, and the Communist forces again outran their supplies.

On January 22, 1951, the fighting resumed, but this time Ridgway attacked. His tactics were traditional, but a radical departure from what had been going on in Korea. The troops advanced overland, not just as columns moving up roads. Each unit was in contact with its flankers. Ridgway had built up the Eighth Army's artillery and armor. The firepower was impressive. Air strikes on the enemy were continuous.

The Chinese launched another offensive with the announcement that they were going to drive the foreigners into the sea. It soon sputtered out. Ridgway countered with "Operation Killer." Its object was to use the U.S. firepower to kill as many Chinese and North Koreans as possible. Gaining territory was not important. MacArthur approved the plan, but added a provision: recapture Seoul. Retaking the South Korean capital would make headlines.

Ridgway spent weeks planning the operation. As it began, MacArthur arrived, surrounded by a horde of correspondents. "I have just ordered a resumption of the offensive," said the man who had been telling Washington his army was about to be pushed into a tiny beachhead and wiped out.

In the first week of Operation Killer, IX Corps killed 5,000 Chinese in the Yang-pyang and Hujin sector while losing few men of its own. Ridgway hoped to push the enemy so closely it could not reorganize and resupply. But the Communists retreated behind a screen of troops who fought ferociously, almost to the last man, to let their comrades reorganize. Operation Killer was followed by Operation Ripper. The ROKs were now functioning as wholly reliable, effective troops. The 1st Battalion of the 2nd ROK Regiment wiped out an enemy battalion without losing a man. Ridgway was pushing north. On March 20, the Americans and their allies were just south of the 38th Parallel when the Joint Chiefs sent a message to MacArthur:

State planning presidential announcement shortly that, with clearing of bulk of South Korea of aggressors, United Nations now prepared to discuss conditions of settlement in Korea. Strong U.N. feeling persists that further diplomatic effort towards settlement should be made before any advance with major forces north of the 38th parallel. Time will be required to determine diplomatic reactions and permit new negotiations that may develop. Recognizing that parallel has no military significance, State has asked JCS what authority you should have to permit sufficient freedom of action for next few weeks to provide security for U.N. forces and maintain contact with enemy. Your recommendations desired.

MacArthur replied that it was "completely impractical to attempt to clear North Korea," and that "My present directives…are adequate to cover the two points raised by the State Department." Nobody asked him "to clear North Korea." So he was apparently ready for the diplomatic moves to begin.

Four days later, MacArthur made a diplomatic move of his own—a bombastic and insulting message to the Chinese, taunting them with their "complete inability to accomplish by force of arms the conquest of Korea." He warned them that the U.N. could expand its military efforts to China's coastal and interior areas, which would "doom Red China to the risk of imminent military collapse." Finally, he appointed himself—not the U.N. or the president of the United States—the master of war and peace. "Within my area of authority as military commander, however, it should be needless to say, I stand ready at any time to confer in the field with the commander-in-chief of the enemy forces in an earnest effort to find any military means whereby the realization of the political objectives of the United Nations in Korea, to which no nation may justly take exception, might be accomplished without further bloodshed."

At best, MacArthur's message was the most blatant example of a military leader defying the civilian government in American history. At worst, it may have caused the death of some 20,000 American soldiers who were killed between that time and the time peace talks were finally concluded.

The immediate result of the message was the firing of the highest ranking, most decorated, and one of the most insubordinate generals in American history. Truman's

Republican opponents tried to make political hay of the incident, but when the Joint Chiefs refused to back up MacArthur and the "old soldier" finally "faded away," there was little hay in the barn.

Ridgway, who had changed the course of the war, was appointed to replace MacArthur. Field command of the Eighth Army went to James A. Van Fleet.

The Chinese and North Koreans began another offensive. It didn't get far. The U.N. army pushed back. By the end of May, the Eighth Army and its allies were well across the 38th Parallel. Yakov Malik, the Soviet ambassador to the U.N., told American diplomat George Kennan that the Chinese and North Koreans would consider peace talks. The talks began in July.

As the peace talks began, so did the heaviest fighting of the war. The Eighth Army attacked the eastern mountains—peaks 6,000 feet above sea level that American newspapers called "hills"—held by the supposedly extinct North Korean Army. These mountains became known as Bloody Ridge, Heartbreak Ridge, and the Punch Bowl. The Punch Bowl, an extinct volcano crater, took its name from its shape. The other ridges got their names from what was involved in taking them.

Finally, Van Fleet was ordered to stop advancing. He stopped, but the fighting went on—a continuous series of company and battalion-sized raids and ambushes, similar to the trench warfare of World War I with mountains. These were punctuated by major Communist offensives which left Chinese and North Korean bodies carpeting the ground, but gained no real estate.

Dwight Eisenhower ran for president promising to visit Korea and end the war. He visited Korea, but the war went on. The Republican myth was that Ike threatened to use the atomic bomb, so the Communists quit. The Truman Administration had talked about using nuclear bombs at the beginning of the war; MacArthur threatened to use them later. The Chinese did not believe the United States would use nuclear weapons, and they were right. The North Koreans probably didn't care either way. On July 27, 1953, half a year after Eisenhower took office and three years, one month, and two days after the war began, the Chinese and North Koreans agreed to a truce. After a long series of offensives were bloodily repulsed, it had dawned on the Communist side that they were not going to reunite Korea.

The credit for that belongs to one man, Matthew Ridgway. If he had not reorganized and rejuvenated MacArthur's disintegrating army, a Communist superpower (the USSR), and soon-to-be superpower (China), would be a rowboat ride from Japan, an industrial powerhouse, and the United States' biggest ally in the Far East. Napoleon said that in war, morale is to the physical as three is to one. Having won their civil war, the Chinese Communists were cocky when they entered Korea. If they had proved the United States to be the "paper tiger" their propaganda said it was, they would be almost confident enough to swim across the Strait of Tsushima.

It is most unlikely that the United States would have allowed Japan to be invaded. And there is only one way it could have stopped such an invasion. World War III would have been the first all-nuclear war.

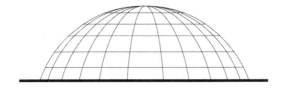

Honorable Mentions

Even the most case-hardened Yankee has to admit that Thomas J. "Stonewall" Jackson was one of the greatest American generals, and that Robert E. Lee was a noble southern gentleman. But this list is not primarily concerned with military talent. And any nobility of spirit shown by these subjects is purely coincidental. The people on this list changed history. Lee, Jackson, and all the Confederates were not trying to change history. Basically, they saw the world changing around them, and they were trying to stop the change. (And in any case, they failed.) Nevertheless, book about the Confederate leaders would be fun to write and fun to read. The Confederate Army contained some extremely interesting characters, especially Stonewall Jackson.

Another war that was rich in suggested candidates was World War II. Among them, George C. Marshall, Dwight D. Eisenhower, George S. Patton, and Douglas MacArthur. Marshall (similar to Robert E. Lee) was the epitome of a Virginia gentleman. He was a superb administrator, but there is no doubt that many others could have done the same job at least well enough to make WWII have the same outcome. Eisenhower was a great combat theater administrator. He did an excellent job of keeping such military prima donnas as Bernard Law Montgomery and George Smith Patton in line. But the power

the Allies were able to deploy against the Germans on the Western Front made the result almost inevitable. That's why Patton, a great combat commander, is not among the 50, either. The same could be said for MacArthur (although he gets a good deal of space in Chapter 50). The leaders who did make it are Yamamoto and Guderian, for inventing combat formations that are still standard, Spruance for recognizing and acting on the decisive moment, and Hitler for starting everything.

A number of other military leaders have been suggested for the list. Here are some of them:

Darius the Great: Darius launched the Persian expedition that led to the Battle of Marathon. That was a great Greek victory, but the Persian king's plan was sheer brilliance. Darius could easily have sent an overwhelming army into Greece, but there were a couple of problems. Such an army could not live off the land in rocky, unfertile Greece. (The Greeks themselves had to import their food.) A Persian army would have to be supplied by sea. But the Northern Aegean is stormy and filled with navigational hazards such as tiny islands and hidden ledges. (A short time before, a storm had destroyed a Persian fleet commanded by Darius's son-in-law, Mardonius, who was invading Thessaly and

Thrace.) And worst of all, the Greeks were a mighty sea power. Just 45 years before the expedition, a fleet from the small Greek city of Phocaea destroyed the navy of mighty Carthage. If all the Greek cities united, there was probably no navy in the world that could withstand them.

But Darius did not ascend the throne of Cyrus with dumb luck. He usurped the throne and reconstructed the disintegrating Persian Empire with a combination of hard fighting and intrigue. He did not aim to swallow Greece in one gulp. He declared war on Athens and Eretria, because, he said, they had helped Ionian cities in Asia Minor when they revolted against Persia. He sent agents to both Greek cities to foment subversion. Then he sent a relatively small force under a Median general named Datis directly across the Aegean to Eretria. As planned, the Eretrian fifth column opened the city's gates to the Persians. Then Datis wrecked the plan. He rounded up the Eretrians and made them slaves. Datis then landed at the plain of Marathon. The idea was to lure the Athenian army away so traitors could open the gates. Somebody flashed a signal from Athens, and the Persians began to embark. Just then, the Athenians attacked. Most of the Persians got away, however, and sailed to Athens. When they got there, the gates were locked, and stayed that way. The traitors, who (after Datis's treatment of Eretria) were a tiny minority, were not going to open the gates when they learned that the Persians had been defeated at Marathon.

A generation later, Darius's son, Xerxes, tried the brute-force method his father had rejected, and it turned out as Darius had foreseen. If Darius had won, he would have changed the world. He lost, and the world changed anyhow, but not the way he wanted it to.

Miltiades: The general who commanded the Athenians at the Battle of Marathon. Marathon was a decisive battle, and it did have a great effect on history. However, there were 10 Athenian generals on the Greek side, and Miltiades was commanding at the time of victory only because it was his turn to do so. Actually, there was very little a general commanding a Greek phalanx could do to change the course of the battle. It's almost certain that Marathon would have turned out the same way if one of the other nine generals were commanding.

Lysander: Lysander was a Spartan admiral during the Peloponnesian War between Athens, Sparta, and their allies. The war lasted from 431 to 404 B.C., and involved most of the Hellenic world, as well as Persia, which subsidized Sparta. Sparta was the supreme power on land, as Athens was at sea. In 404 B.C., the Athenian and Spartan navies were near Aegospotami near the Dardanelles. The Athenians (under Conon) tried for four days in a row to get the more numerous Spartan fleet to leave its anchorage and come out and fight. Lysander ignored the challenges. On the fifth day, the same thing happened, and the Athenians returned to their base, pulled some of their ships up on the beach, shipped their oars, and relaxed. Lysander's fleet, which had remained battle-ready, dashed across the strait, captured all but 20 of the 170 Athenian ships, and killed all the captured seamen.

That ended the war. Sparta (and then Thebes) became the leading power in Greece. The Hellenic world changed for a time, although within a few generations Philip II of Macedon would make those changes irrelevant. And given the feckless conduct of Conon, almost any enemy could have become the victor at Aegospotami.

Scipio Africanus: Scipio is best known for his defeat of Hannibal after the latter's return to Africa. Most military historians, though, find his campaign in Spain, prior to his African trip, more brilliant. He was able to defeat Hannibal because he had a better army, one which included a mass of Numidian cavalry. Winning the Numidians away from the Carthaginians was a diplomatic victory as important as his military victory. But in any case, after staying in Italy 16 years and winning victory after victory, Hannibal proved that he could not conquer Rome. There were too many Italians, and they were too loyal to Rome. Scipio's victory merely confirmed a change that had already been made.

Alaric: The Gothic king sacked Rome for the first time since Brennus and his Gauls in 390 B.C. When Alaric took Rome (A.D. 410), however, Rome was no longer the capital of the Roman Empire. The capital of the Western Empire was Ravenna, which Alaric had unsuccessfully tried to take. The Western Empire was already in the advanced stages of decay during Alaric's lifetime, and his capture of Rome was just one more milestone on the road to extinction. That road was a complicated tangle of betrayal and murder involving (among others) the Emperor Honorius, his sister Placidia, several Gothic kings, the Roman generals Aëtius and Boniface, and Attila the Hun (the most decent of the lot). When Attila died, his empire fragmented. Attila's secretary, Orestes (a Roman who had joined the Huns years before) led an army of Germans and Huns into Ravenna and made his young son, Romulus Agustulus, emperor. Odoacer, a part Hun-part Goth officer, led a mutiny and killed Orestes and deposed Romulus Agustulus. That coup is generally considered the official Fall of Rome.

Tarik ibn Ziyad: Not exactly a household word, but a pretty important character nevertheless. You've heard of the Rock of Gibraltar? That was originally Jebel al Tarik—Tarik's Mountain. Tarik commanded the first Muslim troops to land in Spain. They stayed there for centuries and profoundly changed history. But if Tarik hadn't led them, someone else probably would have, and the result would have been the same.

Richard the Lionhearted: Richard was a great knight, certainly the greatest royal fighting man of his time. Arab mothers are said to have told their children that if they weren't good, *el Malik Rik* would get them. After the fall of Jerusalem, Richard helped retake Acre, then he took his army through a swarm of hostile Muslims to within sight of Jerusalem. But he did not try to take the city, because he knew that—cut off from the coast—a full field army would be required to keep Jerusalem supplied. Hearing that Saladin was besieging Jaffa, he took a galley to the city and, leading no more than 50 knights, waded ashore and routed hundreds of Muslim besiegers. But for all his military prowess, Richard made no significant change. And he was a terrible king: He spent very little of his reign in England.

William Wallace: also known as "Braveheart." Wallace stirs the hearts of all Scottish patriots. He was both brave and shrewd—a good enough general to defeat the much more powerful English. But the English captured him and executed him, and Scottish liberation didn't come until much later.

Timur i Lenk (Timur the Lame): also known as Tamerlane. Timur was a Turkish conqueror and (he claimed) a descendant of Genghis Khan. Timur was almost as good a tactician and strategist as his ancestor and even more bloodthirsty. But aside from conquering many kingdoms in Central Asia, he had no lasting effect on history. He did not, for example, increase the exchange of goods and ideas between East and West.

Gonzalo de Cordoba: Known to his contemporaries as the "Great Captain," Fernandez Gonzalo de Cordoba was a Spanish soldier who won many victories in the Italian Wars between Spain and France. He was notable for the way he incorporated the matchlock arquebus into Spanish infantry formations. He made the Spanish infantry feared throughout Europe. The Italian Wars, though, took place in a period of rapid developments in military technology. After the Great Captain's retirement (because King Ferdinand, who financed Christopher Columbus, feared his popularity), military supremacy shifted back and forth between Spain and France. Gonzalo de Cordoba was a great general, but he didn't make a lasting change in history.

Gustavus Adolphus and Albrecht von Wallenstein: These two are the Gold Dust Twins of the 30 Years' War. They led armies on opposite sides of that horrible conflict. Both were military geniuses. Each came within an eye-blink of unifying the many states of 17th-century Germany. In this case, the geniuses cancelled each other out. Gustavus was killed fighting Wallenstein at the Battle of Lutzen. Wallenstein was assassinated by agents of the emperor he was serving less than a year and a half later. The war dragged on for another 14 years.

Sebastien Le Prestre de Vauban: Vauban was history's greatest military engineer. In designing fortresses and taking fortresses he had no equal. But he merely refined techniques that had been developing for centuries.

Frederick the Great: Frederick established Prussia as a first class military power with his brilliant, if sanguinary tactics and strategy. But his father, Frederick William I, laid the foundations for that by spending an inordinate amount on his army. Prussia's advance in status during Frederick's reign did not amount to a major change—nothing like the change that occurred after the Franco-Prussian War of 1870. As with Vauban, Frederick refined techniques that had been in use for years. His human automatons performed faultlessly in 18th-century linear infantry tactics, and Frederick taught them some new wrinkles, such as his oblique advance. But linear tactics started to become obsolete after Frederick's reign. They were modified in the French and Indian War and the American Revolution. At times in the French Revolution and the Napoleonic Wars they were discarded entirely. And with the advent of the breech-loading rifle, they became suicidal.

Arthur Wellesley, Duke of Wellington: Wellington was a great general, and he defeated Napoleon at Waterloo. But for years, Napoleon had been inadvertently educating his enemies in tactics and strategy. By the time of Waterloo, none of them were as good at these arts as Napoleon, but they had many more men, having adopted the French system of conscription. Without Wellington, Napoleon would still have been overthrown.

Shaka: As the Zulu king, Shaka created a new kind of military organization and dominated South Africa. He certainly changed conditions among the black nations of southern Africa, but in a couple of generations the descendants of European settlers with their rifles and horses complete eradicated Zulu power.

John A. "Jacky" Fisher: Fisher was a moving spirit for modernizing the British Navy during the late 19th and early 20th centuries. He was the ultimate battleship admiral, and because of him the Dreadnought class of ship became the main symbol of national military power. That was the cause of the arms race between Britain and Germany, which was climaxed by the Battle of Jutland. Except for the Battle of Tsushima between Japan and Russia, battleships never made much of a mark on history.

Theodore Roosevelt: Teddy Roosevelt was certainly instrumental in the development of the first American overseas empire. He was one of the hawks behind the Spanish-American War, and as assistant secretary of the navy, arranged to have Commodore George Dewey command America's "China Squadron" and, as soon as war was declared, to proceed to the Philippines. Roosevelt was no "chicken hawk." He led a regiment of dismounted cavalry against Spanish positions in Cuba, although he magnified the accomplishments of his troops by disparaging others (particularly black regular cavalry and infantry troops). The establishment of an overseas empire was of course a major change in American policy, but Roosevelt probably deserves less credit—or blame—for this than President William McKinley.

Herbert Horatio Kitchener: Early in the 20th century, Kitchener was an almost legendary British hero. In the last years of the 19th century, he led the expedition against the Sudanese "Dervishes" who had killed another greatly overrated British hero, Charles George "Chinese" Gordon. (Gordon managed to claim—in the Western World, but not in China—credit for the feats of an American mercenary, Frederick T. Ward,

during the Tai Ping Rebellion.) A few years later, Kitchener ended the last Anglo-Boer War victoriously. He was commander in chief of the British Army at the beginning of World War I. And after he was lost at sea, some British professed to believe that he wasn't really dead and would, similar to King Arthur, return to save the nation in its next hour of need.

A list of Kitchener's accomplishments begs for a few qualifications. Of the Battle of Omdurman, Kitchener's showdown with the "Dervishes," an eyewitness said, "It was not a battle, but an execution." Thousands of Sudanese, armed with swords and spears, trotted toward the British line, while six Maxim machine guns mowed them down. At the end of the battle, 28 British and 20 Egyptians were dead, but 11,000 Dervishes had been killed. The British victory did not require anything approaching genius. In South Africa, the back of Afrikaaner resistance had already been broken by the British field marshal, Lord Roberts. Kitchener's biggest contribution was some of the world's first concentration camps (for Afrikaaner women and children) in which thousands died of disease and malnutrition.

Paul von Hindenburg: Hindenburg, a retired German general, gained fame at the very beginning of World War I when the troops he commanded defeated the invading Russians in the Battle of Tannenburg. The battle was a tactical masterpiece, and Hindenburg earned the reputation of being a genius. Actually, more credit for the victory belongs to Erich Ludendorf, his chief of staff, who advised him. Ludendorf, in turn, took the advice of Col. Max Hoffman, a tall, fat, lazy officer who was reputed to be the least athletic officer in the German Army, but was demonstrably the best tactician. After the failure of von Falkenhayn's attack on Verdun, Hindenburg was moved to the west and replaced Falkenhayn as chief of the Great General Staff. He took Ludendorf with him. Unfortunately for Germany, he left Hoffman behind. That was a good thing for the Allies, because Hoffman would probably have been able to show Ludendorf the mistakes he was making in his 1918 offensive.

Douglas Haig and Erich von Falkenhayn: In 1916, Douglas Haig was commander of the British troops on the Western Front. It was a job he retained all through the war, which resulted in him being feted with the victors in the bloodiest war fought up to that time. In 1916, Haig had a plan to end the war. He had just received reinforcements—thousands of newly enlisted British soldiers. They were members of what was called Kitchener's Army, youths who had flocked to the recruiting offices when the war broke out. Haig was going to use these new troops to break through the German lines in the Somme sector, which had been relatively quiet. To prepare for the attack, Haig concentrated a huge amount of artillery, which dropped three million shells on the German lines the week before the troops went "over the top." Aerial observers reported that the German trenches had been obliterated.

During the last Anglo-Boer War, British generals learned that they could reduce casualties in an attack by having troops advance by rushes in small groups, but that made it harder to control them. Most of the men Haig was using were untested in battle. Since the German opposition had apparently been wiped out by the artillery barrage, and as the troops would be preceded by a "creeping barrage" to take care of any remaining Germans, he ordered his assaulting troops to

walk through the German lines in open order. 100,000 men started for the German lines, 20,000 died on the battlefield, and another 40,000 were wounded, many of the fatally.

When the artillery barrage lifted, the Germans dragged machine guns out of dugouts 20 feet below the surface and fired at the advancing British. Few of them reached the German barbed wire, which, instead of being cut by the artillery, had merely been heaped up in impassable snarls.

The first day of the Battle of the Somme should have shown Haig that he needed another plan. But for the next four months, he kept feeding men to the German machine guns. After four months, the British advanced seven miles but were as far from a breakthrough as when they began. Those seven miles cost the lives of 419,654 men—more dead than the United States was to suffer in all of World War II.

Unfortunately, Haig's performance was typical of World War I generals. It is somewhat remarkable that he continued to command all British forces on the Western front for the rest of the war. That was not true of Erich von Falkenhayn, who replaced von Moltke (the younger) as German chief of staff and de facto commander of German forces on the Western Front. Falkenhayn decided that the way to end the war was to "bleed France white" by attacking the fortress of Verdun. He almost did. But he almost bled Germany white, too. He was eventually relieved of his command and sent to the Eastern Front and then to Turkey.

Mustafa Kemal: Also known as Kemal Ataturk (father of the Turks), he rescued his country from domination by the Greeks after World War I (a fate many Turks would think worse than death) and muscled Turkey out of the renaissance and into the modern world. He certainly made a change in Turkey, but it wasn't a worldwide change.

Vo Ngyen Giap and Fidel Castro: These two are paired because they are intellectual children of Mao Zedong. They took Mao's principles and applied them to different environments. Because they weren't particularly original, and because neither Vietnam nor Cuba compares with China in size or importance, they didn't make the list.

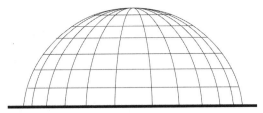

Bibliography

Adcock, F.E. *The Greek and Macedonian Art of War*. Berkeley, Calif.: University of California Press, 1957.

Alexander, Bevin. *Korea: The First War We Lost*. New York: Hippocrene Books, 1986.

Anonymous (Michael Scheuer). *Imperial Hubris*. Dulles, Va.: Brassey's, 2004.

Anonymous (Michael Scheuer). *Through Our Enemies' Eyes*. Dulles, Va.: Brassey's, 2004.

Asprey, Robert B. *War in the Shadows* (2 vol.). Garden City, N.Y.: Doubleday, 1975.

Axelrod, Alan. *America's Wars*. New York: Wiley, 2002.

Ayton, Andrew and J.L. Price. *The Medieval Military Revolution*. New York: Barnes & Noble, 1995.

Beeler, John. *Warfare in England, 1066-1189*. New York: Barnes & Noble, 1996.

Berton, Pierre. *The Invasion of Canada, 1812-1813*. Boston: Little Brown, 1980.

———. *Flames Across the Border: The Canadian-American Tragedy, 1813-1814*. Boston: Little Brown, 1981.

Billings, Malcolm. *The Cross and the Crescent: A History of the Crusades*. New York: Sterling, 1988.

Bradford, Ernle. *The Sword and the Scimitar: The Saga of the Crusades*. New York: Putnam, 1974.

Bussey, Lt. Charles M. *Firefight at Yechon*. Lincoln, Nebr.: University of Nebraska Press, 1991.

Caesar, Julius, Rex Warner (translator). *War Commentaries of Caesar*. New York: New American Library, 1960.

Cannon, John and Ralph Griffiths. *The Oxford Illustrated History of the British Monarchy*. New York: Oxford University Press, 1988.

Catton, Bruce. *A Stillness at Appomatox*. Garden City, N.Y.: Doubleday, 1953.

Chadwick, John. *The Mycenaean World*. New York: Cambridge University Press, 1976.

Chandler, David. *The Art of Warfare on Land*. London: Hamlyn, 1974.

———. *The Dictionary of Battles*. New York: Henry Holt, 1987.

Chiera, Edward. *They Wrote on Clay*. Chicago: University of Chicago Press, 1960.

Cipolla, Carlo M. *Guns, Sails and Empire*. New York: Minerva, 1965.

Clari, Robert of. *The Conquest of Constantinople*. New York: Norton, 1969.

Clausewitz, Carl von. *On War*. Princeton, N.J.: Princeton University Press, 1984 .

Coe, Michael D., at al. *Swords and Hilt Weapons*. New York: Barnes & Noble, 1989.

Connell, Evan S. *Deus Lo Volt*. Washington: Counterpoint. 2000.

Cooper, Matthew. *The German Army 1933-1945*. Lanham, Md.: Scarborough House, 1990.

Cowley, Robert and Geoffrey Parker. *The Reader's Companion to Military History*. Boston: Houghton Mifflin, 1996.

Cottrell, Leonard. *The Anvil of Civilization*. New York: New American Library, 1960.

Creel, Herrlee Glessner. *The Birth of China*. New York: Frederick Ungar, 1961

Clark, Eugene Franklin. *The Secrets of Inchon*. New York: Berkley, 2002.

Crow, John A. *The Epic of Latin America*. Berkeley, Calif.: University of California Press, 1992.

Dawson, Christopher. *The Making of Europe*. New York: Meridian, 1959.

De Beer, Gavin. *Hannibal*. New York: Viking, 1969.

Delbruck, Hans. *History of the Art of War* (4 vol). Lincoln, Nebr.: University of Nebraska Press, 1975.

Derry, T.K. and Trevor I Williams. *A Short History of Technology*. New York: Oxford University Press, 1960.

Descola, Jean. *The Conquistadors*. New York: Viking, 1957.

Diamond, Jared. *Guns, Germs, and Steel*. New York: W.W. Norton, 1999.

Diaz del Castillo, Bernal. *The Bernal Diaz Chronicles*. Garden City, N.Y.: Doubleday, 1956.

Dodge, Theodore Ayrault. *Hannibal*. Cambridge, Mass.: Da Capo. nd.

Duffy, Christopher. *Siege Warfare: The Fortress in the Early Modern World 1494-1600*. New York: Barnes & Noble, 1973.

Duggan, Alfred. *The Cunning of the Dove*. Garden City, N.Y.: Doubleday, 1960.

Dunan, Marcel, ed. Larousse *Encyclopedia of Ancient and Medieval History*. New York: Harper & Row, 1963.

Dupuy, Trevor N., Curt Johnson and David L. Bongard. *The Harper Encyclopedia of Military Biography*. Edison, N.J.: Castle Books, 1992.

Editors of *Life*. *The Epic of Man*. New York: Time Incorporated, 1961.

Einhard and Notker the Stammerer. *Two Lives of Charlemagne*. Baltimore: Penguin, 1969.

Eggenberger, David. *An Encyclopedia of Battles*. New York: Dover, 1985.

Esposito, Colonel Vincent J. *The West Point Atlas of American Wars* (2 vol). New York: Praeger, 1960.

Ezell, Edward C. *Handguns of the World*. New York: Barnes & Noble, 1993.

Falls, Cyril. *A Hundred Years of War*. New York: Collier, 1963.

Fichtenau, Heinrich. *The Carolingian Empire*. New York: Harper & Row, 1964.

Fischer, David Hackett. *Paul Revere's Ride*. New York: Oxford University Press, 1994.

————. *Washington's Crossing*. New York: Oxford University Press, 2004.

Fuller, J.F.C. *A Military History of the Western World* (3 Vol). New York: Da Capo, 1987.

————. *The Conduct of War 1789-1961*. New Brunswick, N.J.: Rutgers University Press, 1961.

————. *The Generalship of Alexander the Great*. New Brunswick, N.J.: Da Capo, 1960.

Ghirshman, R. *Iran*. Baltimore: Pelican, 1961.

Goodrich, L. Carrington. *A Short History of the Chinese People*. New York: Harper & Row, 1963.

Grousset, Rene. *The Rise and Splendour of the Chinese Empire*. Berkeley, Calif.: University of California Press, 1959

Guevara, Ernesto. *Guerrilla Warfare*. New York: Random House, 1961.

Gurney, O.R. *The Hittites*. Baltimore: Penguin, 1969.

Hamilton, Edith. *The Roman Way*. New York: New American Library, 1957.

Hargreaves, Reginald. *Beyond the Rubicon: A History of Early Rome*. New York: New American Library, 1967.

Heaney, Seamus (translator). *Beowulf*. New York: Farrar, Straus and Giroux, 2000.

Herodotus, *The Histories*. (Aubrey de Selincourt translation). Baltimore: Penguin, 1960.

Homer. *The Iliad*. (W.H.D. Rouse translation). New York: New American Library, 1950.

Howarth, David. *Famous Sea Battles*. Boston: Little, Brown, 1981.

Hutchison, Harold F. *King Henry V*. New York: Dorset, 1989.

Joinville & Villehardouin. *Chronicles of the Crusades*. Baltimore: Penguin, 1970.

Keegan, John. *A History of Warfare*. New York: Random House, 1993.

————. *The Illustrated Face of Battle*. New York: Viking, 1989.

————. *The Mask of Command*. New York: Viking, 1987.

————. *The First World War*. New York: Knopf, 1999.

————. *The Second World War*. New York, Penguin, 1990.

Keegan, John and Andrew Wheatcroft. *Who's Who in Military History*. New York: Morrow, 1976.

Ketcham, Richard M. *Saratoga*. London: Pimlico, 1999.

Kippenhahn, Rudolf. *Code Breaking*. Woodstock, N.Y.: Overlook Press, 1999.

Kramer, Samuel Noah. *History Begins at Sumer*. Garden City, N.Y.: Doubleday, 1959.

Kure, Mitsuo. *Samurai*. Rutland, Vt.: Tuttle, 2001.

Lamb, Harold. *Charlemagne*. New York: Bantam, 1958.

————. *Cyrus the Great*. New York: Bantam, 1963.

Lanning, Michael Lee. *The Military 100*. New York: Barnes & Noble, 1996.

Lawrence, T. E. *Seven Pillars of Wisdom*. New York: Dell, 1962.

Layton, Rear Admiral Edwin T. *And I was There*. New York: Morrow, 1985.

Leckie, Robert. *The Wars of America.* Edison, N.J.: Castle Books, 1992.

Leon-Portilla, Miguel. *Broken Spears.* Boston: Beacon Press, 1992.

"Letter from Jedda: Young Osama," *New Yorker*, 12 December 2005, by Steve Coll.

Liddell Hart, B.H. *History of the Second World War.* New York: Putnam's Sons, 1971.

———. *Strategy.* New York: Praeger, 1960.

Lincoln, W. Bruce. *Red Victory.* New York: Simon & Schuster, 1989,

Livy, Aubrey de Selincourt, translator. *The War with Hannibal.* Baltimore: Penguin, 1965.

Lord, Walter. *A Time to Stand.* New York: Bonanza, 1961.

McCoy, Alfred W. *The Politics of Heroin.* Brooklyn, N.Y.: Lawrence Hill, 1991.

McEvedy, Colin. *The Penguin Atlas of Ancient History.* New York: Viking Penguin, 1988.

McNeill, William H. *Plagues and Peoples.* New York: Anchor, 1998.

———. *The Pursuit of Power.* Chicago: University of Chicago Press, 1982.

———. *The Rise of the West.* Chicago: University of Chicago Press, 1963.

McPherson, James M. *Battlecry of Freedom.* New York: Ballantine, 1988.

Machiavelli, Niccolo. *The Art of War.* New York: DaCapo, 1990.

Mahan, Alfred Thayer. *The Influence of Sea Power upon History, 1660-1783.* Williamstown, Mass.: *Corner House.* 1978.

Manchester, William. *American Caesar.* New York: Dell, 1979.

Mao Zedong. *Mao Tse-tung on Guerrilla Warfare.* New York: Praeger, 1961.

Marsden, E.W. *Greek and Roman Artillery: Historical Development.* Oxford: Clarenden Press, 1999.

———. *Greek and Roman Artillery: Technical Treatises.* Oxford: Clarenden Press, 1999.

Megargee, Geoffrey P. Lawrence. *Inside Hitler's High Command.* Kans.: University Press of Kansas, 2000.

Meyer, Karl E. and Shareen Blair Brysac. *Tournament of Shadows.* Washington: Counterpoint, 1999.

Millis, Walter. *Arms and Men.* New York: New American Library, 1958.

Mitsuo Kure. *Samurai.* Rutland, Vt.: Tuttle, 2001.

Montross, Lynn. *War through the Ages.* New York: Harper & Row, 1960.

Morison, Samuel Eliot. *The Two Ocean War.* Boston: Little, Brown, 1963.

Morris, Eric, Curt Johnson, Christopher Chant, and H.P. Willmott. *Weapons and Warfare of the Twentieth Century.* Secaucus, N.J.: Deerbibooks, 1975.

Morrison, Sean. *Armor.* New York: Crowell, 1963.

Moscati, Sabatino. *Ancient Semitic Civilizations.* New York: Putnam, 1957.

Murray, Williamson and Major General Robert H. Scales, Jr. *The Iraq War: A Military History.* Cambridge, Mass.: The Harvard University Press, 2003.

Newman, John. *Bushido.* New York: W.H. Smith, 1989.

Nisson, Martin P. *The Mycenaean Origin of Greek Mythology*. New York: W.W. Norton, 1963.

Nixon, Ivor Gray. *The Rise of the Dorians*. New York: Praeger, 1968.

Oakeshott, R. Ewart. *The Archaeology of Weapons*. New York: Praeger, 1960.

Olmstead, A.T. *History of the Persian Empire*. Chicago: University of Chicago Press, 1960.

Packer, George. *The Assassin's Gate*. New York: Farrar, Straus and Giroux, 2005.

Page, Denys. *History and the Homeric Iliad*. Berkeley, Calif.: University of California Press, 1972.

Palmer, Leonard R. *Mycenaeans and Minoans*. New York: Knopf, 1962.

Payne-Gallwey, Ralph. *The Crossbow*. London: Holland Press, 1986.

Perrin, Noel. *Giving Up the Gun*. Boston: Godine, 1979.

Perroy, Edouard. *The Hundred Years War*. New York: Capricorn, 1965.

Piggott, Stuart (ed). *The Dawn of Civilization*. New York: McGraw-Hill, 1061.

Polybius, Evelyn S. Shuckburgh, translates. *The Histories of Polybius* (2 vol). Bloomington, IN: University of Indiana Press, 1962.

Pope, Dudley. *Guns*. London: Hamlyn, 1969.

Pope, Saxton T. *Bows and Arrows*. Berkeley, Calif.: University of California Press, 1962.

Prange, Gordon. *At Dawn We Slept*. New York: McGraw-Hill, 1981.

———. *Miracle at Midway*. New York: Penguin, 1982.

———. *Dec. 7, 1941*. New York: Wings Books, 1991.

Pratt, Fletcher. *The Battles that Changed History*. Garden City, N.Y.: Doubleday, 1956.

Prescott, William H. *Conquest of Mexico*. Garden City, N.Y.: Blue Ribbon, 1943.

———. *History of the Conquest of Peru*. Philadelphia: Lippincott, 1868.

Preston, Richard A., Sydney F. Wise and Herman O. Werner. *Men in Arms*. New York Praeger. 1962.

"Profusion of Rebel Groups Helps Them Survive in Iraq," *The New York Times*, 2 December 2005, by Dexter Filkins.

Quarles, Benjamin. *The Negro in the American Revolution*. Chapel Hill, N.C.: University of North Carolina Press, 1996.

Raddall, Thomas H. *The Path of Destiny*. New York: Popular Library, 1957.

Regan, Geoffrey. *The Guinness Book of Naval Blunders*. Enfield, England: Guinness, 1994.

Ridgway, Matthew B. *The Korean War*. Garden City, N.Y.: Doubleday, 1967.

Rodgers, W. L. *Greek and Roman Naval Warfare*. Annapolis, Md.: U.S. Naval Institute, 1964.

———. *Naval Warfare Under Oars*. Annapolis, Md.: U.S. Naval Institute, 1967.

Ropp, Theodore. *War in the Modern World*. New York: Collier, 1962.

Runciman, Sir Steven. *History of the Crusades* (3 vol). Cambridge: Cambridge University Press, 1954.

Rusbridger, James and Eric Nave. *Betrayal at Pearl Harbor*. New York: Summit Books, 1991.

Shadid, Anthony. *Night Draws Near*. New York: Henry Holt, 2005.

Singh, Simon. *The Code Book*. New York: Random House, 1999.

Smith, Bradley. *Japan: A History in Art*. Garden City, N.Y.: Doubleday, 1964.

Solomon, Norman. *War Made Easy*. New York: Wiley: 2005.

Solomon, Norman and Reese Erlich. *Target Iraq: What the News Media Don't Tell You*. New York: Context Books, 2003.

Southern, R.W. *The Making of the Middle Ages*. New Haven, CT: Yale University Press, 1962.

Spurr, Russell. *Enter the Dragon*. New York: Newmarket Press, 1988.

Sun Tzu, Samuel B. Griffith (trans.) *The Art of War*. New York: Oxford University Press, 1971.

Talbot, Strobe and Nayan Chandra, eds. *The Age of Terror*. New York: Basic Books, 2001.

Taylor, A.J.P. *The Second World War*. New York: Putnam's Sons, 1975.

Thayer, Charles W. *Guerrilla*. New York: Harper & Row, 1963.

Thayer, George. *The War Business*. New York: Simon and Schuster, 1969.

Thomas, Hugh. *Rivers of Gold*. New York: Random House, 2003.

———. *The Slave Trade*. New York: Simon & Schuster, 1997.

Tuchman, Barbara. *The Guns of August*. New York: Dell, 1963.

Van Crevald, Martin. *Technology and War*. New York: Free Press, 1989.

Van der Vat, Dan. *The Pacific Campaign*. New York: Simon & Schuster, 1991.

Vernadsky, George. *Ancient Russia*. New Haven, Conn.: Yale University Press, 1969.

Webster, T.B.L. *From Mycenae to Homer*. New York: W.W. Norton, 1964.

Weintraub, Stanley. *MacArthur's War: Korea and the Unmaking of an American Hero*. New York: Simon & Schuster, 2000.

Weir, William. *50 Battles that Changed the World*. Franklin Lakes, N.J.: Career Press/New Page, 2001

———. *50 Weapons that Changed Warfare*. Franklin Lakes, N.J.: Career Press/New Page, 2004.

———. *A Well Regulated Militia*. North Haven, Conn.: Archon, 1997.

———. *Fatal Victories*. New York: Avon, 1993.

———. *Soldiers in the Shadows*. Franklin Lakes, N.J.: Career Press/New Page, 2002.

———. *Turning Points in Military History*. New York: Citadel Press, 2005.

Wheal, Elizabeth-Anne, Stephen Pope and James Taylor. *A Dictionary of the Second World War*. New York: Peter Bedrick, 1990.

Wrixon, Fred B. *Codes and Ciphers*. New York: Prentice Hall, 1992

Young, Peter (ed.). *Great Battles of the World on Land, Sea and Air*. New York: Bookthrift, 1978.

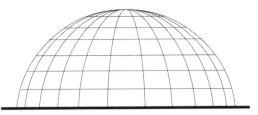

Additional Resources

Amr ibn al-'As

www.answers.com/topic/amr-ibn-al-as

http://en.wikipedia.org/wiki/Amr_ibn_al-As

John Andre (1750-1780)

http://www.si.umich.edu/spies/people.html

Benedict Arnold

www.infoplease.com/ce6/people/A0804793.html

http://en.wikipedia.org/wiki/Benedict_Arnold

www.bnedictarnold.org/

www.ushistory.org/valleyforge/served/arnold.html

The Avars

www,ebcyclopediaofukraine.com/pages/A/V/Avars.htm

http://www.fernweb.pwp.blueyonder.co.uk/mf/avars/htm

www.hyperhistory.com/online_n2/connections_n2/avars1.html

The Black Hole of Calcutta

http://en.wikipedia.org/wiki/Black_hole_of_Calcutta

www.sscnet.ucla.edu/southasia/History/British/Blackh.html

http://www.straightdope.com/maillbag/mblackhole.html

http://www.jimloy.com/history/calcutta.html

Chandragupta Maurya

www.indhistory.com/chandragupta;-maurya.html

www.infoplease.com/ce6/people/A0811323.html

www.indhistory.cp,/chandragupta-maurya.html

www.infoplease.com/ce6/people/A0811323.html

Robert Clive

www.bbc.co.uk/radio4/history/empire/episodes/episode_25.shtml
www.encyclopedia.com/html/C/Clive-R1o.asp
www.bbc.co.uk/shropshire/content/articles/2005/03/29/robert_clive_feature.shtm
www.fordham.edu/hasall/mod/1757plassey.html
http://www.sscnet.ucla.edu/southasia/History/British/Clive.html
http://en.wikipedia.or/wiki/Robert_Clive

Cyrus the Great

http://fordham.edu/halsall/ancient/539cyrus1.html
http://www.iranchamber.com/history/cyrus/cyrus_charter.php
http://en.wikipedia.org/wiki/Cyrus_the_Great
http://www.farsinet.com/cyrus/cyrus_just_ruler.html

Giulio Douhet

http://education.yahoo.com/reference/encyclopedia/entry/Douhet-G
http://en.wikipedia.org/wiki/Giulio_Douhet
www.comandosupremo.com/Douhet.html

Joan of Arc

www.newadvent.org/cathen/08409c.htm

Khalid ibn al-Walid

http://www.britannica.com/eb/article-9045249

Heraclius

www.nipissingu.ca/department/history/MUHLBERGER/ORB/OVC5S2.HTM

Alfred Thayer Mahan

http://en.wikipedia.org/wiki/Alfred_Thayer_Mahan
http://americanhistory.about.com/library/prm/blreluctantseaman.htm
http://college.hmco.com./history/readerscomp/rcah/html/ah_055600_mahanalfredt.htm
www.bartleby.com/65/ma/Mahan-Al.html
www.infoplease.com/ce6/people/A0831198.html

Muhammad

http://en.wikiquote.org/wiki/Muhammad

http://www.fordham.edu/halsall/med/watt.html

www2.sjsu.edu/faculty/watkins/seapeoples.htm

www.fordham.edu/halsall/med/donner.html

Qin Shih Huang

http://college.hmco.com/history/readerscomp/mil/html/mh_010400_chinshihhuan.htm

http://college.hmco.com/history/readerscomp/mil/html/mh_010400_chinshihhuan.html

www.factmonster.com/ce6/people/A0811890.html

www.hyperhistory.com/online_n2/people_n2/ppersons2_n2/shihuangti.html

www.wsu.edu/~dee/CHEMPIRE/CHIN.HTM

Sargon of Akkad

www.publicbookshelf.org/public_html/The_ Story_of_the_Greatest-_Nations

www.zyworld.com/Assyrian/Sargon%20the%Great.htm

www.mazzaroth.com/ChapterFour/SargonDidHeExist.htm

http://en.wikipedia.org/wiki/Sargon_of_Akkad

www.hyperhistory.net/apwh/bios/b1sargon.htm

http://history-world.org/sargon_the_great.htm

www.lexiline.com/lexiline/lexi57.htm

www.historyguide.org/ancient/sargon.html

Satsuma Rebellion

http://en.wikipedia.org/wiki/Satsuma_Rebellion

www.taisho.com/satsuma.html

www.willamette.edu/~cgrady/events.html

http://sun.menloschool.org/~sportman/westernstudies/second/24/2003/eblock/danaj/

The Sea Peoples

www.artsales.com/ARTistory/Ancient_Ships/17_sea_peoples.html

www.artsales.com/ARTistory/Ancient_Ships/17_sea_peoples.html

www2.sjsu.edu/faculty/watkins/seapeoples/htm

http://ancienthistory.about.com/od/hittites/f/seapeople.htm

www.absoluteastronomy.com/encyclopedia/S/Se/Sea_Peoples.htm

The Sea Peoples (continued)

http://encyclopedia.laaborlawtalk.com/Sea_Peoples

http://encyclopedia.laborlawtalk.com/Sea_Peoples

www.absoluteastronomy.com/encyclopedia/S/Se/Sea_Peoples.htm

http://rapidttp.com/milhist/vo1074ic.html

http://nefertiti.iwebland.com/sea_peoples.htm

http://ancienthistory.about.com/od/hittites/fl/seapeople.htm

Seleucus I

www.infoplease.com/ce6/people/A0844353.html

http://en.wikipedia.org/wiki/Seleucus_I_Nicator

The Seljuks of Rum

www.geocities.com/egfroth1/Seljuks.htm?200519

Shang and Zhou Dynasties

http://asianspiritgallery.com/china_shang.html

Sun Tzu

www.en.wikipedia.org/wiki/Sun_Tzu

http://en.wikipedia.org/wiki/Sun_Tzu

Togo Heihachiro

http://en.wikipedia.or/wiki/Togo_Heihachiro

www.arthistoryclub.com/art_history/Heihachiro_Togo

Yi Sun-sin

www.shipsonstamps.org/Topics/htm/turtle.htm

http://my.netian.com/~fprky/yiss.htm

www.nhkick.com/Chung.html

http://en.wikipedia.org/wiki/Yi_Sun_Shin

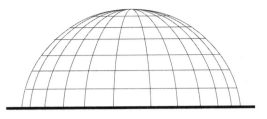

Index

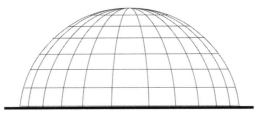

About the Author

William Weir has been a newspaper reporter, a military policeman, an army combat correspondent in the Korean War, a public relations specialist for a large telephone company, and a freelance magazine writer specializing in crime and military subjects. He has written some 50 articles for publications ranging from the *New York Times* to *Connecticut Magazine*. He has written nine previous books: *Written with Lead: Legendary American Gunfights and Gunfighters* (1992), *Fatal Victories* (1993), *In the Shadow of the Dope Fiend: America's War on Drugs* (1995), *A Well Regulated Militia: The Battle Over Gun Control* (1997), *50 Battles That Changed the World* (2001), *Soldiers in the Shadows: Unknown Warriors Who Changed the Course of History* (2002), *The Encyclopedia of African American Military History* (2004), *50 Weapons That Changed Warfare* (2005), and *Turning Points in Military History* (2005). Three of the books have been reprinted in paperback (*Fatal Victories* twice), and three in hardcover. *50 Battles* has been published in Portuguese, Czech, Polish, Korean, and Chinese. *50 Weapons* has also been published in Czech, and *Turning Points* will be published in Polish. It, like *Fatal Victories*, will also be sold by the Military Book Club. Weir and his wife, Anne, live in Connecticut and take pride in the achievements of their three adult children.